UNDERSTANDING OTHERS

Also by Dominick LaCapra

Emile Durkheim: Sociologist and Philosopher (1972, 1985, 2001)

A Preface to Sartre (1978)

"Madame Bovary" on Trial (1982)

[as coeditor, with Steven L. Kaplan] *Modern European Intellectual History: Reappraisals and New Perspectives* (1982)

Rethinking Intellectual History: Texts, Contexts, Language (1983)

History & Criticism (1985)

History, Politics, and the Novel (1987)

Soundings in Critical Theory (1989)

[as editor] *The Bounds of Race: Perspectives on Hegemony and Resistance* (1991)

Representing the Holocaust: History, Theory, Trauma (1994)

History and Memory after Auschwitz (1998)

History and Reading: Tocqueville, Foucault, French Studies (2000)

Writing History, Writing Trauma (2001, 2014)

History in Transit: Experience, Identity, Critical Theory (2004)

History and Its Limits: Human, Animal, Violence (2009)

History, Literature, Critical Theory (2013)

UNDERSTANDING OTHERS

PEOPLES, ANIMALS, PASTS

Dominick LaCapra

CORNELL UNIVERSITY PRESS
Ithaca and London

First published 2018 by Cornell University Press

Library of Congress Cataloging-in-Publication Data

Names: LaCapra, Dominick, 1939– author.
Title: Understanding others : peoples, animals, pasts / Dominick LaCapra.
Description: Ithaca : Cornell University Press, 2018. | Includes bibliographical references and index.
Identifiers: LCCN 2018006953 (print) | LCCN 2018007920 (ebook) | ISBN 9781501724909 (pdf) | ISBN 9781501724916 (ret) | ISBN 9781501724893 | ISBN 9781501724893 (cloth) | ISBN 9781501724923 (pbk.)

Subjects: LCSH: Other (Philosophy) | Empathy—Philosophy. | Compassion—Philosophy. | Humanities—Philosophy.
Classification: LCC BD213 (ebook) | LCC BD213 .L325 2018 (print) | DDC 190—dc23
LC record available at https://lccn.loc.gov/2018006953

To the many "rescue" animals with whom we have shared life for over forty years

It must not be supposed . . . that transference is created by analysis and does not occur apart from it. Transference is merely uncovered and isolated by analysis. It is a universal phenomenon of the human mind, it decides the success of all medical influence, and in fact dominates the whole of each person's relations to his human environment.

Sigmund Freud, *An Autobiographical Study* (1925)

We're all in this together.

Senator Bernie Sanders (2016)

Why rob a bank when you can own one?

Mackie Messer in Bertolt Brecht and Kurt Weill, *The Threepenny Opera* (1928)

A melancholy point of view, for it bases the world order on a lie.

Franz Kafka, "Before the Law" (1915)

Pessimism of the intellect, optimism of the will.

Antonio Gramsci, letter from prison (1929)

CONTENTS

UNDERSTANDING OTHERS

Introduction

The title of this book indicates my concern with an inquiry into the possibilities and limits of understanding as well as of relating in practice to others, especially in specific historical contexts. This inquiry crucially includes an attempt to come to terms with problems such as transference, projection, victimization, and scapegoating. It would be an understatement to say that the other, including the other within, has been a concern of critical thought for quite some time. Perhaps the most influential notion of the other (or others) within has been Sigmund Freud's understanding of unconscious processes. Emmanuel Levinas's notion of an absolute, totally other, which he finds basic to one's infinite ethical responsibility toward others, has also become prevalent, especially in terms of Jacques Derrida's adoption of it with respect to every other who is asserted to be totally other.[1]

---

1. One noteworthy aspect of Levinas's perspective and perhaps of Derrida's as well is that the importance, indeed the infinite value of the other—even when the ways of the other might be found to be opaque, mysterious, or even repulsive—was brought home to him by the treatment of Jews during the Holocaust. (For an insightful, contextually sensitive analysis of Levinas's thought over time, see Samuel Moyn, *Origins of the Other: Emmanuel Levinas between Revelation and Ethics* [Ithaca: Cornell University Press, 2005]). But both Levinas's and Derrida's approaches tend to stay, however provocatively or deconstructively, related to monotheistic traditions, notably Judaism. The historical importance of these traditions is obvious and insistent. But, as should be evident, I valorize other traditions or tendencies notably with respect to indigenous cultures (only at times significant in Derrida) and explicitly raise questions about Derrida's turn to messianicity.

I find to be of particular heuristic value the Freudian idea that in every other (as in oneself), there is something other, in the form of unconscious processes that limit the fulfillment of the classical dictum "Know thyself," while qualifying—but not entirely disqualifying—the applicability of the ideal of individual identity, agency, and responsibility. The attempt to expel this other within, which problematizes identity and causes anxiety in the self, and to project it onto a discrete other, is one dimension of the process of scapegoating that creates a clear-cut binary opposition between self and other (or "us" and "them").

In Freud alterity or otherness is linked to the role of transference, which signals the mutual but differential implication of the self in others. Transference has an inherently social dimension in its bearing on mutual implication that in a sense brings primary heteronomy and the tendency to repeat, at times compulsively. It also is a basis of empathy or compassion, indeed care and love, and, in a negative form, of hatred, animosity, scapegoating, and violence. It makes identity and relative autonomy regulative ideals that may not attain fulfillment but that may be sufficiently achieved to allow for moral responsibility and political agency. Transference as self-implication, involving a tendency to repeat, is most evident and perhaps most forceful with respect to one's relation to authority and idealized figures, real or fantasized. It may also offer a broader perspective on the issue of participant observation, significant in anthropology and pronounced in the life and work of Frank Hamilton Cushing. And it has links with Jacques Derrida's approach to deconstruction and with M. M. Bakhtin's inquiry into dialogization in language use.

Freud denied a role in the unconscious for "ordinary" or chronological time. But the case is different for uncanny forms of temporality such as the return of the repressed, belated effects, and compulsive repetition. The latter seem to suspend time and, in post-traumatic symptoms such as recurrent dreams, involve a captivating sense of full presence or the feeling that one is back there reliving a past that seems intemporal and is existentially more "real" than any actual present or future. A challenge is to see how transference and the repetition compulsion may be cogently argued to be at work or at play in various areas of both individual and collective life, perhaps even in governmental policies and social action. A difficult question concerning transference is how and in what ways it is possible to repeat after the fact, or belatedly reexperience and reenact, something as profoundly traumatic and seemingly alien as aspects of the Holocaust or other extreme events involving violence, scapegoating, and abuse, perhaps events one has never directly experienced oneself. And how can one come to terms with and, to some extent, work through, such possibly incapacitating experiences in ways that enable the understanding of others—other peoples, animals, and pasts—not simply as alien entities or as projections of the self?

There may still be historical work to do on events of the Holocaust itself. But there is also the important issue of its aftermath, including its at times belatedly traumatic effects on children and intimates of perpetrators, victims, and others involved in it. This aftermath also raises the question of relations both actual and theoretical to other possibly traumatic phenomena such as abuse, racism, scapegoating, and colonialism. Attention to trauma is not restricted to, but in recent thought may often be epitomized by, the Holocaust and its aftermath. But trauma in general has aftereffects and is attended by the issue of its contestable representation in various areas (such as historiography, film, literature, and other forms of art) and its at times questionable uses in politics and more generally in society and culture.

Understood in more or less revisionary ways, psychoanalysis is not a psychology in any conventional sense. Rather it is a form of critical theory whose basic concepts (transference as well as trauma, repression, dissociation, denial, repetition, displacement, condensation, projection, incorporation, acting out, working over, and working through) are best understood as undercutting the opposition between individual and society and as individuated or collectivized in different ways in various contexts. Most significantly, basic psychoanalytic concepts signal the mutual implication and interaction of the individual and the social as well as pointing to the role of political thought and action (notably as a crucial dimension of working through problems that call for compassion and respect for otherness or difference but are not simply psychic). All of the various procedures and defense mechanisms discussed by Freud are quite significant. They play differential roles in different times and places and may have analogues (such as exorcism) that cannot simply be reduced to them. I find the tendency to divert and displace or "pivot and project" to be almost compulsively pronounced in recent political and social events, and hence at times place special emphasis on it.

As regards transference, the historian is not in a unique position, although certain techniques may serve as safeguards. Objectification is one such technique, as is its complement, contextualization. But, taken to an extreme, such techniques may involve the denial of transference, which, despite denial, may nonetheless take place in uncontrolled forms. This is not the place to analyze the work of various historians in this regard.[2] But one notable

---

2. On the role of transference in historiography, see, for example, my analyses of important historians such as Carlo Ginzburg, Carl Schorske, and Robert Darnton in *History & Criticism* (Ithaca: Cornell University Press, 1985). For the specific problem of transference in historiography of the Holocaust and related areas, see my *Representing the Holocaust: History, Theory, Trauma* (Ithaca: Cornell University Press, 1994). For representation in Holocaust film and art, including Lanzmann's important 1985 film *Shoah*, see my *History and Memory after Auschwitz* (Ithaca: Cornell University Press, 1998). More recent works return to these issues, notably *Writing History, Writing Trauma* (2001;

example of repetition with minimal change with respect to a seemingly ob-jectified study is Andreas Hillgruber's *Zweierlei Untergang: Die Zerschlagung der Deutschen Reiches und das Ende des europäischen Judentums*.[3] In it Hillgruber argues that the historian studying these two "downfalls" must take the puta-tive perspective of the German nation as a whole (excluding the victims) and empathize with Germans in the east (where Hillgruber himself came from), notably German soldiers fighting the invading Russians on the eastern front. Germans on the eastern front may well deserve empathy or compassion as victims of killing, rape, and plunder by invading Russians. But, in general-izing in an exclusionary manner and focusing on the military, Hillgruber repeats in his own historical discourse what he construes as German perspec-tives during the war, even going to the point of setting up a dubious equiva-lence between the devastation of the Reich (*Zerschlagung* is a very charged term) and the euphemistically termed "end" of Jewry in Europe. (Jewry did not "end." Jews were rounded up, confined, tortured, and killed, and their culture—or *Judentum*—was attacked and to a significant extent destroyed, fortunately and in spite of declared Nazi intentions, not to the point of bring-ing them or it to an end.)

To give a different example, while Lawrence Langer is technically not a historian, his *Holocaust Testimonies: The Ruins of Memory*[4] is an important book for historians among others, and Langer's relation to survivor testimo-nies is transferential to the point of identification and sacralization, including the insistently melancholic and almost dogmatic denial of the possibility for survivors to work through the past at least in the sense of rebuilding a vi-able post-Holocaust life. In Langer there is a sense in which victims cannot become survivors but must remain shattered victims. There is something similar in Claude Lanzmann, whose interest and highly affective, perhaps overly participatory response in his iconic 1985 film *Shoah* are devoted to the victim and not the survivor or only the survivor who can relive and, for the purposes of Lanzmann's film, reenact or act out victimization. But *Shoah* is a film of unquestionably major importance. And Langer may be overreacting

Baltimore: Johns Hopkins University Press, 2014 [with a new preface]), *History and Its Limits: Human, Animal, Violence* (Ithaca: Cornell University Press, 2009), and *History, Literature, Critical Theory* (Ithaca: Cornell University Press, 2013), esp. chaps. 4 and 5.

3. Andreas Hillgruber, *Zweierlei Untergang: Die Zerschlagung der Deutschen Reiches und das Ende des europäischen Judentums* (Berlin: Siedler, 1986). For a discussion of Hillgruber, see my *Representing the Holocaust*, 51–53. *Untergang* is the same word used by Oswald Spengler in what is translated as *The Decline of the West*.

4. Lawrence Langer, *Holocaust Testimonies: The Ruins of Memory* (New Haven: Yale University Press, 1991).

to what he plausibly sees as Charles Taylor's extended neo-Hegelian placebo in *Sources of the Self*,[5] where the Holocaust becomes little more than a blip in the history of a putatively onward-and-upward course of increasing Western justice and mercy.[6]

In my judgment, one may indeed represent important dimensions of the Holocaust and of the experience of victims and perpetrators during it without assuming that this is an easy or unproblematic undertaking or that it adequately renders that experience. Like many others, I find the idea that the Holocaust or traumatic experience during it is utterly unrepresentable to be dubious, and it is typically associated with the noli-me-tangere view that it is taboo, sacred, or sublime. Silence about traumatic, "unspeakable" events and one's responses to them (including feelings of "guilt" or disorientation they may evoke) may understandably be widespread in survivors for a variety of reasons. As has been widely noticed, such silence may be a deeply felt form of respect that can attain religious or postsecular status, perhaps related to bonds with lost intimates. But it may also be both manipulated politically in self-interested fashion and serve to intensify at times fantasy-laden post-traumatic symptoms in the children or intimates of survivors, even for generations to come if that silence is not worked through at least in terms of being addressed in some viable manner.[7] Especially in those born later whose relation to victims may be more remote, one may have the familiar paradox "Whereof one cannot speak, thereof one cannot keep silent," the paradox of believing one can or should say nothing about certain events or experiences and finding oneself able to talk about nothing else, if only on the "meta"-level of endlessly rehearsing why one must keep silent.

The psychoanalytic concept of "working through," which counteracts acting out and the repetition compulsion, implies a modulated form of repetition that engages transferential co-implication and resists compulsion and closure, yet comes with critical and self-critical judgment, enabling possible, and possibly more desirable, futures. Working through also involves opening the self to consideration and respect for, and at least limited understanding of, others as others not reduced to one's own narcissistic projective or incorporative identifications. In this sense, it is required for moral as well as political responsibility and can be seen to have an ethical and political import, or even to involve social and political work. It is not confined to psychological

5. Charles Taylor, *Sources of the Self* (Cambridge, MA: Harvard University Press, 1989).
6. On Langer, see my *Representing the Holocaust*, 194–200; on Taylor, 183–87.
7. See, for example, Gary Weissman, *Fantasies of Witnessing: Postwar Efforts to Experience the Holocaust* (Ithaca: Cornell University Press, 2004).

response, a clinical context, or the one-on-one psychoanalytic relation. Nor should it be restricted to a "talking cure," since it may not bring a full cure but require continual work on the self and on relations with others. And it may well involve acts and practices that are not "talk" or narrowly linguistic (for example, laughter, weeping, song, music, and bodily movements including dance, painting, and other art forms). It is in this sense that I have employed the concept of working through in earlier work and shall continue to do so in this book. Moreover, my approach to Sigmund Freud, as to Jacques Derrida or Mikhail Bakhtin—three figures whose thought plays an important role in the following pages—has been and continues to be selective and in part critical, not mimetic or dogmatic. I would nonetheless insist that a continuing interest in the thought of such important figures is not an old-fashioned fad or a fixation on the past. What is "faddish" or fixated is not the belief that there is still much of value in their work as well as in that of other significant thinkers and writers of the past. It is rather the continual quest for something new, which easily becomes an academic, professional, or artistic variant of planned obsolescence. The challenge is to see how what is of lasting value in past thought may be rethought and turned in directions that are not simply forms of mechanical repetition or defensive objectification.

The principal "others" I address from various perspectives are other animals, other peoples (notably Jews and Zunis, respectively, in relation to the Holocaust and to colonialism, along with possibly collusive and intrusive anthropological inquisitiveness), and one's own as well as others' pasts, especially insofar as they bear on and indeed may still be alive in or haunt the present. In historiography, it has become a cliché to say that the past is a foreign country. But this foreignness may uncannily recur with variations in the present, for example, in the form of disconcerting repetitions and sacrificial or quasi-sacrificial forces that are typically and deceptively situated outside "modernity" and construed as irrational atavisms. Hence, for example, approaches to the Holocaust have often been divided between construing the genocide as the result of modernizing forces (bureaucracy, alienation, and the industrialization of mass murder—probably the dominant historiographical approach) or as an effect of resurgent "irrationality," notably in the form of the return of quasi-religious desires for purification and redemption (a less prominent but still active concern in historiography and related disciplines). It has become increasingly obvious that these two approaches are not mutually exclusive but historically and existentially intertwined and that the emphasis on instrumental rationality obviates the role of other forces that are deemed premodern and irrational only at the risk of underestimating their importance and their more or less displaced and distorted operation in "modernity." One should also be sensitive to the ways processes active in the Holocaust, such as quasi-sacrificial desires for purification, self-justification, and even redemption or salvation, may not be unique to the desire to get rid of (*entfernen*) Jews but found in other prejudicial, scapegoating phenomena as well, which may at times go to violent, indeed genocidal or near-genocidal extremes. "Ethnic cleansing" may have both instrumentally rational dimensions (such as "turf" wars and the possession of land, jobs, and resources) and less instrumental, even quasi-ritual aspects (such as the sense of contamination from contact with certain others, particularly sexual contact, engendering demands for segregation, expulsion, or extermination).

Another form of alterity or otherness running through the analyses in this book is that which emerges from the division of labor or of spheres of activity, notably as this process applies to disciplines such as historiography, social science, philosophy, and literary criticism. There has of course long been a call for inter- or cross-disciplinarity as a requirement in the study of complex problems and processes. But this call may be honored in good part in name only, at times as a voice crying in the wilderness. Academic departments remain rather sharply differentiated, and individuals who cross disciplinary lines must not only (as well they should) be conversant with practices and protocols within other disciplines but also be able to embrace divided identities that may create distrust in colleagues seeking secure self-definition and identity (say, as a historian, philosopher, or literary critic). Such distrust may be prominent even in a theoretical orientation claiming to deconstruct or severely question the viability of unmarked or undivided identity, closure, and totalization. And whatever the dominant or prevalent theoretical or methodological tendencies in a discipline, the day-to-day interaction among colleagues brings practical forms of affiliation and of discourse that have an effect on thinking, writing, interpersonal interaction, and the education of students.

It is rare that a literature, philosophy, or even political science department will hire someone with a degree in history, and even more rare that a history department will hire someone with a degree in literary studies, philosophy, or even political science. Prizes such as book awards tend to be intra- rather than interdisciplinary, although some prize-winning books may of course have interdisciplinary dimensions. A continued source of debate is just how firm or secure disciplinary lines should be, as well as where a given inter- or cross-disciplinary concentration (such as critical theory, intellectual history, and historiographical theory or "metahistory") best belongs. I also touch on the question of the extent to which historians themselves in the United States, England, and France read and try to understand one another across national boundaries. In what follows, lines between and within disciplines shall be crossed in ways that I hope prove to be thought provoking, open to debate, and even controversial but not undertaken for the sake of a shock effect that soon becomes all too predictable. Moreover, protocols, especially pronounced in professional history, may be breached, for example, with respect to footnotes that go beyond providing references for assertions and offer at times supplementary or even divergent perspectives, extending or displacing a point made in the principal body of the text.

I have earlier written on certain topics revisited in this book, and I attempt to treat them in ways that do not replicate but rather significantly vary, inflect, and go beyond what I have argued before. This is especially true of the problems of history, memory, the Holocaust, and other animals as well as the posthuman and the postsecular. I also comment on the electoral campaign and initial phase of the administration of Donald Trump, which contain elements that, unfortunately, are both timely and of continued relevance to the basic problems I treat. I try to make as explicit and clear as possible the respects in which I employ selectively and at times significantly revise Derrida's deconstruction and Freud's psychoanalysis as well as the "dialogism" elaborated by Mikhail Bakhtin. In some ways, the results are distinctive and my own responsibility, especially with respect to their bearing on historiography. At times I enter different areas, as in the discussion of Frank Hamilton Cushing and his "adventures" in Zuni. Cushing spent over four years in Zuni. He became a close associate of its "Governor" and even a member of its prestigious religious society of the Bow. But Zuni and other indigenous peoples remain divided or at times ambivalent about his role at Zuni, often seeing it in contrasting terms of intrusive betrayal or attempted empathic understanding. The chapter points to the tensions in Cushing's role as an "other" or "outsider" who became at least to some extent an important "insider." It also explores the relations between the still controversial anthropological "method" of participant observation and the psychoanalytic concept of transference. Indeed, in Cushing's relations with the Zuni, one has a striking case of the promises and pitfalls of being with and trying to understand others, a case that still poses challenges for the Zuni, other indigenous peoples, and those who attempt to be compassionate yet critically self-conscious commentators.

It is evident that otherness or alterity wears many masks, only some of which I shall explore here.[8] Furthermore, many of those to whom I refer

8. For an important study that expands inquiry into understanding and relating to "others" beyond the parameters explored in the present book and includes the mentally disabled, "wild"

(such as Frank Hamilton Cushing, Edward S. Curtis, and George Custer) are controversial in ways I do not explicitly explore but often point to even while indicating why I find such figures worth careful study. I would add that, like history, anthropology has long existed with a tense if not combative relation between its social-scientific and humanistic tendencies. The former, especially via an association with archaeology, can veer toward scientism or at least empirical and monographic narrowness. And the humanistic pull has at times gone in the direction of extremely speculative, abstract theoreticism. A new look at a figure such as Cushing may help to revive an interest in the history of anthropology and to rekindle a more challenging interaction between humanistic and social-scientific orientations (as well as between theory and research) in anthropological and ethnographic studies. It may even point to anthropology's posthumanist and postsecular possibilities, notably in terms of relations with other animals and a rethinking of indigenous spirituality, including the role of the fetish and the katsina (or kachina).[9] An especially challenging feature of Cushing is the way his thought and practice tend to be an embarrassment to professional anthropologists and historians who do not simply exclude or marginalize him with respect to their field of concern. The reason may well be that he insistently enacts or even acts out transferential relations in forms of participant observation, and the latter are often if not typically avoided, repressed, or denied as part and parcel of important forms of professionalization and disciplinary practice that separate sharply between self and other, observer and observed, or past and present.

The chapter on history and literature takes the form of a review essay or dialogic exchange with the important book of Ivan Jablonka, *L'histoire est une littérature contemporaine: Manifeste pour les sciences sociales*.[10] It also provides an instance of what I defend in intellectual and cultural history: an extended critical analysis and attempt to understand specific texts and artifacts (as well as their larger contexts of production and reception). Jablonka seeks something other than a mere combination of history, social

---

children, infants, people with neurological disorders, and angels, as well as artificial intelligences, see James Berger, *The Disarticulate: Language, Disability, and the Narratives of Modernity* (New York: New York University Press, 2014). Berger explores how such "others" play a crucial role in much significant modern thought and literature.

   9. The katsina is a carving made from the root of the cottonwood tree. It represents one or more of the over 300 spirits in the religion of the Pueblo peoples. It was traditionally used to teach aspects of religion to children too young to participate in religious practices. It is also represented and enacted by masked dancers during ceremonial dances. (The often preferred recent transliteration is "katsina," but "kachina" is employed earlier in the literature and at times today as well.)

   10. Ivan Jablonka, *L'histoire est une littérature contemporaine: Manifeste pour les sciences sociales* (Paris: Éditions du Seuil, Librairie du XXIe siècle, 2012).

science, and literature. He would like history, itself understood as a social science, to be a literature of the real world. He is also interested in literature informed not only by the results but, more important, by the forms of reasoning and inquiry of history and related social sciences (notably anthropology and sociology). Hence he makes a challenging attempt to coordinate history, literature, and social science in an understanding of history that avoids dichotomies yet also distinguishes sharply between literature and fiction. He both approximates history and literature and distances history from fiction that is not heuristically and methodologically in the service of historical inquiry.

There is no linear development among the chapters of this book, but instead cross-references, which may at times involve returning to earlier points or discussions. This approach hopefully generates a sense of the interacting forces that provide connective tissue for the argument. The largest ambition of this book is to further the development and effectiveness of a "posthumanist" (or other than narrowly human) frame of reference that situates and limits the human in a broader ecological and existential context. This is the context in which any defense of the humanities is best understood. The recent emphasis on the importance of STEM disciplines (science, technology, engineering, and mathematics) has at times, even increasingly, come with the idea that the humanities must be made "practical" on the model of a STEM discipline and otherwise are to be denigrated if not dismissed as useless. When they take the latter turn, the praise and funding of STEM disciplines go beyond what is desirable and turn away from key problems that bear on understanding, critical thought, and implications for the present and future. What eventuates may well find its place in the type of ultraconservatism or even neoliberalism that defends runaway exploitation of nature and other animals and sees the world only as the repository of resources to be privatized and consumed in ways that putatively serve "human interests." The recently prevalent concept of the Anthropocene is helpful in indicating the increased impact of humans on the rest of nature, evident in the issue of global warming. This impact may indicate a human footprint that threatens to stamp out whatever does not fit its mold or accord with its directives, a footprint that easily becomes counterproductive and self-destructive. The concept of the Anthropocene itself should not legitimate anthropocentrism but instead function as an indicator of human impact on the world that is to be called into question when it becomes self-centered and exploitative. One consequence is that theories of evolution should not be taken as a secularization of the great chain of being that overtly or covertly places the human at its pinnacle and functions to justify human uses and abuses of other beings and the environment itself.[11]

A key aspect of the dominance of a narrow, exclusivist humanism, which may be further narrowed from "speciesism" to chauvinistic nationalism and racism, is the increasing division of the population, both within countries and across the world, into a small class of the very wealthy and an overwhelming number of the poor, with a shrinking of the middle class. In the United States, one seems to have had a modified (and perhaps soon-to-be exaggerated) return to the "Gilded Age" with its privileged class of the superrich, its drive toward privatization (including even highways and prisons), and its unregulated or deregulated economic and financial system. Recently one has even witnessed the emergence of extremely conservative and authoritarian if not neofascist tendencies with significant popular support. Indeed one frequently invoked statistic has some sixty odd individuals owning as much wealth as the entire bottom half of the world's population, and within the United States, attention has at times turned from the wealthiest 1% to the superprivileged 1/10 of 1%. Whatever the precise statistics may be, extreme inequality is blatantly obvious, and it is a scandal that has been focused on by both Pope Francis and Bernie Sanders, a conjunction that may remind us that one of the first Jewish democratic socialists was Jesus Christ. Recent events also remind us that a large group of people may not act or vote in their own rational best interest but be moved not only by warranted grievances but also by affective and ideological, indeed phantasmatic and hateful, forces, including modes of prejudice and scapegoating. My conviction is that a sustained

---

11. One recent development in biology is the ability to edit genetic sequences, accelerate evolution, eliminate certain genes, and enable others to proliferate both in the laboratory and in "the wild." The consequences are exhilarating and intimidating, permitting both the possible extirpation of certain diseases (such as malaria or Lyme disease) and the triggering of untold devastation. Fortunately, some scientists (notably Kevin Esvelt of MIT) now recognize that science is not a self-enclosed activity without responsibility for consequences but a practice bound up with broadly ecological, ethical, and political concerns that require responsible attention in any experiment or innovation. See, for example, the informative article by Michael Specter, "Rewriting the Code of Life," *New Yorker*, January 2, 2017, 34–43. It is noteworthy, as Specter observes, that Esvelt faced impediments in his career due to the cross-disciplinary and in part public-oriented quality of his work. "Despite his awards, publications, and influential mentors, Esvelt struggled to find a position that would help him achieve his goals as a scientist and as a public educator. To many institutions, he seemed like a strange hybrid. He has certainly demonstrated great talent as a researcher, but he had also decided to become a sort of proselytizer. He long ago concluded that telling the story of science, and the choices it presents, is just as valuable as anything he might accomplish in a lab" (37). Esvelt pointed to the example of Carl Sagan as an important but unjustifiably looked-down-upon scientist with an agenda comparable to his own.

concern for other peoples, other times, and other-than-human beings forms the larger frame of reference in which an insistence on economic, social, and ecological issues as they affect humans must be seen in order to be better understood and addressed. A crucial threshold shall have been crossed when such a concern has a prominent place on political agendas of movements and parties.

On the cover of this book is a photograph of a katsina carving by Aaron Honyumptewa. The katsina is a Yowe or "Priestkiller." Despite their legendary reputation as a people of peace, the Hopi, like other Pueblo peoples, including the Zuni, nonetheless at times took part in internal and external conflict, notably in the seventeenth century, culminating in the Pueblo Revolt of 1680. (The carver, Aaron Honyumptewa, is, he reported, Hopi and Picuris, and when I purchased the katsina from him at the 2015 Indian Market in Santa Fe, he stated that the Indian in the katsina was not a Hopi but a member of another tribe who had been engaged by the Hopi to undertake the violent act, which he asserted they refrained from performing themselves. He also said that the katsina had shocked some of his Catholic Hispanic neighbors, and it was certainly the center of much attention and some controversy at the preview the evening before the beginning of the market.)

The 1680 revolt was directed against the Spanish conquistadors and their clerical wing, who had at times attempted to destroy native religious practices, including kivas and katsinas. Echoes and ghosts of the conflict have not entirely disappeared, especially surrounding the annual fiesta in Santa Fe celebrating the 1692 reentry (*Entrada*) of the Spanish under Antonio de Vargas after the violent suppression of the Pueblo Revolt. Efforts have been made to make the celebration more inclusive, at times by seeing the reentry and reconquest, through distorting rose-colored glasses, as peaceful events, at other times by attempting to frame critically the reconquest and shift the fiesta in the direction of a celebration of possible peace and cooperation in the present and future. A step in this direction in certain cities and states (including Santa Fe, Berkeley, Denver, Alaska, and Vermont) has been supplementing and contesting Columbus Day by (re)naming the same day Indigenous Peoples Day, a gesture that is itself both politically correct and arguably quite simply correct.

The katsina represents an Indian about to kill, perhaps to sacrifice, a Franciscan. The Franciscans along with other orders often functioned as the clerical component of conquest. They were going to build a church in Hopi as part of their missionary activity in converting Indians to Christianity, a church that the Hopi did not want. The katsina seems to capture the killing of a Franciscan, whether actual or legendary, in a moment of suspended animation. One is tempted to see it with Western eyes as analogous to the Laocoön statue or perhaps to paintings of the arrested sacrifice of Isaac by Abraham (for example, Caravaggio's of 1603). (Aaron's father, the celebrated artist and carver Stetson Honyumptewa, who was at the same booth as his son at the Indian Market, appeared to agree with the aptness of the analogy I drew between his son's carving and representations of the sacrificial scene [or Akedah] involving Isaac and Abraham.)[12] The katsina might also be seen as indicating the extreme breakdown of an attempt to understand the other, a counterpart to the failure of the West and its dominant religion to understand the spiritual practices it tried to delegitimate, supersede, and get rid of, whether by extirpation or assimilation.[13]

Conversion literally may mean the turning of the other into the self or the same, often with the sacrifice or constriction of understanding in the interest of control and assimilation, themselves at times entailing the "sacrifice" of indigenous peoples and their cultures. Conversion might even be seen as an attempt to pluck out the eye that offends you rather than to arrive at some sense, however inadequate, of the perspective from which it sees. The Indian

---

12. A significant difference is that, in the katsina as opposed to the biblical account, there is no ram with its horns tangled in the bushes, as if prepackaged to serve as (an often forgotten or ignored) sacrificial substitute for Abraham's son.

13. It is noteworthy that a guide I once had at Acoma, another Pueblo people, took pains to point out that, in her opinion, the church there was not welcome and that the view from it was directed toward the portable toilets just below. I would, however, also note that, despite the status of Christianity as the religion of the conquerors, relations between native practices and Christianity are at times interactive and not always antithetical. Catholicism has at times attempted to allow for the coexistence of its own and native rituals and images. Noteworthy in this respect are the murals of katsinas above the stations of the cross in the Church of Our Lady of Guadalupe in Zuni, New Mexico. (The Zuni are also a Pueblo people. Their practices are close to those of the Hopi, but they generally do not sell or even display their katsina carvings. For example, fetish carver Max Laate is quoted as saying: "I didn't want to carve kachinas anymore. They are religious and I didn't want to do that. I could make kachinas as a gift, but not for sale, for if you do that you are selling part of your self and your life will shorten." Quoted in Marian Rodee and James Ostler, *The Fetish Carvers of Zuni*, rev. ed. [Albuquerque, NM: The Maxwell Museum of Anthropology, the University of New Mexico, 1995], 89.) The striking katsina murals in the Church of Our Lady of Guadalupe (along with other images such as a Christ figure wrapped in Zuni blankets, which is placed above the altar) were painted over a twenty-five-year period in the late twentieth century, with the permission of the parish priest, by the artist Alex Seotowa, assisted by his two sons, Kenneth and Edwin. Alex Seotowa, who attended parochial school, describes himself as "a Catholic who is also a 'cultural practitioner' of Zuni traditions." He sees parallels between Catholic and Zuni practices and tries to elicit the shared spirituality in both. For him katsinas are intermediaries similar to guardian angels. See the story by Gustav Niebuhr in the *New York Times*, January 29, 1995 (http://www.nytimes.com/1995/01/29/us/zunis-mix-traditions-with-icons-of-church.html [accessed May 18, 2016]). Note that while Hopi carvers do sell katsina carvings, some of them, such as Stetson Honyumptewa, feel that katsinas have spiritual significance and that they as carvers work within a tradition in which religion plays an important role.

of the katsina is saying no to conversion in what may be the most decisive way possible. In this book, I seek ways other than conversion, killing, or sacrificing others, as in his own way did the artist who carved the Yowe katsina, while nonetheless bringing out the violence of the confrontation where killing went disproportionately in the other direction.

Note also that some Zuni wanted to do to Frank Hamilton Cushing what is being done to the Franciscan. Cushing the anthropologist did not seek to convert the Zuni; indeed he wanted to protect and even become one of them, at least up to a point. But he intruded on their way of life and did things they found unacceptable, manifestly intrusive, and perhaps sacrilegious and appropriative, such as drawing and taking notes during their ceremonies and sacred practices. During my own visits to Zuni, if it seemed appropriate, I have broached the question of the memory of Cushing among the Zuni. I typically have been met with an uneasy, ambivalent response, somewhere between an uncomfortable laugh and a dismissive gesture, which may show that Cushing is still a live issue and that the divisions in the tribe as well as within some of its members during his time there have not entirely disappeared.

By the way, early in my career, I considered seriously becoming either a priest (when I was in a parochial grammar and then high school—I like to think a priest of the Dan and Phil Berrigan or the Michel de Certeau rather than the militantly converting variety) or later an anthropologist (having studied in Paris during the 1960s with Claude Lévi-Strauss).[14] In a sense, religion and anthropology were paths not taken in which I have nonetheless maintained a strong if at times critical interest.

---

14. De Certeau, whom I got to know toward the end of his life, shared, I think, the critical orientation I pursue in this book. In contrast to the view that postulates a dichotomous opposition between past and present or between religion and secularity, he was extremely sensitive to the issue of (at times disconcerting) displacements (or repetitions with change) over historical time. As he explicitly puts it, "Born as a historian within religious history, and formed by the dialect of that discipline, I asked myself what role religious production and institutions might have had in the organization of the modern 'scriptural' society [which includes historiography based exclusively or even predominantly on written archives—DLC] that has replaced them by transforming them. Archaeology [in Freud's and perhaps Foucault's sense—DLC] was the way by which I sought to specify the return of the repressed, a system of Scriptures which modernity has *made* into an absent body, without being able to eliminate it. This 'analysis' allowed me to recognize in current labors a 'past, accumulated' and still-influential labor. In this fashion, which made continuities and distortions appear within systems of *practice,* I was also the subject of my own analysis" (Michel de Certeau, *The Writing of History,* trans. Tom Conley [1975; New York: Columbia University Press, 1988], 14). One may recognize in the last statement an affirmation of the role of transference in the basic sense of the co-implication of self and other, including the scholar in relation to his or her text or "object" of study, which raises the issue of displacement distinguished from dichotomous opposition (or simple replacement and "epistemological break") over time.

I have intimated that conversion is a form of sacrifice of the other for the sake of the self or the same. All too often it accompanies an overly homogeneous rather than self-questioning idea of one's own identity. One thing I have tried to understand critically throughout my work is the practice of materially or symbolically sacrificing the other, including the other within, whom, for the sake of one's own material or spiritual advantage, one does not try to understand or to engage in other than self-centered, identity-reinforcing ways. And I have contended that there is an objectionable form of disciplinary or departmental identity politics that may become sacrificial for the sake of internal solidarity or fellow feeling (even for the sake of a fantasy of an academic department as one big happy family). In any case, the imposition of solidarity or consensus, along with the exclusion or expulsion of others with whom you disagree, is often detrimental both to the intellectual vitality of the academy and to the understanding of problems that themselves cut across disciplines and contest disciplinary identities in ways not amenable to an additive interdisciplinarity. (If it does not affect ways of conceiving problems and underlying frames of reference, adding history to anthropology or literature, for example, may be a calculation in which one plus one equals not two but instead less than one.) Here understanding, insofar as it is appropriative or narrowly instrumental and fails to recognize and respect its own limits, is itself open to criticism.

These pages were written or revised under a cloud of oppressive topicality with respect to the key issues they address. The 2016 presidential campaign and the initial months of the presidency of Donald Trump were marked by extreme disarray and dangerous tendencies that warrant attention in that they unfortunately resonate with major themes of this book. Some readers may find jarring or inappropriate my periodic references to Donald Trump and aspects of his campaign and the beginning of his "reign" as president. But these references to the early phase of the at-times unpredictable unfolding of the Trump era bear directly on problems that are very much at issue throughout this book, problems such as the role of authoritarianism, prejudice, racism, misogyny, scapegoating, ethnic profiling, ultranationalism, anti-immigrant animus, and hostility toward "weakness." These problems should not be relegated to other times, peoples, and places. Phenomena in and around the Trump campaign and the beginning of his administration (phenomena that do not show signs of abating) have brought home the force of a return of extreme reactions with the urgency of a clear-and-present danger. Trump has shown himself to be the personification of the other that others typically keep within as a repository of repressed or suppressed tendencies. He has expressed, enacted, or authorized, if not aided and abetted, such tendencies in an aggressive and blatant form.[15] His popular support, which ranged from one-third to almost one-half of the electorate, raises complex and disturbing questions about the state of the nation, including the large number of Republicans in Congress who continued public endorsement of him at least in the interest of furthering an anti–New Deal agenda and retaining power.[16]

A few prominent series of incidents warrant special mention as evidence of the kind of misogyny, prejudice, scapegoating, and authoritarianism Trump supports or furthers. One comes from his campaign, and the others during his first six months in office. A little over a week before the November 8 election, a now famous or infamous *Access Hollywood* video emerged showing a fifty-nine-year-old Trump bantering with Billy Bush and bragging about the way his celebrity status enabled him to do whatever he liked with women, including grabbing them by their private parts (for which Trump used a vulgar term). When a series of women emerged soon after to testify to their own experiences with Trump, a number of them indicated clearly that Trump's assertions in the video referred to his actual behavior with them. Trump immediately threatened to sue them after the election, but this—like other threats or claims, for example, the assertion that he would disclose his tax returns after the election—proved to be campaign "rhetoric" that was little more than intimidation or hot air. He was more attached to fulfilling his more extreme, misguided promises, such as building a wall between the United States and Mexico, restricting or even banning immigration from certain Muslim-majority countries, and rolling back regulations on the private sector, including those on fossil fuel production and on banks where the earlier weakness of regulations contributed significantly to the financial crisis of 2008. Trump has had a positive and pronounced investment in the term "extreme," as in "extreme vetting" of immigrants, a term that obscures the role of existing and often effective procedures and easily shades into "excessive," opening the way to harassment and even torture.

On August 11 and 12, 2017, toward the end of Trump's first half year as president, a large, militant, "Unite the Right" demonstration was held in Charlottesville, Virginia, composed of far- (or "alt"-) right groups (some

---

15. In contrast to the tack taken by some Trump apologists, the point here is not what his friends think or whether Trump is really a bigot in his "heart of hearts." It is rather what he says and what his behavior manifests. These are not simply externalities or problems of communication and "optics." Especially in a public figure, they are part and parcel of what he is and what he represents.

16. A stunning statistic is that Trump received the vote of 63 percent of white men and 53 percent of white women.

armed and armor-clad). The constellation included white supremacists (or nationalists), racists, the KKK, and neo-Nazis. They were opposed by an even larger group of counter-demonstrators that included activist antifascists as well as many antiracist, peaceful participants, including a significant number of clergy. Reportedly apprehensive about numerous right-wingers who were more heavily armed than the police, the latter stayed on the sidelines during outbreaks of violence and intervened to dissipate the crowd only after many skirmishes. Most commentators, including certain Republicans in Congress (even Senators Orrin Hatch and Marco Rubio), saw the violence as provoked by the far-right groups who were the organizers of the demonstration. In an extreme incident, an automobile driven by James Alex Fields, an exponent of white supremacist and racist views, was intentionally directed into a group of counter-demonstrators, killing one person and injuring twenty others. President Trump commented weakly or even evasively on the events only late in the day when he condemned "in the strongest possible terms this egregious display of hatred, bigotry, and violence on many sides. On many sides." His largely scripted, deceptively "many-sided" comments seemed inspired by the views of far-right figures in his own administration (including Stephen Bannon, Stephen Miller, and Sebastian Gorka [characterized by Dana Milbank of the *Washington Post* as Trump's "id"]) along with others coming from Breitbart or Fox media and in line with views of supporters whose presence was evident among the demonstrators (a number of whom wore Trump's signature MAGA ["Make America Great Again"] caps). In marked contrast to Trump's former comments on Muslim-related violence, which was dwarfed in the United States by home-grown acts of violence and terror, he did not present what had occurred as a form of domestic terrorism fomented by the far right. The former KKK leader David Duke, a vocal Trump supporter present at the demonstration (about whom Trump claimed not to know anything when told of his support during the campaign), was interviewed as expressing the view that people like himself had voted for Trump to enact what was affirmed by "Unite the Right" demonstrators. In a tweet following Trump's remarks, he advised Trump to "remember it was White Americans who put you in the presidency, not radical leftists." Many others on the "alt-right" saw Trump's amalgamating comment and accompanying tweets as in effect not only omitting any specific criticism of them but endorsing their actions.[17]

---

17. See Joe Heim et al., "One Dead as Car Strikes Crowds amid Protests of White Nationalist Gathering in Charlottesville; Two Police Die in Helicopter Crash," *Washington Post*, August 13, 2017, https://www.washingtonpost.com/local/fights-in-advance-of-saturday-protest-in-charlottesville/2017/08/12/155fb636-7f13-11e7-83c7-5bd5460f0d7e_story.html?utm_term=.38b271dca0ac

On August 14, two days after the events, Trump, under pressure from various quarters, atypically adhered to a prepared script. Subsequent to an enumeration of what he saw as the successes of the economy during the first half year of his presidency, he at last mentioned the groups specifically responsible for the racism, hatred, and violence in Charlottesville, to wit, white supremacists, the KKK, and neo-Nazis. He did not mention the "alt-right" or the role in his White House of Stephen Bannon (who as its director had declared Breitbart to be the "platform" of the alt-right) and others, despite the rising call for the dismissal of Bannon as a top adviser.

However, immediately evoking widespread condemnation is the way Trump reverted to type and seemed spontaneously to express what his scripted comments a day earlier had thinly veiled. In a press conference on August 15, Trump doubled down in turning to false equivalency by blaming "both sides" for the violence, referring to what he termed the "alt-left," and even finding "a lot of people" among the far right who were for Trump at the demonstration "to innocently protest" (with no reference to white supremacists, KKK, and neo-Nazis as prominent presences among "a lot of people"). He also failed to mention that many of the far-right demonstrators had come from out of state armed and ready for violence. The open question at this juncture was whether various figures, including Trump's Republican supporters in Congress and in the media, who were ready to part ways with Trump's rash and irresponsible words, were also willing to name Trump as their purveyor and to distance themselves from him as well as, ostensibly, from what he was propounding.[18]

Yet Trump also has a wily, self-aggrandizing ability to promote himself while confusing others and to leave them in doubt about whether they are witnessing a clever strategy, an unbalanced floundering, or a disorienting fusion of both. He has been praised for his deceptive ability to appear as

---

(accessed August 13, 2017); and Amy B. Wang, "One Group Loved Trump's Remarks about Charlottesville: White Supremacists," *Washington Post*, August 13, 2017, https://www.washingtonpost.com/news/post-nation/wp/2017/08/13/one-group-loved-trumps-remarks-about-charlottesville-white-supremacists/?utm_term=.04c45f65142d (accessed August 13, 2017).

18. On August 22, in the wake of the events in Charlottesville, Trump held what many saw as an inappropriate campaign rally in Phoenix, returning to the site of his first major event during the campaign. His speech in Phoenix contained many false or misleading statements; regarding the events in Charlottesville on Saturday, August 12. He quite simply and directly said: "We condemn in the strongest possible terms this egregious display of hatred, bigotry and violence"—but he failed to include the crucial, leveling qualification "on many sides. On many sides." See Chris Clizza, "Donald Trump's 57 Most Outrageous Quotes from his Arizona Speech," *CNN Politics*, August 23, 2017, http://www.cnn.com/2017/08/23/politics/donald-trump-arizona/index.html (accessed August 23, 2017).

a straight-talking "outsider" and to speak directly to the needs and desires of his audience. But all too often this ability reinforces scapegoating and prejudice, even taking the form of shockingly uncensored, tendentious, or even mendacious, immature behavior. He often seems like a paradigm case of "acting out" with little or no attempt to "work through" difficult problems and dubious propensities. In a seeming paradox, the more outlandish the falsehood or lie and the more it is brazenly repeated, the greater the probability it will be believed or accepted by those who share one's proclivities and prejudices but on their own may be unable or unwilling to flout well-established conventions or contravene facts in a flagrant manner.

Perhaps the most notorious but far from the only instance is Trump's key if not principal role in spreading the extreme, arguably racist falsehoods of the so-called birther movement in an attempt to delegitimate Barack Obama as president. Despite conclusive evidence to the contrary, Trump and other "birthers" denied Barack Obama's American citizenship and became fixated on the issue of producing his birth certificate. In important ways, this orientation was similar to the fixation on Hillary Clinton's almost compulsively discussed hacked emails, disseminated on a daily basis before the election by WikiLeaks, which served as a conduit for those (including the Russian government) opposed to Clinton and favoring Trump. The targeting of Clinton's emails, often diminishing the importance of other issues (such as repeated and at times normalizing reports of instances of Trump's outlandish behavior), was shared by Trump, his followers, his Republican allies, and at times the media, including mainstream outlets.

Trump feels he must always be in the right and refuses to admit "mistakes," which typically are not simple mistakes but highly charged, often prejudicial acts or assertions. For him such an admission would be tantamount to displaying a sign of "weakness" characteristic of a "loser." Trump invariably wants to be a "winner" and at times will not acknowledge losses or tries to "spin" them as in reality victories. Hence he tends to "double down" or intensify insistence on false claims, at best surrounding them with cagey reservations, evident diversions, or at times actual or imagined scare quotes allowing projection away from himself onto others. Never to admit "mistakes," prejudicial distortions, or losses is to preclude learning from experience or changing one's proclivities, notably with respect to the institutional and normative requirements of an office such as the U.S. presidency (in contradistinction to that of the aspiring dictator à la Vladimir Putin or his analogues). Trump also does not seem to realize that behaving as if one were above the law is not a legitimate form of executive privilege. As a "reality TV" star and throughout the presidential campaign into his presidency,

Trump has often appeared to be a man possessed, in his fantasy-laden animus against supposedly threatening, alien others and in his consuming need for the uncritical support of adulatory associates and of large cheering crowds to assure his popularity and identity. His seemingly addictive need for campaign rallies, which were continued even after he won the election, pointed both to a dangerously effective political tactic, stirring up his "base," and to an ego-enhancing scene in which speaker and audience could bind together in a regressive, emotive expression of hate, scapegoating, and at times near-violent elation.[19]

Trump's interminable series of campaign rallies could at times evoke toxic, violent sentiments in an enthusiastic crowd. Animosity was often directed at an enclosed group of reporters, assailed in one instance by shouts sounding like "USA" but with some chanting "Jew S A." Federal circuit courts allowed the continuance of two suits against Trump for provocation to violence. On April 1, 2017, a U.S. district judge in Kentucky allowed plaintiffs to move forward with a suit brought by three protesters who were assaulted at a Trump campaign rally in Kentucky by members of the audience (one of whom was a known member of a white nationalist group) after Trump had called out from the podium: "Get 'em out of here." The judge found that Trump had "at least implicitly encouraged the use of violence or lawless action."[20] At a rally in Iowa on February 1, 2016, Trump told the crowd: "There may be somebody with tomatoes in the audience. So if you see somebody getting ready to throw a tomato, knock the crap out of them, would you? Seriously. Okay? Just knock the hell—I promise you, I will pay for the legal fees. I promise, I promise. It won't be so much 'cause the courts agree with us too." Trump later reneged on the promise.[21]

Without drawing direct causal lines, one may also mention the assault on *Guardian* reporter Ben Jacobs on May 24, 2017, by billionaire Montana

---

19. A scarcely credible adulatory incident was the first full meeting of Trump's cabinet in mid-July. Like a self-satisfied, dictatorial schoolmaster, Trump went around the large table, expecting and receiving servile encomia from cabinet members, who poured out not only childish praise but, in the case of (soon-to-be-dismissed) chief of staff Reince Priebus, an expression of feeling blessed by serving the Trump agenda. See Julie Hirschfeld Davis, "Trump's Cabinet, with a Prod, Extols the 'Blessing' of Serving Him," *New York Times,* June 12, 2017, https://www.nytimes.com/2017/06/12/us/politics/trump-boasts-of-record-setting-pace-of-activity.html?mcubz=0 (accessed June 13, 2017).

20. See Alice Ollstein, "Judge: Trump Incited Violence against Protesters at Kentucky Rally," *TPM News,* April 1, 2017, http://talkingpointsmemo.com/news/trump-rally-violence-court-incitemet (accessed April 2, 2017).

21. See Sam Reisman, "Trump Tells Crowd to 'Knock the Crap Out' of Protesters, Offers to Pay Legal Fees," *Mediate,* February 1, 2016, http://www.mediaite.com/online/trump-tells-crowd-to-knock-the-crap-out-of-protesters-offers-to-pay-legal-fees/.

Republican candidate for Congress, Greg Gianforte. The incident, which left Jacobs visibly shaken, was spun and falsified by Gianforte's campaign manager to appear as if it had been provoked by the aggressive behavior of a "liberal" reporter. The record was set straight both by an audiotape and by multiple witnesses to the event, including three reporters for Fox News, who testified to Gianforte's throat-grabbing, body-slamming, punch-throwing explosion. The latter's reaction was evoked by a once-repeated, mild-mannered question asking how Gianforte responded to the Congressional Budget Office's just released (and largely negative) report on the Republican health care act, a report Gianforte had earlier said he was waiting to see. Gianforte was charged by a local sheriff, who had donated to his campaign, with misdemeanor assault, and an "understanding" judge spared him any jail time, fined him $385, and sentenced him to community service and twenty hours of sessions for anger management. In what was apparently not intended as an ironic gesture, Gianforte pledged to donate $50,000 to the Committee to Protect Journalists. Trump on his late May tour abroad said in passing: "Great win in Montana."[22] Soon after, a more extreme act of violence, which evoked significantly different responses than the Gianforte incident, was the shooting and wounding of Republican Congressman and House Majority Whip Steve Scalise as well as four others, including two local police officers assigned to protect Scalise. The mass shooting took place at a baseball practice session in Arlington, Virginia, in preparation for a charity game the following day. The shooter, killed by the wounded police officers, was identified as James T. Hodgkinson, a sixty-six-year-old resident of Illinois and reportedly an anti-Trump supporter of Bernie Sanders. Sanders as well as other members of Congress and President Trump strongly condemned the action. Trump called for unity, while Sanders is reported as saying that "real change can only come about through nonviolent action." A shocking statistic is that in the United States in 2017 up to the above case, in 165 days there had been 154 mass shootings of four or more people (195 if the shooter is

22. See Matt Volz, "APNewsBreak: Gianforte to Plead Guilty to Assault Charge," *Washington Post,* June 9, 2107, https://www.washingtonpost.com/national/apnewsbreak-gianforte-to-plead-guilty-to-assault-charge/2017/06/09/6039ec42-4d5b-11e7-987c-42ab5745db2e_story.html?utm_term=.8d42f2455b49 (accessed June 10, 2017), Jessica Taylor, "Republican Gianforte Wins Montana House Race despite Assault Charge," *NPR,* May 26, 2017, http://www.npr.org/2017/05/26/530103144/republican-gianforte-wins-montana-house-race-amid-assault-charge (accessed May 26, 2017); and Sam Levin and Julia Carrie Wong, "Greg Gianforte Sentenced to Community Service for Assaulting *Guardian* Reporter," *The Guardian,* June 12, 2017, https://www.theguardian.com/us-news/2017/jun/12/republican-greg-gianforte-sentenced-assaulting-guardian-reporter (accessed June 13, 2017).

included), which could in one sense be taken as a continual form of domestic terrorism.[23]

As should become evident in the course of this book, the question is not whether there are serious fault-lines in existing social structures, or genuine sources of discontent, evident in the depressed economic conditions of significant segments of the population and epitomized in the contaminated drinking water of Flint, Michigan. Rather the question is how one is to address these problems in other than discriminatory and exacerbating ways. One thing the Trump phenomenon has illustrated is that political correctness may in certain situations be correct as well as a deterrent to public manifestations of what would be objectionable even on a private level. And a virtue of not allowing hatred and insult to be expressed and even celebrated or cheered in public discourse is that kept to oneself such twisted sentiments may at least remain shamefaced.

Not all of Trump's irate and at times belligerent followers accept his prejudices. And, despite evident unwillingness to place themselves in question by admitting ways Trump may have deceived them, notably with respect to the promise of returning jobs in declining or increasingly automated industries, as well as medical care and tax reforms supposedly benefiting them, many of his supporters may warrant empathy. Empathy or compassion may be called for especially when supporters are victims of injustice and suffer from actual hardship or unfairness as well as from ideological self-deception, notably about what they will actually get from a President Trump and his combination of establishment affiliates and far- or (euphemistically termed) "alt-right" operatives. Trump and his "surrogates" at times did not explicitly fend off the latter and might solicit or encourage them (with Trump even appointing former Breitbart CEO Stephen Bannon as a principal security adviser). Establishment Republicans, whom Trump and his "movement" explicitly excoriated and rejected but who often, even after undergoing Trump's scorn and putting forth "never-Trump" rhetoric, quickly resurfaced, at times as compliant rationalizers or sycophants, in order to retain power and pursue a long-standing anti–New Deal agenda.[24] Despite compassion for those

---

23. See Michael D. Shear et al., "Steve Scalise among 5 Shot at Baseball Field; Suspect Is Dead," *New York Times,* June 14, 2017, https://www.nytimes.com/2017/06/14/us/steve-scalise-congress-shot-alexandria-virginia.html?mcubz=0 (accessed June 14, 2017); and Christopher Ingraham, "The GOP Baseball Shooting Is the 154th Mass Shooting This Year," *Washington Post,* June 14, 2017, https://www.washingtonpost.com/news/wonk/wp/2017/06/14/the-gop-baseball-shooting-is-the-154th-mass-shooting-this-year/?utm_term=.6953f13a2ffb (accessed June 14, 2017).

24. For an analysis of the growing obstructionism, extremism, and rejection of compromise in the Republican Party that helped prepare the way for Trump's electoral victory, see the bipartisan

with cause for real grievances, the question remains whether what Trump and certain of his followers at times stand for, as clearly expressed during his campaign and his early actions as president, does not deserve acceptance or affirmation but calls instead for criticism, resistance, and organized opposition.

In the initial stage of Trump's presidency in early 2017, one could still hope for a shift in orientation and an opportunity to applaud its success. But his words and behavior in this period were not promising.[25] One inauspicious sign was that Trump resisted resolving his own conflicts of interest or disclosing his tax returns, which might have helped to indicate the nature and extent of his business dealings, obligations, debts, and other involvements and provide some idea of how his acts as president might serve these interests, notably with respect to Russian and other foreign financial or government-related institutions. Among his cabinet members and close advisers are billionaires,

---

study of Thomas E. Mann and Norman J. Ornstein, *It's Even Worse Than It Was*, new and expanded ed. (2012; New York: Basic Books, 2016). It is important not to focus all attention on Trump the objectionable individual because this would deflect attention from the Republican Party and the way in which it turned into a wayward breeding ground in which Trump could become the extreme but well-fertilized and insufficiently opposed outcome. See, for example, Alex Pareen, "This Is Normal," *Fusion*, June 29, 2017, http://fusion.kinja.com/this-is-normal-1796496747 (accessed July 2, 2017). The more complex issue is what motivates members of the public who continued to support Trump to varying degrees, including those who voted him into office and the more restricted group that identifies with him to the point of not being turned away whatever he says or does.

25. On the relation between Trump and Stephen Bannon, see Joshua Green, *Devil's Bargain: Steve Bannon, Donald Trump, and the Storming of the Presidency* (New York: Penguin Books, 2017). At the February 23, 2017, annual meeting of the Conservative Political Action Conference (CPAC), Bannon emerged from the shadows to give a rare public speech. He enunciated basic foundations of his own ideology and to a significant extent that of the Trump administration. They included economic nationalism (in Trump's own preferred term, "America first"), national sovereignty (including shows of strength, intensive competition with other nations, and defense of supposedly Western values), identification of the "corporatist, global media" as the opposition party (for Trump, "the enemy of the people"), protection of the borders with respect to immigrants to preserve "our culture" and "reason for being," and "the deconstruction of the administrative state." The latter implied extreme deregulation of the privatized economy and the appointment as cabinet heads of individuals committed to dismantling their own agencies. (See Max Fisher, "Bannon's Vision of a 'Deconstruction of the Administrative State'," *New York Times*, February 25, 2017, A13.) Bannon, who has indicated a predilection for Lenin and Satan, conflated deconstruction with dismantling, disruption, and destruction, a notion that is very different from Derrida's use of deconstruction (as well as my own). Under pressure from the recently appointed National Security Advisor, Lieutenant General H. R. McMaster, Bannon was removed from his official position on the NSC on April 5, 2017, but he apparently retains influence over Trump on an unofficial basis. Bannon like some others (even in more liberal or progressive circles) dichotomizes between economic and identity politics. But an economic nationalism conjoined with discrimination in immigration policy is itself a form of white (even white supremacist) identity politics. And a fixation on jobs is misleading if it stresses statistics in the abstract and ignores the quality of jobs and the question of to whom it is that more desirable jobs are being channeled.

multimillionaires, generals, and family members (such as daughter Ivanka and her very wealthy husband, Jared Kushner), including both denizens of the "Wall Street swamp" he deceptively promised to drain and certain individuals who have indicated dedication to undermining, deregulating, and privatizing what they are supposed to protect or regulate (the environment, the disadvantaged, public education, a less prejudicial prison system, financial institutions, health care, and even diplomacy).[26]

At this juncture, I shall turn from a discussion of particular features of the beginning of the Trump phenomenon that accord with key aspects of my overall argument and return to them only briefly in the course of my account. I shall conclude this introduction by stressing more general considerations, beginning with a fittingly parodic allusion to a pointed moment in Samuel Beckett's *Murphy* when the narrator informs the reader that the time has come to discuss what must be called, for want of a better word, the protagonist's mind—his way of thinking and its relation to practices he advocates. Trump is in basic ways an exponent of thought that resists criticism and self-criticism. Insofar as critical thinking is an ideal of the humanities, especially for those who affirm the role of critical reflection in humanistic research, Trump, like his associates, is no advocate of the humanities. His use of language is nondialogic and instrumental, aimed at bullying his adversaries or seducing, convincing, and playing into or aggravating the preconceptions of followers. (It is disheartening that these preconceptions, reinforced by an uncritical attachment to or identification with the leader, may be so ingrained that nothing Trump does seems able to shake them, at least in his "base" comprised of upwards of 30 percent of the electorate. Many of these seem unconcerned or ignorant about the nature of threats to a constitutional democracy either domestically in the behavior of Trump and his associates or in the incursions into the democratic process by Russia or other hostile foreign powers.)

Trump seems always to be campaigning and has but one basic speech, which he repeats time and again, often seeing a prepared script as a distraction and adding variations to his set piece that often amount to recently heard, unfounded claims picked up from right-wing media. His manner of addressing an audience is a dubious, cajoling kind of call-and-response, requiring not critical engagement but mutual affective reinforcement of foregone

---

26. Ironically, the three generals in Trump's cabinet—Secretary of Defense James Mattis, National Security Advisor H. R. McMaster, and (for a time) Chief of Staff John F. Kelly—have been widely seen as three of the saner, more "adult," and diplomatic figures who may help to restrain Trump's more erratic and extreme tendencies.

conclusions and prejudices. It is often punctuated by chants (the most famous of which are "Build the wall," with respect to Mexico, and "Lock her up," referring to Hillary Clinton). Here one might see an affinity between the reality TV star, a role Trump continued to play, and the TV evangelist, both of whom may be con artists or hucksters, attesting to the confluence of certain variants of evangelical religion, unregulated capitalism, and right-wing politics, along with elements of a social-Darwinist, winners-versus-losers ideology. (The latter traits also appear in a more sober and seemingly respectable form in Vice President Mike Pence, who has referred to himself as first a Christian, second a conservative, and third a Republican.)[27] Trump detests criticism of himself or his policies and demands loyalty of his associates, often leading them to defend assertions that are indefensible, at times by "walking them back" and (mis)translating them into less manifestly false or offensive statements. The intellectual contortions of his associates or surrogates in trying to make him credible, notably adviser Kellyanne Conway and press secretary Sean Spicer (replaced as of July 21, 2017, by the even more diversionary, dismissive, professedly evangelical Sarah Huckabee Sanders), may be destined to become legendary.[28]

---

27. Trump has had widespread support especially from right-wing white "evangelicals," including Jerry Falwell and his son. Even after the disclosure of the *Access Hollywood* video and the president's questionable responses to the events of August 12, 2017, in Charlottesville, and despite his abandonment by leaders in the corporate and artistic worlds, he by and large kept the adherence of his hand-picked council of foremost evangelicals. One current speculation was that evangelicals cared less about Christian morality in general (of which Trump was hardly an exemplar) than about affinities with the far-right Tea Party, appointment of conservative Supreme Court justices like Neil Gorsuch, and antiabortion and other right-wing policies. See, for example, Joanna Walters and Sam Morris, "Trump's Evangelical Panel Remains Intact as Others Disband," *The Guardian,* August 19, 2017, https://www.theguardian.com/us-news/2017/aug/18/donald-trump-evangelicals-charlottes ville (accessed August 19, 2017). One should not conflate largely white evangelical apologists for Trump with evangelicals who in word and deed manifested other than merely rhetorical support for essential religious and moral principles bound up with the civil rights movement, notably Bishop William Barber of North Carolina, for whom Trump's evangelical supporters were hypocrites who misappropriated the term "evangelical."

28. The typical role of yes-man Pence has been to stand, literally or figuratively, behind Trump and to shake his head up and down in approval of whatever it is Trump says, however dubious, as if to confer on the president's words approval, legitimacy, or even benediction. On Pence's questionable connections with Christian supremacy movements and in particular with Erik Prince, founder of the government services and security firm Blackwater, brother of Betsy DeVos, and like her, a major contributor to the Trump campaign, see Jeremy Scahill, "Mike Pence Will Be the Most Powerful Christian Supremacist in U.S. History," *The Intercept,* November 16, 2016, https://theintercept.com/2016/11/15/mike-pence-will-be-the-most-powerful-christian-supremacist-in-us-history/ (accessed May 17, 2017). Like some other commentators, Scahill places in question the "reasonable-adult-cum-innocent-bystander" status often ascribed to Pence, for example, in the case of knowledge about Mike Flynn and contacts with Russia. See also Adam Entous et al., "Blackwater Founder Held Secret Seychelles Meeting to Establish Trump-Putin Back Channel," *Washington Post,*

For Trump, as for Carl Schmitt (who metamorphosed from Weimar critic and constitution builder into leading Nazi jurist), the basic political binary divides friends from enemies, notably the loyal from the disloyal. One may well argue that this opposition, or at least distinction, applies at best to personal relations. Its extension to politics is dangerous, for it places loyalty over competence and personalizes issues that should be resolved on other grounds, both principled and pragmatic. Trump, on the contrary, values most highly the loyalty of his friends cum political associates (for example, in the appointment of the irascible and inflammatory General Michael Flynn as a chief security adviser, a post from which Trump was constrained against the grain to dismiss him, reportedly because of a lie Flynn told to Vice President Mike Pence concerning Flynn's behavior with respect to undeclared contacts with problematic Russians, including Russian ambassador Sergey Kislyak, seen by U.S. intelligence agencies as associated with Russian intelligence networks—not the behavior itself, which Trump defended along with Flynn's "nice-guy" status and suitability for the role of top security adviser).[29] Trump typically rewards loyalty, at times despite the limited or nonexistent competence of the recipient in the pertinent area (for example, that of Flynn, Ben Carson in housing, Rick Perry in energy, or arguably even Jeff [Jeffrey Beauregard]

April 3, 2017, https://www.washingtonpost.com/world/national-security/blackwater-founder-held-secret-seychelles-meeting-to-establish-trump-putin-back-channel/2017/04/03/95908a08-1648-11e7-ada0-1489b735b3a3_story.html?utm_term=.0aef7fec2c32 (accessed May 15, 2017); and Ursula Faw, "Mike Pence Is Toast: Anonymous Letter to WaPo Shows the Role of Eric [*sic*] Prince in Trump-Russia, *Daily Kos*, May 26, 2917, http://www.dailykos.com/stories/2017/5/26/1666425/-Mike-Pence-Is-Toast-Anonymous-Letter-To-WaPo-Shows-The-Role-Of-Eric-Prince-In-Trump-Russia (accessed May 27, 2017). While carefully avoiding any direct confrontation, Pence, toward the end of the initial six months of the Trump presidency, began distancing himself from Trump on certain issues (such as the veracity of reports concerning Russian interference in the electoral process) and was widely seen as beginning to lay a more independent basis for his own political future.

29. Flynn, who felt he had been made into a scapegoat, resurfaced on March 30, 2017, apparently offering to testify before relevant congressional investigating committees and federal agencies if he were offered immunity from possible criminal prosecution. See Mark Mazzatti and Matthew Rosenberg, "Michael Flynn to Testify before Congress in Exchange for Immunity," *New York Times*, March 30, 2017, https://www.nytimes.com/2017/03/30/us/politics/michael-flynn-congress-immunity-russia.html?_r=0 (accessed March 31, 2017). There was no immediate acceptance of his offer. It is tempting to suspect that Trump's attachment to Flynn may be due less to the latter's "nice-guy" appeal than to the possibility that Flynn may be able to disclose things, especially about the involvement of Trump and associates with the Russians, that Trump would very much prefer to conceal. Others involved in the Trump campaign who had questionable ties to Russia or other foreign entities included early adviser Carter Page, campaign manager for three months in 2016 Paul Manafort (who had received considerable sums from Russia and other foreign governments), and Jeff Sessions with respect to conversations with the Russian ambassador Sergey Kislyak not disclosed during testimony before a Senate committee concerning his appointment as attorney general. Flynn himself, whom Trump never stopped supporting, had to register retrospectively as a foreign agent because of his ties with Turkey as well as his undisclosed reception of money from Turkey and Russia.

Sessions, the extremely controversial attorney general, an early member of the Trump team who had to recuse himself in any investigation of the campaign because of his involvement in it and, in the eyes of many, because he had lied under oath to Congress about his communications with the Russian ambassador). Given Trump's narcissism, it is less often a question of his loyalty to others than of theirs to him.[30] The counterpart to rewarding loyalty is condemnation and revenge aimed at critics or perceived opponents, including the mainstream media, members of which Trump terms "enemies of the people." These words hark back, intentionally or not, to lethal views run amok in the terroristic phase of the French Revolution and in the purges by dictators such as Hitler and Stalin. It is also noteworthy that Hitler demanded that each member of the German armed forces (*Wehrmacht*) swear an oath of personal allegiance to him and not to the constitution, an oath that became effective on August 2, 1934, when Hitler combined the offices of president and chancellor. Trump's demands remain informal, but it is arguable that he tends to see his role not so much as a constitutional president but as a would-be dictator or at least an order-shouting, hire-and-fire, authoritarian CEO of a big corporation (an attitude shared by his security adviser Bannon).

A favorite technique of "argument," common to Trump and his "surrogates" or associates, might be termed "pivot and project." The technique or tactic is to avoid the critical question being addressed to you (notably by representatives of the media), pivot toward a preferred, often endlessly repeated "talking point" that undermines your opponent or adversary (such as Clinton's emails or putative "crookedness" and the reporting of possible collusion of Trump associates with Russians interfering in the election as fake media news about a fake or fabricated story), and project onto that opponent what is typical of your own approach (such as lying, disseminating "fake news," or victimizing others). Trump is, in popular terms, a prototypical "con artist" who makes hollow promises, dissembles and manifests other than compassionate concern for the suffering and needs of others, and relies on the distorted ideas spread by far-right, often conspiracy theory–inspired, "nonmainstream" but often closely followed media. Yet he seemingly has

---

30. In July 2017, Trump started to berate his first major campaign supporter in the Senate, Jeff Sessions, indicating that the latter should resign. The reason was Sessions's self-recusal in the Russia investigation and other matters related to the campaign in which Sessions had an important role. Trump believed that, by recusing himself, Sessions was "weak" and "disloyal," failing to "protect" Trump against investigation, notably by Special Counsel Robert Mueller. Commentators who were not Trump surrogates or uncritical supporters found that Sessions had taken the obvious proper course of action and that Trump once again (as in his firing of FBI Director James Comey over what Trump termed "the Russia thing") was seemingly trying to obstruct justice.

been able to convince his followers that he not only listens to and fully under-stands their plaints, indeed "feels their pain," but alone stands forth as their heartfelt spokesperson and even their savior. Well known from the practice of authoritarians and dictators is the "big-lie" technique or frequent repeti-tion of false, misleading, often egregious (mis)statements, especially con-cerning something beyond the purview or the ordinary experience of people and backed by seeming authority. This technique may well in time have the effect of making falsehoods or lies be taken as true, at least by those whose preconceptions and narcissistic needs induce them to identify with, believe in, and reinforce the credibility of a hollow idol as leader.[31]

A particular but perhaps symptomatic and paradigmatic feature of Trump's thought process and his way of communicating with others, notably his de-voted followers, is his reliance on "tweets." These media bites are confined to 140 characters. Trump's tweets are important because they reveal basic ways his mind "works," including when they are outrageous and insulting at-tacks on critics that are fit for inclusion in scandal-mongering tabloids such as the Trump-friendly *National Enquirer* (owned and run by Trump's longtime friend and supporter David Pecker).[32] Trump believes that the "tweet" mode of communication creates a sense of immediacy in his contact with others,

---

31. See the cautionary accounts in Federico Finchelstein, *From Fascism to Populism* (Oakland: University of California Press) and in Timothy Snyder, *On Tyranny: Twenty Lessons from the Twenti-eth Century* (New York: Penguin Random House, 2017). A fact-checking article entitled "President Trump's List of False and Misleading Claims Tops 1,000," by Glenn Kessler, Michelle Ye Hee, and Meg Kelly, appeared in the *Washington Post*, August 22, 2017, https://www.washingtonpost.com/news/fact-checker/wp/2017/08/22/president-trumps-list-of-false-and-misleading-claims-tops-1000/?utm_term=.e314e19b6e63 (accessed August 23, 2017). It noted that, as of the date of the article's publication, the president averaged nearly five false or misleading claims a day. More than thirty had been repeated three times or more, including the statement that the Affordable Care Act was "essentially dead" (repeated fifty times). The more outlandish falsehoods came from rehashed campaign rhetoric and included the claims that Hillary Clinton gave 20 percent of the U.S. uranium supply to Russia and that the deputy FBI director got $700,000 from Clinton. Many of the repeats were contentions that had been previously debunked and were easily determined to be false or misleading by anyone concerned about ascertaining the truth. Increasingly reported on has been the role in disseminating "fake news," often furnished by Russian operatives, of unregulated and misleadingly self-styled "neutral" (yet profit-oriented) media platforms, notably the at-times unholy techno-trinity of Facebook, Google, and Twitter.

32. See Jeffrey Toobin, "The *National Enquirer*'s Fervor for Trump," *New Yorker*, July 3, 2017, http://www.newyorker.com/magazine/2017/07/03/the-national-enquirers-fervor-for-trump (ac-cessed July 3, 2017). Pecker has apparently blocked the publication in his journal of any material det-rimental to Trump, including a story about his affair (during his marriage to his wife Melania) with a former *Playboy* Playmate of the Year. Without sufficient confirmation of details, it has emerged that Trump may at times receive assistance on his tweets from affiliates. But the tweets arguably indicate his associative, uncensored, often fact-free way of thinking and in any case are put forward publicly in his name. They are also taken legally as his pronouncements, which affiliates at times try to "gentrify" or spin and twist as somehow plausible or credible.

and it transcends or even fends off conventional media, such as television or newspapers, whether printed or online. The tweet, however, may also be unmediated by fact checks or critical thought and self-criticism. A Trump tweet is not comparable to a well-crafted, thoughtful aphorism or epigram, and Trump is not a Montaigne or Nietzsche for the common man. He typically tweets what first comes to a self-centered mind fed by prejudices and preconceptions. And he may simply repeat unchecked and unfounded allegations of right-wing media hosts who are Trump fans and may well trade in conspiracy theories (Alex Jones, Mark Levin, or Sean Hannity, for example). Trump's uncritical listening or occasional reading seems largely confined to right-wing media, especially the Breitbart and Fox networks, whose slanted "talking points" he often simply repeats. With respect to the "mainstream" media that are typically scapegoated, he tends to sacrifice the messengers by blaming them for whatever negative news they broadcast about him. Projection is rampant in that he is inclined to blame the media, as he blames others (especially critics and perceived adversaries), for what typifies to a far greater extent his own behavior, such as a reliance on unsubstantiated assertions or even "fake news." However unfounded or offensive their content may be, his tweets are presumably followed by millions, many of whom seem to take him at his word (or at least "seriously" if not "literally," in a self-serving opposition misleadingly invoked during the campaign and continued into the Trump presidency). Moreover, conventional media are constrained to follow and comment on his tweets, especially when they are the sole source for learning his views on various issues. (Some supporters, such as House Speaker Paul Ryan, claim not to pay any attention to them, which is tantamount to saying they do not care what he says or does so long as he subscribes to their own agenda.) Clamping down on the dissemination of news, typical of autocracies, has also taken the form of not holding press conferences or holding them only infrequently or at times in restricted or even closed sessions that may not be filmed or even recorded.

A salient feature of the tweet is that it requires a very short attention span and does not allow for extended thought, prominently including questioning give-and-take and critical or self-critical reflection. Trump's tweets are typically hit-and-run comments that are one-way, nondialogic, at times insulting pronouncements. His tweets often become a form of cyber bullying reminiscent of the onstage bullying that allowed Trump to play the strong man he admired in Putin, enabling him to blow away his Republican rivals for the presidential nomination. Trump apparently does not read books or extended pieces of writing. The tweet may typify his thought and perhaps be symptomatic of thought and attention for a significant number of others in a media-drenched, speed-obsessed environment where analogues of the tweet are phenomena such as talking points, "bullets," channel surfing, skimming, and perhaps even fast food (for which Trump has a declared penchant).

Although I attempt to make them pertinent to the larger issues discussed in the book, comments concerning Trump and his team must at times be time bound and provisional, in good part because what seems like a hastily assembled (or dissembled), ramshackle saga, with elements of the spy story, the film noir, and absurdist theater, continues to have various twists and turns on an almost daily basis.[33] But basic patterns and possibilities seemed well established in the initial months of the Trump presidency as well as the campaign, and many of them enact to a dangerous degree how not to understand and treat others.

A version of chapter 3 appeared in *History and Theory* 55 (October 2016): 371–95, and a version of chapter 5 appeared in *History and Theory* 56 (March 2017): 98–113. A version of chapter 6 appeared in *Do the Humanities*

---

33. A major event after the firing of James Comey was the appointment of Robert Mueller as special counsel to investigate possible relations between the Trump team and Russian affiliates, notably in the attempt to sway the election against Clinton. Mueller soon became the more focused object of Trump's obsessive animus with respect to the Russia investigation, including an apparent desire to fire Mueller. This desire was counteracted on many fronts, including congressional efforts to protect Mueller. Many Trump associates were apparent objects of inquiry or investigation by Mueller and FBI agents, including Michael Flynn, Paul Manafort, Donald Trump Jr., and Jared Kushner as well as possibly Trump himself. See, for example, Amber Phillips, "Jared Kushner Trying to Secretly Talk to the Russians Is the Biggest Billow of Smoke Yet," *Washington Post*, May 26, 2017, https://www.washingtonpost.com/news/the-fix/wp/2017/05/26/jared-kushner-trying-to-se cretly-talk-to-the-russians-is-the-biggest-billow-of-smoke-yet/?utm_term=.62815d904496 (accessed May 27, 2017). According to Reuters, FBI investigators were examining whether Russians suggested to Kushner or other Trump aides that financing people with ties to Trump would be facilitated by relaxing economic sanctions against Russia. See Natasha Bertrand, "'This Is Off the Map': Former Intelligence Officials Say the Reported Kushner-Russia Plan Is Unlike Anything They've Ever Seen," *Business Insider*, May 28, 2017, http://www.businessinsider.com/jared-kushner-backchannel-plan-russia-flynn-2017-5. See as well the intricate web of associations discussed in Matt Apuzzo et al., "Trump Jr. Was Told in Email of Russian Effort to Aid Campaign," *New York Times*, July 10, 2017, https://www.nytimes.com/2017/07/10/us/politics/donald-trump-jr-russia-email-candidacy.html?mcubz=0 (accessed July 11, 2017). As commentators never tire of saying, all this and more constitute circumstantial evidence that may amount to nothing yet may lead to a great deal. Still, one may be inclined to speculate that there was so much smoke surrounding Trump, especially concerning the Russia issue, that if there were no fire, Trump would at least have to go down as one of the foremost magicians in history—at least as a master of trompe l'oeil. Still, what seemed obvious was a kind of purloined-letter situation in which the most blatant and dubious acts were out in the open and at times obscured by a frantic quest for new details or instances. For example, to all appearances there was evidence of an attempted obstruction of justice when, in a televised interview on May 11 with Lester Holt on NBC (preceded the day before by an unprecedented meeting in the Oval Office with Russian diplomats Kislyak and Sergey Lavrov where Trump reportedly expressed similar sentiments, including the feeling that he had taken pressure off by getting rid of Comey), Trump ostentatiously declared that he had made the decision to fire Comey because of "the Russia thing" being investigated under the FBI director's supervision.

Have to Be Useful? ed. G. Peter Lepage, Carolyn (Biddy) Martin, and Mohsen Mostafavi (Ithaca: Cornell University Press, 2006), 75–85.

Ivan Jablonka's book, discussed in chapter 5, is being translated by Nathan Bracher and published by Cornell University Press under the title *History Is a Contemporary Literature: Manifesto for the Social Sciences*. Jablonka has added a new preface written in part in response to the earlier published version of chapter 5. I did not see the new preface before writing the present book.

For their careful readings and suggestions, I would like to thank Jane Pedersen, Mahinder S. Kingra, and two anonymous readers for Cornell University Press. I would also like to thank Sara Ferguson and Marian Rogers for their very helpful editorial assistance.

CHAPTER 1

History, Deconstruction, and Working through the Past

For certain commentators, deconstruction is a dead issue or at least a thing of the past, rendered irrelevant in good part by the Paul de Man affair and responses to it. I would like to argue that, despite criticisms one may make of how the de Man controversy was handled by a significant number both of de Man's supporters, alas including Derrida, and of his at times dismissive critics, there are important respects in which there are features of deconstruction, and of Derrida's thought in particular, that remain relevant to important problems.[1] One prominent initiative I would stress as making deconstruction especially pertinent historically, ethically, and politically is its questioning of binary oppositions that are related to a quest for purity and unproblematic identity. Binaries are crucial to the workings of a scapegoat mechanism whereby anxiety and insecurity in the self or the self's group are projected outward onto vulnerable others—others

---

1. For my own early discussion of the de Man affair and some important responses to it, including Derrida's, see *Representing the Holocaust: History, Theory, Trauma* (Ithaca: Cornell University Press, 1994), chap. 4. For a perceptive discussion and defense of the role of deconstruction in history, see Ethan Kleinberg, "Haunting History: Deconstruction and the Spirit of Revision," *History and Theory* 46 (December 2007): 113–43. See also Kleinberg's book *Haunting History: For a Deconstructive Approach to the Past* (Stanford: Stanford University Press, 2017). See as well the informative, archivally based, contextual analyses in Edward Baring, *The Young Derrida and French Philosophy* (New York: Cambridge University Press, 2011).

who may well be seen as the detested cause of degeneration or pollution. Scapegoating depends on decisive binary oppositions, notably between self and other, and in a feedback loop it is instrumental in generating or reinforcing such invidious oppositions. Policing, violence, and the building of real or symbolic walls may of course be employed socially and politically to underwrite and lend credence to binarism in general and scapegoating in particular.

In contrast to pure binaries, Derrida proposed a generalized trace structure and the mutual but power-laden, asymmetrical marking of putative opposites. This view is epitomized in his often misinterpreted statement "Il n'y a pas de hors-texte"—There is no outside-the-text. Contrary to a prevalent misconstruction, this statement implies, in terms of a generalized trace structure, not that there is nothing of significance outside texts in the ordinary sense but instead the importance of a relational network in which there is no unproblematic, unmarked, nonimplicated, formalistic inside-the-text either. I do not read Derrida (and I do not think Derrida reads Derrida) as reinforcing an inside / outside binary by eliminating or even suspending reference or context. Instead he is inviting an attempt to rethink their relations to texts, language, and signifying practices in general. He is manifestly not making an argument for the self-referential autonomy of the text or the idea that it is sufficient for a reader (including an intellectual historian, philosopher, or literary critic) to confine research to reading a text in isolation from all other considerations, although he typically does point (at times in a contestable way, as in the de Man affair) to the complexities of at least certain texts and the way they set in motion a multiplicity of tensely related forces.

As late as 2016, a noted intellectual historian could repeat once again a misleading understanding of Derrida, which one might have thought to be thoroughly discredited, especially since he refers to my own work as supporting his understanding, even though he goes on, in a self-contradictory fashion, to discuss my efforts as focusing on "cultural context . . . at the expense of an understanding of the argument of the texts themselves."[2] Richard

---

2. Richard Whatmore, *What Is Intellectual History?* (Cambridge: Polity Press, 2016), 34. Despite its general title, Whatmore's book is by and large an exposition and defense of the methods of the so-called Cambridge school, whose leading figures include his oft-cited pair, Quentin Skinner and John Pocock. They and other affiliates of this school, who focus on political history and theory, represent what is for Whatmore genuine intellectual history. He provides informed glosses of Skinner and Pocock but, despite his occasional mention of other approaches, one may still ask what more can and should be said about currents in recent approaches to intellectual history. The work of prominent intellectual and cultural historians more or less of Whatmore's generation, notably in the United States, by and large does not follow Whatmore's agenda. See, for example, the contributions to *Rethinking Modern European Intellectual History,* ed. Darrin McMahon and Samuel Moyn (Oxford: Oxford University Press, 2014).

Whatmore writes that Derrida "questioned the placing of texts in historical contexts. As Derrida wrote, texts functioned in the absence of their author and could be understood by the scrutiny of the text alone. This approach was famously summarized in the second part of his book *De la grammatologie* (1967): 'Il n'y a pas de hors-texte (there is nothing outside the text)' " (33).[3] Although one might well question this translation, which would apply rather to "Il n'y a rien hors du texte," Whatmore may not have read closely and with sufficient understanding the texts and arguments to which he here refers. It is a non sequitur to infer from "the absence of the author" that texts could be "understood by the scrutiny of the text alone." Instead Derrida's famously misread statement implies the recontextualization of texts over time that accompanies rereadings and uses over which an author has no definitive control such as proprietary intentionality.[4]

Whatmore does not address the contrast between two divergent approaches to intellectual history. The Cambridge school attempts to reconstruct the thought or "conversations" of the past, on which it "eavesdrops," by combining a study of presumably intentional meaning and the discursive context in which that meaning was elaborated and debated, especially in terms of idioms or paradigms supposedly distinctive of a past time. Quite important is a reaffirmation of philology and extensive erudition, which may even be taken not only as valuable, pertinent practices but also more problematically as the constituents of a specific, even self-sufficient historical methodology. Here one has a reformulation of the ideal of fully objective knowledge of the past in its own terms and for its own sake, although Skinner in his later works indicated that his approach might have practical value insofar as we might learn from exchanges in the past that may have been forgotten or downplayed but can still say something to us and our problems if only in terms of a contrast between that past and the challenge of the present and future. The latter perspective to some extent introduces a Benjaminian twist, which I find valuable, into a seemingly rather conventional and unilaterally objectifying frame of reference.

---

3. Without quoting the original, John Banville could also write: "As Jacques Derrida notoriously asserted, all is 'text,' and beyond the text there is nothing." Banville, "Philip Marlowe's Revolution," *New York Review of Books*, October 27, 2016, 38.

4. One may recognize the important ethical and legal role of intention when questions of responsibility are at issue. Still, even in the absence of one's own intentional action, one may bear a variable degree of responsibility and liability for the effects of actions or practices of ancestors or preceding generations to the extent that one benefits from them, for example, concerning the expropriation of land, resources, and possessions from subjugated and oppressed peoples.

The approach I have defended does not coincide with Derrida's but draws critically and selectively from it and also from others (notably Freud and M. M. Bakhtin). Like historians in general, I recognize the value of the attempt to reconstruct the past, its discourses, and its arguments. But, like Derrida among others, I do not see this attempt as self-sufficient or unproblematic. In attempting to elucidate this issue, it is indeed important to affirm the role in historiography of truth claims, accurate assertions, and rigorous attempts to validate them. But it is too simple and even misleading to believe one can put forth a fully objective reconstruction of what occurred in the past that separates the objectified past sharply from the present. Discursive contexts are significant, but they may well be multiple, especially in the case of complex texts, and the determination of which contexts are most pertinent to a text or utterance is not a foregone conclusion. Idioms or paradigms are debatable constructs in relation to which texts or utterances are not simple instantiations but rather uses of language or signifying practices that may modify, contest, or at times have a transformative effect on putative contexts, idioms, or paradigms. Moreover, there are problems of "translation," both literal and figurative, in rendering the past and in making it more or less understandable to groups in the present. One has here the question of what Bakhtin termed "responsive understanding" and what Derrida approached in terms of opening a reading that does not dismiss traditional methods such as contextualization but problematizes them in recognizing not the inevitability of a unilaterally projective or radically constructive presentism, but the demands of a self-implicating interchange with a nonhomogeneous past and with whatever is taken as other (such as pasts, peoples, and animals).

As Derrida insisted, increasingly in a critical exchange with the thought of Freud, language is worked over by various forces, at times escaping the intention of the author and taking texts in unanticipated directions and allowing for belated recognitions. I would add that a formulation of intention is itself often retrospective, belated, and dialogic, notably when one disagrees with an interpretation of what is being asserted or explored (for example, the meaning of "Il n'y a pas de hors-texte"). A basic point about intention is that, in public discourse, including legal proceedings, if you know what you are doing and are aware of probable consequences, then your act is prima facie intentional. Intention here is not a question of internal states or acts, for example, peering into a mind or soul (including one's own) to see what was "really" meant or wanted. Those in the Cambridge school certainly recognize unintended consequences in history, but they may not coherently relate such consequences to language use or signifying practices in the past itself but take them primarily as later acts of unilateral appropriation if not highway

robbery of what exists as the proprietary domain of clear and distinct autho-
rial intention. There may well be illegitimate attempts to evade intention
and the responsibility for statements or other acts that attend it, but such
attempts do not account for all the complexities that the issue of intention
entails. Moreover, the texts, discourses, and practices of those in the past or,
more generally, in other times and places may themselves be quite intricate,
internally divided, and contested. Something similar may be said for the present, perhaps with special insistence, since (the problematic) "we" are part of
that present and have sometimes intensely affective and evaluatively charged
investments in what is happening in it and to us.

Here we enter the difficult terrain of the following: (1) What Freud addressed in terms of transference, bringing the mutual implication of self
and others and involving a tendency to repeat. Transference (positive, negative, and ambivalent) includes but is not limited to parents and children
or analysts and analysands. Moreover, transference is a relational concept
not restricted to individual psychology or to the one-on-one clinical relation. I would also contend that transference is not confined to relations with
people in contrast to texts or animals (for example, a text like the Bible [and
many others] or an animal, especially one considered as part of the family
or even as being a person). There is a crucial social dimension to the concept
of transference. And, as Freud intimated, there is what might be termed a
conflict-laden *general economy of transference* to some extent controlled in, but
not confined to, the clinical relation. (2) What Bakhtin discussed as the internally dialogized, polyphonic, often conflictual, and possibly carnivalized
dimension of texts and discourses (not to be confused with conventional
dialogues between discrete individuals or characters often amounting to a
nondialogic exchange of stereotypes, clichés, or "talking points").[5] (3) What

---

5. For example, in Flaubert's *Madame Bovary,* the "dialogues" between Emma and Léon or between the priest Bournisien and the pharmacist Homais are nondialogic exchanges of clichés. But
they are set or positioned in the text by the narrator in a dialogized way through the often ironic or
parodic as well as empathic modulations of free indirect style, which I read as an internally dialogized process relating the narrator, in modulations of proximity and distance, to various objects of
narration, some of which are not people, for example, Emma Bovary's hand or Charles's hat. But,
as Bakhtin notes in *Problems of Dostoevsky's Poetics*, ed. and trans. Caryl Emerson, intro. Wayne C.
Booth (1963; Minneapolis: University of Minnesota Press, 1984), a dialogue is most powerful and
revealing when the words of one interlocutor make explicit what the other has already internally said
to him- or herself but in a covert manner that is denied or resisted, as in the exchange in *The Brothers
Karamazov* between Alyosha and Ivan concerning the guilt of the latter in the killing of their father
(255–56). Moreover, actual dialogue with another person was, for Dostoevsky, the only mode of
self-disclosure and communication (or even communion) without evasive loopholes (248–49). I also
would note that in Camus's *The Fall,* structurally similar to Dostoevsky's *Notes from Underground,*
the narrator engages in a duplicitous, internally dialogized monologue inducing the complicity of

Derrida investigated in terms of a trace or "textual" structure that could also be seen as a general network of differential co-implications. Deconstruction and self-deconstruction applied to internally self-questioning or "dialogized" texts and discourses that could claim unity and identity only through a problematic movement of idealization and analytic reduction.

One may also note the relation among Derrida, Freud, and Bakhtin on the issue of binary oppositions. In Derrida, binaries mutually mark one another. Indeed one of a pair of opposites is the "same" as the other but as differed and deferred, a notion that may be taken to open the question of the variable nature of distinctions that are not taken to be binaries.[6] In Freud there is an ambivalent relation between basic concepts, which he explored notably with respect to the uncanny and the interaction of affects such as love and hate.[7] Bakhtin argued that, in contrast to at least the aspiration of monological statements, dialogical and especially carnivalized image, language use, or practice structurally

> strives to encompass and unite within itself both poles of becoming or both members of an antithesis: birth-death, youth-old age, top-bottom, face-backside, praise-abuse, affirmation-repudiation, tragic-comic and so forth, while the upper pole of a two-in-one image is reflected in the lower, after the manner of figures in playing cards. It could be

---

the assumed interlocutor (or the analogously situated reader) but leaving gaps where the other may resist and answer back. (For further discussion of these issues I would refer the reader to my *Madame Bovary on Trial* (Ithaca: Cornell University Press, 1982), esp. chap. 6, to *History, Politics, and the Novel* (Ithaca: Cornell University Press, 1987) on *Notes from Underground* (chap. 2), and to *History and Memory after Auschwitz* (Ithaca: Cornell University Press, 1998) for *The Fall* (chap. 3).

6. See Jacques Derrida, *Margins of Philosophy*, trans. Alan Bass (1972; University of Chicago Press, 1982), chap. 1, *"Différance."*

7. See especially Freud, *The Uncanny*, trans. David McLintock, intro. Hugh Naughton (1919; New York: Penguin Books, 2003). "Among the various shades of meaning that are recorded for the word *heimlich* is one in which it merges with its formal antonym, *unheimlich*, so that what is called *heimlich* becomes *unheimlich*. . . . This reminds us that the word *heimlich* is not unambiguous, but belongs to two sets of ideas, which are not mutually contradictory, but very different from each other—the one relating to what is familiar and comfortable, the other to what is concealed and kept hidden. *Unheimlich* is the antonym of *heimlich* only in the latter's first sense, not in its second. . . . The term 'uncanny' *(unheimlich)* applies to everything that was intended to remain secret, hidden away, and has come into the open" (132). For Freud, the uncanny refers to the return of the repressed and, in the first instance, to the mother's genitals or womb, the initial home *(Heim)* to which one strives to return (as the "mad" musical genius Leverkühn in Mann's *Doctor Faustus* indeed does once he succumbs to a coma and seeks refuge with his aged mother). Freud also observes that the uncanny is often associated with the demonic. It may be pertinent to observe that in Dostoevsky's *Brothers Karamazov* and in Mann's *Doctor Faustus* it is the devil who appears like a phantom-like projection and uncannily quotes the returning repressed words of the extremely disturbed protagonist (be it Ivan or Leverkühn) to himself. See also my discussion of the uncanny and the problem of its relation to the sublime in *History and Its Limits: Human, Animal, Violence* (Ithaca: Cornell University Press, 2009), 85–89.

expressed this way: opposites come together, look at one another, are reflected in one another, know and understand one another. . . . And in just this way could one define the basic principle of Dostoevsky's art. Everything in his world lives on the very border of its opposite. Love lives on the very border of hate, knows and understands it, and hate lives on the border of love and also understands it. . . . Faith lives on the very border of atheism, sees itself there and understands it, and atheism lives on the border of faith and understands it. . . . Love for life neighbors upon a thirst for self-destruction. . . . Purity and chastity understand vice and sensuality.[8]

As I shall later indicate, what is crucial is not to allow the deconstruction of binary oppositions and the affirmation of a certain kind of ambivalence to eventuate in the generalization of ordinary ambiguity or equivocation and the disintegration of all distinctions, especially on ethical and political levels. Nor does the critique of absolute foundations, related to the deconstruction of binary oppositions, imply such disintegration or the idea that "anything goes." Rather it poses problems in terms of contestable but possibly convincing and cogent distinctions and arguments instead of dogmatic beliefs.

The foregoing problems indicate the importance of self-reflexive vigilance in historians and other analysts in terms of an attempt to attend to and explicitly elucidate, insofar as possible, the affective and evaluative or "ideological" investments we have in our own discursive practices, investments that may be more or less opaque to us and not entirely controlled by intentions. These investments may even function to question our own identity and claims to autonomy. Hence one may always ask the question, Am I now sounding like, or being ventriloquized by, my parent or mentor? In ways worth investigating, emulators of Derrida, Lacan, or Foucault (among others) may at times seem to undertake or undergo stylistic identity theft, a kind of possession by the style and voice of the other. Needless to say, issues become more complex when one attends to the rhetoric of discourse and usage in all its variations from irony and parody (or self-parody) to testimonial affirmations, indications of concern, and statements of belief. A turn to psychoanalysis at its most fruitful points to an effort to address complexities of language and life with concepts and procedures that touch on dimensions of self and society often glossed over in the reconstruction of past utterances and idioms, notably when focused only on intentions and, more generally,

8. Bakhtin, *Problems of Dostoevsky's Poetics*, 176.

on conscious practices.[9] This psychoanalytic turn is evident in Derrida but resisted in the Bakhtin circle, which, at least in V. N. Volosinov's *Freudianism: A Critical Sketch*,[10] did not explore possible relations between a Bakhtinian orientation and Freud's thought, but saw Freud in restricted terms, emphasizing what was taken to be Freud's neglect of historical specificity and the role of language in culture along with his reliance on ahistorical biological reductionism (a partially valid but very limited perspective on Freud).[11]

Trauma has a distinctive role here in its affective impact and disorientation of language and life, and its effects pose problems with respect to the disconcerting, compulsive, unintentional irruptions of the past into the present and future. It may also induce extreme confusion and the inability to make distinctions and cogent judgments. This intrusive traumatic past may be experienced, however misleadingly, as more present, pressing, and real than current circumstances. This past eludes unproblematic representation and untroubled styles. It has to be worked on and through (as well as played out in jokes, laughter, and other performative processes such as song and dance). Working on and through does not imply the achievement of closure and full identity or autonomy. It points instead to a self-implicating process in the attempt to reconstruct the past in ways that may raise questions for the present and create openings to often unpredictable but to some extent shapable futures. One aspect of this process is to move from dichotomies or fully decisive binary oppositions to more flexible and subtle distinctions or differences that exist on a spectrum from the scarcely discernible to the quite strong and at times decisive distinction that allows for decisions and judgments. I would note here that a professional advantage and disadvantage of the approach of the Cambridge school (in this respect to some extent like the New Criticism) is that, despite differences among its affiliates that may be more or less significant, it does provide a secure matrix or methodology that can be taught and learned in a rather conventional manner and enable scholars to take up research projects that promise success, at least in the eyes of those who accept its premises. The comparable advantage and disadvantage

---

9. Many people may not realize when they are using free indirect style rather than, say, direct quotation or attempted objective reporting of the sort "he or she said." Moreover, the distinction between mention and use may not be recognized whether intentionally or not. For example, a mention of another's use of insult may be taken as engaging or using the insult in one's own voice. But it may also be the case that one's own use of insult may be disguised or glossed as mention.

10. Trans. I. R. Titunik and ed. with, and including an appendix by, Neal H. Bruss (Bloomington: Indiana University Press, 1987). Volosinov's long essay was first published in 1927.

11. In his own work, Lacan countered at least two of these criticisms, and one may argue about the role of historical specificity in theoretical discourse. (I am in favor of it—and not simply as an instance of some putatively universal concept or structure such as the "real.")

of what might be called a more dialogic and self-critical approach is that one certainly interacts with and may well learn from the practice of others, but one may not readily, if at all, provide protocols or models for scholars to share or follow, especially if one's goal is to bring out aspects of the past and our relation to it that are exploratory, open to contestation, less than obvious, and generative of questions for the implicated, responsive reader and scholar.

I have intimated that, in a textual or trace structure (including but not to be identified with a literal text), seeming opposites that mutually mark one another could be deceptively made to appear pure or integral through questionable projection of anxiety-producing or uncanny elements onto the utterly separate and distinct other. This projective procedure has unfortunately been very prevalent in history.[12] Derrida famously explored this process with respect to the loaded difference between the oral and the written, important for the myth of the oral community as unaffected by the difficulties projected exclusively onto so-called literate cultures, notably conflict and violence.[13]

Pure opposition and difference are also at play in other, typically hierarchical yet reversible binaries such as that between the inside and the outside, nature and culture, text and context, space and time, male and female, Aryan and Jew, colonizer and colonized, the secular and the religious, history and memory, the philosophical or the social-scientific and the literary, and so forth. The typical move is to locate the source of anxiety only in the presumably cut-off and alienated, often demonized other. In a certain form of authoritarian "populism," quite important in the recent past (for example, in Donald Trump and his followers), there is a sharp binary between us and them: we the people (or the "real" people) and the others or aliens who really

12. As intimated earlier, the procedure was very evident in the 2016 presidential campaign, especially among Donald Trump and his "surrogates," where the marching order seemed to be pivot away from an embarrassing question, turn to your preferred "talking points," and project repeatedly, accusing your accuser of what you are accused, such as lying or assault on vulnerable others (notably abused women).

13. The binary between the written and the oral may be reversed, with the written as the dominant or privileged category, as has been the case with the "publish or perish" dictum in the academy or the preference for written documents in historiography along with the tendency to avoid, or see as typically unreliable, testimony and memory. This reversal has blatantly prejudicial effects for peoples whose culture relies on oral traditions and memory, notably indigenous peoples but also other oppressed groups for whom testimony is crucial. These effects have been drastic in the case of American Indians and Australian Aborigines whose claims to land or even whose very historical and legal existence has been subjected to unrealistic demands for written documentation and whose oral traditions have often, especially until very recently, been dismissed as unreliable and inadmissible in legal proceedings. (These crucial points have often been ignored in at times dismissive discussions of memory and oral testimony by historians.)

do not count and are inimical to a true society and polity. Some groups may be particularly vilified components of "the others" (traditionally Jews but also certain foreigners or aliens within or without, such as undocumented or "illegal" immigrants, for example, Mexicans and Muslims). A decidedly undemocratic element enters the picture in the conviction that the others are not to be seen as parts of a democracy in which there may well be conflicts over differences in policy or opinion. Instead others are crooked and corrupt, participants in or beneficiaries of a "swamp" that has to be cleaned up. They "rig" the system even when one benefits from that system, including ways it may be "rigged" to favor the wealthy and powerful or be manipulated to one's advantage by ostensible enemies or opponents (such as the Russians who themselves should not be demonized despite the orientation of certain questionable leaders). Identification with a charismatic leader and his message, which pretends to convey the authentic voice of the people, may bring the feeling that even those in disadvantaged circumstances are valued as "the people" and may seek revenge on a dubiously circumscribed establishment that does not include seeming insiders (certain billionaires and corporate executives who support the pseudopopulist leader).

One issue raised here is whether processes of extreme analysis at times function as questionable rituals of purification possibly related to forms of scapegoating, victimization, and at times sacrificial violence. Such processes of extreme analysis might include the formation of often useful ideal types or models *when they serve certain functions,* such as an invidious quest for identity and exceptionalism, including the ideology of a chosen people or the uniqueness of the West as opposed to the rest. (The latter is arguably operative in Max Weber's methodological reliance on ideal types geared to demonstrating the presumed uniqueness of the West.) Extreme analytic purification or "cleansing" may be active as well in disciplinary identity politics based on a debatable hard-and-fast opposition between fields or disciplines such as history, philosophy, and literary studies.[14] Sharp oppositions may also be operative in the quest for the uniqueness, privileged, even "chosen" status of the human being in contradistinction to all other animals, often deceptively condensed into "the" animal. The latter is one area in which Derrida's

---

14. There have been many attempts to divide these fields, for example, by separating history from literary studies or philosophy, the separation at times taken as definitive of the "real" historian or the "historian's historian." I obviously maintain that historiography should take an interest in literature and itself have literary and philosophical dimensions without being conflated with fiction or a traditional philosophy of history. And a special object of attention for intellectual historians should be unexamined or implicit assumptions and frames of reference, for example, anthropocentrism both in the past and in oneself.

later work has a bearing on critical animal studies and the critique of anthropocentrism. Important in this respect is the attempt to go beyond the human in expanding the scope of concern, compassion, justice, and generosity. For example, an issue here is whether the concept of genocide or even crimes against humanity should be extended to other species and not restricted to humans. The implication is that anthropocentric humanism, including human-rights discourse, may dubiously base itself on a typically concealed, exclusionary, possibly violent scapegoating and sacrificial mechanism with respect to animals or "the" animal as other. One might attempt a history of humanism that, unlike existing anthropocentric histories, includes rather than marginalizes or neglects the role of other animals, which is common in history in general, however deprovincialized, global, or total it claims to be.[15]

Deconstruction (via such notions as *différance* and supplementarity) tends to valorize at least certain hybrids and hyphenated composites or even to see them, in history and culture, as generative and reproducible. Of course, certain composites are undesirable, for example, a leader who is a combination of Hitler and Stalin or, perhaps more to the point in the recent past, Mussolini, Berlusconi, and Putin. Nonetheless, in culture pure entities, including the purely "human" or the "real" man or woman (and so forth), are a contestable result of pruning, processing, and policing. Cultural hybrids can reproduce, and this may cause anxiety in those wedded to strict disciplinary and generic boundaries. A closely related notion is that in history one begins in medias res or in an in-between positioning with more clear-cut identities, positions, beginnings, and endings as more or less attainable heuristic fictions or contestable projects. One might even propose that the human is the being-in-process that cannot fully know itself but that over time and space has sought, in repeated yet variable ways, an identity based on a decisive criterion that opposes the human in binaristic fashion to the other, notably "the" animal, typically in a manner that justifies doing violence to that other (capturing, experimenting on, killing, and eating it). Fortunately, this quest for the decisive criterion that certifies and privileges human identity has been brought into question by what may be an increasing number of people.

Before proceeding with an argument related to the above points, I would parenthetically observe that one may ask whether Derrida adequately confronted the problem of how what I have sketched and in certain respects endorsed as his orientation could be related to his later emphasis on

---

15. This neglect or marginalization occurs even in noteworthy studies, such as Lynn Hunt, *Inventing Human Rights: A History* (New York: W. W. Norton, 2007) and Samuel Moyn, *The Last Utopia: Human Rights in History* (Cambridge, MA: Harvard University Press, 2010).

messianicity and the view that every other is totally other (*tout autre est tout autre*). The latter view seems to conflate every other with a radically transcendent, hidden God (and vice versa). And every other seems to be situated *hors-texte* or beyond an implication in the mutual marking of a network-like trace structure. My own response to this view is to argue that every other is not totally other but rather that in every other (as in oneself), there is "something" other, perhaps radically (I hesitate to say totally) other. This "other" is treated by Freud in terms of unconscious processes, which place a nonfixatable limit on self-understanding and transparent communication (or an ideal speech situation). Still, how to interpret Derrida's messianicity is open to question, and the trace-structure / totally-other problem is a (perhaps postsecular) variant of the immanence / transcendence question that has a claim to being the paradigmatic aporia or double bind of Christianity and perhaps of the so-called Western tradition. (In Christianity, the question is whether God is in the world or otherworldly and transcendent, or possibly both.) Arguably, this problem has been displaced onto the issue of whether meaning is inherent in signs or arbitrary and in a sense transcendent with respect to them (what may be a misleading binary).[16]

Some (for example, John Caputo) have seen Derrida as a paradoxically religious thinker (offering a "religion without religion") while others (for example, Martin Hägglund) have maintained that he is a "radical atheist."[17] Despite his predilection to refer primarily to monotheistic religions and his latter-day emphasis on messianicity, it is at least conceivable to see a dimension of Derrida's thought as pointing to an atheistic religiousness—a religion not without religion but without a supreme deity. It is important to note that in the Durkheimian tradition (from which Derrida in part draws, for example, via Marcel Mauss and Georges Bataille), it is the role of the sacred and not God or a belief in a theistic being that is the crux of religion. The sacred and its displacements in more secular contexts may be a crucial dimension of a generalized trace structure, force field, or relational network. And it is noteworthy that the "totally other" (for those who affirm this notion, for

---

16. One might argue (as does Derrida in *De la grammatologie*) that in historical uses of language (*langage*), one has a process of motivation and demotivation of signs in relation to meaning with, at the limit, a demotivated or "anasemic" sign appearing to have arbitrary meaning. Here Derrida is not simply a follower of Saussure concerning the arbitrariness of the signifier.

17. See John D. Caputo, *The Prayers and Tears of Jacques Derrida: Religion without Religion* (Bloomington: Indiana University Press, 1997) and John D. Caputo and Gianni Vattimo, *After the Death of God,* ed. Jeffrey W. Robbins, with an afterword by Gabriel Vahanian (New York: Columbia University Press, 2007). See also Martin Hägglund, *Radical Atheism: Derrida and the Time of Life* (Stanford: Stanford University Press, 2008). See also Edward Baring and Peter Gordon, eds., *The Trace of God: Derrida and Religion* (New York: Fordham University Press, 2015).

example, Levinas, Kierkegaard, or Derrida) may be a sublimely paradoxical, anxiety-producing, unsettling vis-à-vis in a so-called "relation without relation." The God of Kierkegaard's *Fear and Trembling* is not a very cozy being or one to be invoked in a simplistic "do-you-believe-in" type question. One might even argue that, in *Fear and Trembling,* not only Abraham but God is on trial or being tested to an extent Kierkegaard may have resisted seeing. The obvious but bewildering question the text brings to mind is, What kind of a God would command the sacrifice of one's child, and, more manifestly, is Abraham mad to think he does?[18]

Aside from what are arguably its (post)secular analogues or even displacements, such as the "real," the "archaic heritage of guilt," or constitutive melancholy, original sin itself has recently made a comeback, perhaps as one aspect of the postsecular turn in recent thought.[19] An appeal to original sin seems to give thought a profundity or depth, often via a return to Augustine and Paul, for example, in the work of Alan Jacobs in his noteworthy *Original Sin.*[20] Jacobs in orthodox fashion traces original sin to the inheritance of guilt from Adam's fall that is transmitted to all who come after him, even comparing such transmission to genetic processes and construing it as pointing toward the need for redemption through Christ's self-sacrifice. More unexpectedly perhaps, Jacobs emphasizes its egalitarian nature in figuring all humans as fallen or corrupt in a manner that counters claims to exceptionalism or the inherent singularity or chosenness of certain groups or individuals. He also notes that in Reinhold Niebuhr, who stressed original sin early in the twentieth century, this egalitarianism was throughout his life linked not to conservatism as it is in many thinkers (for example, T. S. Eliot) but to progressive politics and social activism. But to give original sin a structural and foundational status is a high, dogmatic price to pay for egalitarianism and even progressivism, which result only from a commendable but questionable construction of original sin that is relatively uncommon.

Short of agreeing with Jacobs, one may perhaps see original sin (and its analogues) in nondoctrinal or dogmatic terms as pointing to the precariousness of life and to an "originary," repeated possibility, tendency, or even

---

18. I would nonetheless note that, in terms of the argument I am trying to develop, there may be a mind-boggling sense in which the universe is infinite. But that does not mean that we are infinite or oriented toward a presumably infinite or totally other "other," however deferred or to come (*à venir*).

19. I am indicating in passing what is subject to argument: that notions such as Lacan's real, Freud's archaic heritage of guilt, and constitutive melancholy (for example, in Judith Butler's *Psychic Life of Power* [Stanford: Stanford University Press, 1997], esp. 197–98) are—or function as—displacements of original sin or its consequences.

20. Alan Jacobs, *Original Sin: A Cultural History* (New York: HarperCollins, 2008).

propensity to transgress or do "evil" that limits progress or perfectibility and points to the ambivalent duality or split nature of the human being as both good and bad. But this problematic status is different from seeing original sin as derivative of Adam's fall or more generally as a founding trauma or an inherent, universal, quasi-transcendental structure of which specific events, acts, or processes are instantiations. One way to see original sin (perhaps as well as its analogues) is as a condensation of the inter- or transgenerational transmission of trauma in given traditions, stemming from extreme, often violent transgression and generating feelings of guilt over generations. This process is rendered mythically when its source is pinpointed in terms of the fall of Adam (or an analogous event such as Freud's primal crime), with original sin (or a heritage of guilt), hypostatized as foundational. In brief, original sin (or its analogues) should not be seen as a solution or an answer but as a notion that poses problems and raises questions calling for critical inquiry.

One argument worth making is that the deconstruction of binary oppositions should not be taken to imply the disintegration or effacement of all distinctions or the generalization of what Primo Levi termed the gray zone. With this generalization (criticized by Levi but arguably enacted by Giorgio Agamben), everyone indiscriminately becomes complicitous as a perpetrator-victim. By contrast, what the deconstruction of binary opposites makes more not less demanding is the problem of rearticulation and articulatory practices (including institutions). And crucial to articulation is the role of distinctions or differences. Along with the problem of distinctions or differences and their articulation comes the issue of rethinking distinctions in terms of their relative strength or weakness both in fact and in right. In other words, pure binaries are distinctions taken to an extreme, and while all distinctions are problematic, some distinctions are not only more problematic but more indefensible and harmful than others. Defensible distinctions and their articulation are necessary for cogent thought and practice, including practical reason, judgment, and social action. And they raise the question of whether existing institutions and practices bound up with invidious distinctions or differences, especially certain binaries or dichotomies, are dubious if not disastrous and should be subject to change in ethically and politically desirable directions.

Without pretending that I have comprehensive answers to this enormous range of issues, I would nonetheless offer only a few examples of how one might address a key problem in the wake of deconstruction concerning distinctions or differences and their articulation in thought and practice. I would note that Derrida does not take the path I am indicating, although at points his thought intersects with it. But the path I would defend does not go in the

direction of messianicity, the "mystical" foundation of authority, an idea of
originary peformative violence (or a *coup de force*) that presumably precedes
norms and laws, what seem to be decisionist leaps of faith, or a notion of
"undeconstructible" justice as infinitely other and always to come (*à venir*),
although I would agree that any claim to have definitively established a just
order is open to challenge, and that particularly difficult decisions may be
supported by more or less cogent and convincing arguments but not decisively founded in certainty or simply derived from programmatic principles.[21]

An important distinction in Primo Levi and others is that between perpetrators and victims, including its relation to the "gray zone," where the distinction is not a binary but involves various degrees of complicity between
perpetration and victimization. As intimated above, such complicity does
not invalidate the distinction but renders it problematic in certain cases while
nonetheless retaining its strength in others. In the Holocaust there were
many cases of both perpetrators who were not in any pertinent sense victims and victims who were in no significant sense perpetrators or complicit
in perpetration as "bystanders" (a dubious term insofar as it indiscriminately
connotes innocence or indifference instead of possible degrees of complicity
whether as active cooperation or passive acceptance if not affirmation). The
suffering and even the traumatization of certain perpetrators or accomplices
should be recognized, as in the case of German victims of Allied bombing
raids or even military or SS men or women who underwent traumatization
and subsequent symptoms from their own acts of abuse toward others. But
they should not be seen in terms of equivalency with abused victims or even
as victims or survivors of the Holocaust in an ethically or political pertinent
sense. Victims of bombing were affected by at times excessive or at least debatable actions of the Allies seeking victory, while traumatized perpetrators
abusing victims were harmed by their own abusive behavior and its effects.
(Especially noteworthy are possible harmful effects upon the descendants
of perpetrators.) Even the violence against Germans on the eastern front,

---

21. See Jacques Derrida, "The Force of Law: The 'Mystical' Foundation of Authority," *Cardozo
Law Review* 11 (1990): 920–1045. It is also included in Drucilla Cornell et al. eds., *Deconstruction and
the Possibility of Justice* (New York: Routledge, 1992). See also my commentary on Derrida's essay (not
included in the Drucilla Cornell volume), which was given on the version of the essay presented at
a conference at Cardozo Law School, "Violence, Justice, and the Force of Law," *Cardozo Law Review*
11 (1990): 1065–78. As I have noted elsewhere, Derrida's essay did not as yet include the footnotes
and "Post-scriptum" on Nazism and the "final solution" (973–74 and 1040–46), of which I was not
made aware before the publication of the volume. See also my discussions in *History and Reading:
Tocqueville, Foucault, French Studies* (Toronto: Toronto University Press, 2000), 216–223, and *History
and Its Limits*, 98–102. See also Derrida's *The Gift of Death*, trans. David Wills (1992; Chicago: University of Chicago Press, 1995).

including extensive rapes, as objectionable as this was, is equated or weighed with respect to the genocide and abuse of the Holocaust only in a very questionable form of book balancing that typically has functioned in an apologetic manner. And perpetrators who may be traumatized by their actions do not ipso facto become victims in the pertinent ethical, political, and legal senses.

One also has here the problem of the role of empathy or compassion in understanding. Empathy with respect to victims is often unproblematic, and the shutting off or blockage of empathy may itself often be a precondition for perpetration and for active or passive complicity in victimizing others. (Such blockage may in time become a matter of habituation or hardness.) The role of empathy in understanding perpetrators or even certain complicitous figures in the gray zone is open to debate, as is the very meaning of empathy or compassion itself. I have criticized the conflation of empathy with identification and argued that empathy is an imaginative, intellectual, and emotional rapport with the other as other that does not imply an ability to take the place of, or speak for, the other. It might rather be understood as putting oneself in the other's position without taking the other's place—a distinction that recognizes difference. Insofar as there is an element of identification in empathy, it may be best captured in Kaja Silverman's tense, even oxymoronic notion of heteropathic identification.[22] As I take it, this would be an internally divided identification that does not eliminate or subsume difference. It is to be contrasted with incorporative or projective identification, which undermines understanding of others by assimilating them to the self. I would see a role for empathy with the perpetrator at least in the sense of recognizing the possibility of certain actions or experiences for oneself under certain conditions. It may be impossible to determine the degree of that possibility unless one is actually in a comparable position, but it is in no sense desirable to seek out that position in order to acquire greater certainty about one's capabilities or propensities. Instead recognizing the possibility for oneself would rather be related to a heightened awareness that would increase vigilance and help counteract any tendencies toward inadmissible actions or beliefs that one may harbor, perhaps as an unconscious effect of growing up or living in certain contexts or of identification with the aggressor. A somewhat similar problem arises with respect to the many shades in the gray zone, although here many of us may have had experiences in which we have in fact found or placed ourselves in ambiguous situations and

---

22. See Kaja Silverman, *Threshold of the Visible World* (New York: Routledge, 1996).

not acted in ways of which we would be proud. In the case of those placed by victimizers in double binds not of their own making, as was the situation of significant numbers of victims in the Holocaust, as well as in other fraught situations (for example, harkis in Algeria or Vietnamese cooperating with French or American occupying forces), one may well be inclined to share Primo Levi's suspension of judgment with respect to Jewish councils or Sonderkommandos.

A difficult aspect of empathy is related to one's response to transferential co-implication with others, which itself may be seen as a precondition of empathy. Empathy may be taken in a relatively objectifying or vague if seemingly unobjectionable sense to imply trying to elicit how others "see" things, especially in terms of the stories they tell themselves to explain and justify their actions. But empathy may also be understood in ways that accentuate, even overextend, that co-implication, as may occur in Dilthey's influential notion of feeling one's way into another, even reexperiencing what the other has experienced. But would this be desirable with respect, say, to the excruciatingly traumatic and possibly incapacitating experience of certain victims such as *Muselmänner* or others undergoing compulsive reliving that renders impossible agency and responsibility in the present and future? I have argued that empathy is indeed called for in such cases but would ideally eventuate in a noncompulsive form of empathic unsettlement whose nature would vary and could not be determined with precision. At the opposite end of the spectrum, is there a sense in which one may resist such empathy with respect to certain perpetrators, not only Hitler or Himmler but ruthless abusers in less exalted positions—resistance that counters violence or elation in victimizing others and may not be objectionably callous or defensive but instead a self-conscious attestation to certain values? One may even ask whether all others deserve empathy. At present, especially in Trumpland, a proximity to the orientation of perpetrators or identification with the "winning" aggressor and with abusive, prejudiced behavior may be too much of a temptation for some if not many, rather than a seemingly alien experience that has to be put forward and familiarized. It may well be too simple and facile to assume the liberal cosmopolitan status as one's default position. In any case, empathy or compassion should be distinguished from affirming, accepting, or forgiving, which require critical judgment that does not negate empathy but cannot be conflated with it. In general, empathy or compassion may be necessary but never enough for informed understanding or for viable social and political action.

An example to which I have already alluded suggests that the entire network of distinctions between humans and other animals warrants extensive, careful rethinking in nonbinary ways having historical, ethical, and political implications. With respect to victimization and violence, which I take to be key problems, there may well be situations in which the distinction between perpetrator and victim is very strong, as in the majority of cases in the Holocaust, where the gray zone is relatively restricted and brought about primarily by the policies of perpetrators that placed victims in double binds and attempted to make them accomplices in their own oppression. There are other situations in which the gray zone may be much larger, although marked differences in power would skew the gray zone in very important ways with the brunt of responsibility for its genesis and functioning generally attributable primarily to the more powerful. Our recent wars and our extended financial crisis, aggravating an excessive gap between the very rich and others, not only the middle class but crucially the very poor, offer vast fields for discriminating analyses of rather dark gray zones where decisive judgments (and jail time) are at times warranted.

A further point, not restricted to the problem of the gray zone, is that many crucial distinctions are analytic. Certain distinctions may not delimit concrete cases or situations (for example, a box of red in contrast to a box of green crayons) but apply to situations in debatable and differential ways. A problematic but, I think, defensible analytic distinction I have made and elaborated elsewhere is between structural and historical trauma, related respectively to the absence of foundational certainties or absolutes (an absence often taken or mistaken as a traumatic loss) and to losses of specific historical beings and entities.[23] The two may coincide in empirical phenomena, but simply collapsing or denying the distinction between the two can be misleading. It may lead to a quest for a putatively lost but actually absent absolute (for example, a paradise lost or the conflict-free *Volksgemeinschaft* and similar utopias or absolute foundations, including the once great but now supposedly lost America). This quest stems from a confused fantasy that may possibly induce the experience of the "loss" of what you never had or even could possibly have, with the putative "loss" often blamed on despised, typically scapegoated others. Or, alternatively, the collapse of the distinction between structural and historical trauma may lead to a draining of specificity from historical losses construed only in terms of highly abstract theory (arguably including certain forms of trauma theory). Specificity is also at risk when losses are treated as instantiations of some structural absence or

---

23. See my *Writing History, Writing Trauma* (2001; Baltimore: Johns Hopkins University Press, 2014 [with a new preface]), chap. 2. I would note that the absence of foundational certainties or absolutes may be taken not as traumatic but as challenging yet liberating, as I think Nietzsche argued.

transhistorical construct such as the Fall, original sin, constitutive lack, the Lacanian "real," or an idea of history per se as trauma. I would not universalize structural trauma (including the "real") or give it a quasi-transcendental status, but lend it at most a qualified credibility at least within the so-called Western tradition where the notion of the Fall (or some analogue) as a foundational trauma has played a prominent role as a belief related to certain practices. The notion of structural trauma might also be related to the importance of foundational traumas in general, including the Holocaust or 9/11—traumas where catastrophic historical events are given structural or paradigmatic significance—traumas that should and at times do problematize identity but paradoxically may also become the at times invidious and politically dangerous ground of group as well as individual identity used to justify dubious acts or policies (as alas has happened with both the Holocaust and 9/11).

The belief in the full objectivity of historical research, often correlated with an idea of the archive of written documents as the bedrock of such objectivity, may at times function as another instance of hypostatizing an absence or seeking certainty or an absolute foundation where none is available. At the very least, archival research may be privileged to an inordinate extent. To make these assertions is not to downgrade the importance and the value of archives and meticulous archival work. But historiography should not be confined (as it often is) to the translation of archives into narratives. And the written archive should not be given indiscriminate preference in history over the oral and memory. Such a restrictive construction of history (or historiography) has at least three pitfalls. First, as already intimated, it downplays or even denigrates the significance of memory, testimony, and oral history—an attitude that functions to the detriment of victims and oppressed peoples, notably those for whom oral traditions or testimonies are crucial. It may thus replicate colonial or postcolonial practices that have made tendentious and discriminatory use of the demand for written archival proof. Second, an exclusive emphasis on written archives obscures the value of research drawing on published or other available sources (documentaries or films, for example). It simultaneously obscures more "archival" or less manifest, even secret and uncanny, dimensions of such available sources. (The "archival" or less manifest aspects of what is out in the open has of course been a special concern of deconstructive and psychoanalytic readings.) And privileging conventional archives may occlude the problematic features of archives themselves.[24] Third, it overly restricts to narrative (both theoretically and

---

24. I touch on some of these aspects in chapter 3.

practically) modes of articulation in historiography or at least privileges narrative to the detriment of analysis, description, argumentation, and essays (often relegated to the second-class status of "think pieces"). By contrast, one can recognize the value of narrative but not devalue other modes of research and presentation in historical inquiry as well as in other practices such as fiction, poetry, and film, which are also important in attempts to come to terms with problems, including trauma. One possible effect of the hierarchy that places archival research and narrative at its pinnacle is to elevate those doing this type of work, typically downplaying the significance of other approaches, notably forms of intellectual and cultural history, particularly those that recognize the importance of literature, art, and philosophy.

The emphasis on revenants and hauntology in the later Derrida takes his deconstruction of absolute origins or foundations in a newer direction and in one sense generalizes the role of possessive forces or "ghosts" from the past that are accentuated in trauma and its aftereffects. (Like some others, such as Nicolas Abraham or Toni Morrison, I find especially significant the insight that the ghost or revenant may be seen as a haunting post-traumatic effect.) I would suggest that objectivity in a nonabsolute sense might be recast as the result of careful, critical, and self-critical research and argument that resist unmediated identification, symptomatic repetition, and acting out possession by the past but rather try to account for and counter, especially with respect to highly charged problems, the inevitable transferential tendency to incorporate or project into the other (or the object of research) whatever suits one's often unacknowledged or even unconscious propensities, ideologies, and desires. Such a concept of objectivity does not entail the collapse of the strong distinction between truth (or warrantable assertion) and falsehood. Nor does it authorize playing fast and loose with facts or a so-called post-factual discourse, which may be a misleading euphemism for meretricious claims, misleading propaganda, or downright lies, as in certain forms of recent political rhetoric or "fake news" as well as in past formations such as fascism.[25] Yet there is a sense in which the historically situated (including

---

25. An aspect of the tactic of pivoting from the one who is criticized to the putative faults of the other, whom one opposes, is related to the so-called post-factual or post-truth phenomenon. The latter may include the belief that the function of dissembling or lies is the exposure of the hypocrisy and elitist complacency of its objects, be they the mainstream media or establishment political figures, such as Hillary Clinton. In this sense, pivoting may be understood and defended, however dubiously, not in its relation to projection, which may nonetheless be operative and important, but as a twisted path to telling a certain truth about the other—the other as hypocritical emperor without clothes. Yet truth may also be suspended or subverted insofar as the one who does the disclosing or exposing is a specific type of "troll" who pretends to be beyond norms in doing things, such as shaming or victimizing, for the sake both of disrupting what is seen as the established order and of a cynical laugh at the expense of its hapless victim as well as all others who are benighted enough to take normativity,

historians) are always trying to reconstruct, understand, and analyze the past on contested ground and in dialogic, at times self-questioning, relation to its haunting, transgenerational ghosts as well as to other inquirers past and present, both inside and, ideally, also outside one's own discipline.

The campaign and the initial phase of the presidency of Donald Trump signaled the importance of a set of distinctions that one might have assumed to be obvious, distinctions that are strong and pronounced. One of them is between fact and fiction along with truth and falsehood. The supposed advent of the so-called post-truth or post-fact era has appeared to upset or even dismantle this distinction on which not only history but everyday life is based. A warrantable assertion, justifiably taken to affirm a true fact, is one that is confirmed or substantiated by evidence beyond a reasonable doubt. A falsehood asserts what is untrue and without a demonstrable basis in fact. A fiction asserts neither a fact nor a falsehood. It becomes a falsehood when it is not framed as fiction but is asserted as a true fact. In science and in history, there is a role for heuristic fictions that do not masquerade as facts but may be useful in research into facts and their interpretation or theorization. A heuristically fictive model or ideal type, for example, the concept of the Renaissance, of economic man, or of instrumental rationality, may be quite useful in orienting inquiry, including inquiry into ways its reference to empirical reality or facts is not inclusive and exhaustive. Moreover, a fiction in the sense of a novel or play may include facts or offer a reading or interpretation of historical processes. But that does not make it tantamount to a factual account or a type of historical research even if it involves and may fruitfully interact or raise multidirectional questions with respect to the latter.

Readings, interpretations, and theories may call for further differentiations, but one thing they share is that they cannot be confirmed in the way or with the degree of conviction that applies to certain facts, for example, the fact that Barack Obama was born in the United States. Assuming that there is a high degree of accuracy in the procedures used to arrive at it, one can assert that the inaugural address of Donald Trump had an audience attending it estimated to be approximately 250,000 people. One can also assert that there is extremely little or no evidence for the claim that 3 or so million fraudulent voters cast ballots for Hillary Clinton that account for the margin of her popular victory in the 2016 presidential election. Despite evidence, Trump and certain of his supporters have insisted that there are doubts about Obama's

legality, and ethics seriously. On the recent phenomenon of the troll, especially on the Internet, see, for example, Whitney Phillips, *This Is Why We Can't Have Nice Things: Mapping the Relationship between Online Trolling and Mainstream Culture* (Cambridge, MA: MIT Press, 2016).

citizenship, the attendance at Trump's inaugural address, or even the role of fraudulent voters for Clinton in the 2016 election, as well as making other unsubstantiated and misleading claims (for example, the claim that Obama "tapped" phones in Trump Tower during the presidential campaign).

Sean Spicer, Trump's former press secretary, has stated that Trump has believed and continues to believe in fraudulent voters responsible for Clinton's large margin in the popular vote. What is it to believe in the truth or the factual status of a claim that is proved to be groundless? Is it like believing in the virgin birth of Christ or the triune personhood of God? Apparently not, since the latter as articles of faith could not be proved true or untrue and are beyond ordinary understanding, while the assertion concerning millions of fraudulent voters for Clinton is presumably based on empirical evidence. But it cannot be shown empirically to be true, and one might cogently conclude that it is false. If one continues to "believe" it, it is plausible to look for other grounds for the "belief," such as the way claims about fraudulent voters may function as a diversion from, or cover for, the role of fraudulent or dubious types of voter exclusion, such as decreasing the number of polling places, gerrymandering districts, or restricting times for voting in a manner that is prejudicial to certain groups, such as African Americans.[26] Trump has had the power, usually on the basis of a fly-by-night, ill-considered tweet, to send others scurrying, sometimes for days on end, trying to confirm or disconfirm implausible or irrelevant allegations and assertions, often garnered uncritically from pro-Trump, unreliable sources. Indeed the general question concerning so-called post-factual or post-truth assertions or beliefs is whether and how they function ideologically in questionable and even illegitimate fashion, often as diversionary falsehoods or, when intended to deceive, as lies. There are more difficult dimensions of the complex relations whose rudiments I have traced, but it is critical, and perhaps a dangerous

---

26. Pending before the Supreme Court is a case concerning the gerrymandering of voting districts on a partisan-political basis. A lower court struck down such a practice with respect to Wisconsin. The contentious point is apparently how much partisanship is too much. See Ariane de Vogue and Daniella Diaz, "Supreme Court to Hear Partisan Gerrymandering Case," *CNN Politics,* June 20, 2017, http://www.cnn.com/2017/06/19/politics/supreme-court-partisan-gerrymandering/index.html (accessed June 23, 2017). The Associated Press has reported that a new statistical method for detecting the degree of political gerrymandering has been developed. The analysis found four times as many states with Republican-skewed state legislative districts than Democratic ones. In the two dozen most populated states, there were nearly three times as many with Republican-tilted U.S. House districts. The result was that in 2016 Republicans won as many as twenty-two additional House seats over what would have been expected based on the average vote share in congressional districts across the country. See David A. Lane, "Analysis Shows Gerrymandering Aided GOP in 2016," Associated Press, reprinted in the *Santa Fe New Mexican,* June 25, 2017, A-1 and A-8.

and embarrassing sign of a cultural and political crisis, that one insist on basic points that run counter to the tactics of deceptive "con artists" who undermine the important function of confidence and trust in a polity and a society. It is of course conceivable that a con artist will be so immersed in self-deception or tied in ideological knots that he or she may con him- or herself to the point of confusion and self-deception, perhaps becoming a so-called pathological liar. But it is also likely that the abuse of the confidence and the exploitation of the credulity of others (crucial in the big-lie technique) is, at least in great measure, a tactic or ploy of self-aggrandizement, power seeking, and the dismantling of democratic institutions. Falsehoods or lies may also be acceptable or even valuable to a group following (indeed having intense transferential bonds prompting identification with) a leader because the falsehoods or lies reinforce preconceptions or prejudices and thus the bases of identity and solidarity within the like-minded group and hostility toward others taken as opponents or enemies. But it is worth stressing that Trump cannot bring himself to accept or admit defeat, loss, or "mistakes." As already intimated, defeat must be magically transmuted into (or "spun" as) a win, and a loss or mistake must be seen as a winning strategy. The "very sad" result is a topsy-turvy, narcissistic, confidence game for hucksters and falsifiers, applauded by those who cannot face the fact that they have been conned. If it registers that one's idol is hollow and deceptive, then the façade may crumble, and one's self-assured identity may give way with it, perhaps disclosing one's destructive and self-destructive tendencies.

I would also note a significant distinction or difference between deconstruction and critique in general—one between procedures both of which may be called for in certain cases. But the distinction or difference brings into question an indiscriminate notion of the nature of all texts (or practices and institutions) as inviting deconstruction. Deconstruction may be seen as closely related to immanent critique (for example, in Theodor Adorno), and it depends on the existence of different, mutually contestatory, self-questioning tendencies or forces in the object of study. For example, one may counter an objectionable practice, such as discrimination or the disproportionate incarceration of African Americans, by confronting the practice with established principles of American democracy ostensibly affirmed by those who discriminate. And, in a different register, one may argue that a text by, or more generally the thought of, Freud has within it the wherewithal to render dubious Freud's own misogynistic or reductive tendencies. But a predominantly one-dimensional, monological, ideologically saturated practice or text may not to a significant degree harbor internally contestatory or self-questioning forces, although it may be rife with equivocations, eva-sions, and self-contradictions. For example, an anti-Semitic tract might pres-ent Jews both as vermin or pests (the lowest of the low) and as all-powerful, world-historical, conspiratorial forces manipulating the economy in both capitalism and communism. In another context, a rambling speech by Trump, insulting women, judges, the disabled, or Mexicans and casting the media as the enemy of the people, would not merit deconstruction. It would rather call for critique.

Of importance here is the role of fantasy in ideology that may harbor contradictory elements and shape both belief and practice in ways that foster victimization to the point of abuse and violence. While insisting on the role of reality and reality testing, something psychoanalysis does is to lead one to recognize the importance of fantasy and projection in construing or miscon-struing problems, notably in fact-resistant prejudices. In certain situations, a fact is like a snowball smashing against a sold brick wall of prejudice. To try to deconstruct a text or practice that is ideologically saturated and structured through fixated, rigidified, at times violently policed prejudices, binaries, and stereotypes is something like a category mistake, and it may lend itself to a dubious rewriting of history. I have indicated in the past that I think this occurs in Derrida's own (as well as others') attempt to overcomplicate and deconstruct a March 4, 1941, anti-Semitic article by the young Paul de Man, appearing in the major Belgian newspaper *Le Soir*, in a manner that at times evades what calls for criticism and rewrites history, transforming collabora-tion into resistance.

One key issue of historical interest, which I can address only briefly, is temporality. In both Derrida and Freud, as well as some others, temporality is rethought in terms of displacement or repetition with change, at times drastic or traumatic change. I find this approach to temporality to be of great heuristic value and to offer a more accurate and subtle understanding of relations over time than does the simple opposition between continuity and discontinuity (including the epistemological break), for example, with respect to secularization. In secularization, what are usually taken as the reli-gious and the secular are interacting forces whose instantiations are complex constellations linking the past, present, and future. This applies, for example, to the quasi-sacrificial dimension of victimization when believed to bring, through violence, regeneration or redemption of the perpetrator. Language itself—jazz in music in an even more ostensible way—is an institution or practice that involves repetition with change, and an innovative or improvis-ing initiative brings about significant change in repetitive patterns—change that may be disruptive or at times revolutionary in nature. Hence change with respect to repetition may at times be decisive or even traumatic, including on an experiential level when one undergoes deconversion and a loss of faith or perhaps a conversion to a different, "secular" faith such as Marxism or even deconstruction or psychoanalysis when taken as an all-encompassing commitment if not ideology. Such a view of temporality as displacement (or repetition with variable degrees of change) situates periodization and period concepts not as altogether useless but as pragmatic and problematic ideal types that should not function to obscure countertendencies in a given period or series of texts even when the countertendencies are subdominant or subdued but may in time come to have a more prominent if not dominant status. Chronology nonetheless remains important not as the universal logic of time but as a scaffolding for a narrative, which may still be marked by repetition with variation. Chronology is also pertinent for the specification of the relative importance of certain events, for example, the significance of de Man's anti-Semitic article published in March 1941 compared with a much less discussed and perhaps more significant one published in August 1942 after the roundup and deportation of Jews had begun in Belgium. De Man's own response or nonresponse to his early writings, involving at most disclosure to a few intimates, more generally became a lifelong secret or object of concealment, perhaps existing in a twilight zone between suppression, repression, and encryption. One might further speculate that it had some relation to his recurrent preoccupation with the problem of falling and fallenness and perhaps with the density or even cryptic, haunting, and haunted nature of significant aspects of his style of writing.

I would note that the interest of Derrida and Freud in the marginal, apparently insignificant or small object can be related to displacement whereby that marginal object may be the locus of extremely "cathected" or charged issues so significant that one avoids direct contact with them. In a sense the significant is repeated in almost indiscernible or seemingly unimportant form in the little object, the footnote or aside, for example. Such a view may generate a swerve in reading practices that purposely avoid what seems obvious in order to focus on the less obvious, the more thought-provoking, or even the hidden or secret in a text or a tradition. Of course, this view must be qualified in a number of ways. What seems obvious in other cultures or in the past—or even to one group of readers in the present—may not be obvious to present readers or a set of them. It may even appear to be alien or uncanny. Part of the work of reading and interpretation is to ferret out what was seemingly obvious as well as what it marginalized, repressed, or avoided, and how such a constellation changed or operated in other times and places. Moreover, what seemed obvious may be contested or contestable even within a con-temporaneous frame of reference, and there may well be differences or divi-sions in any culture about what goes without saying or passes as obvious and self-evident. What is presented as obvious or self-evident in a text, tradition, or culture may in fact not be all that obvious. It is commonplace to observe that an insistent initiative of critical thought and of experimental art is to defamiliarize what is generally taken as obvious and to open different possi-bilities in understanding or vision. A further consideration is that the striving to produce the unexpected, disconcerting insight may induce a through-the-looking-glass effect whereby a strong reading (or misreading) is undertaken not as an explicit rewriting but as a procedure that goes beyond responsive-ness and becomes arbitrary, projective, and wish fulfilling. Such a possibility may be ineradicable, but it underscores the importance of contestation, argu-ment, and (self-)critical judgment in evaluating various readings.

As already noted, transference, as I use the term in a revisionary sense, stresses co-implication, including the implication of the "observer," such as the historian, in the observed. It includes affective involvement and the ten-dency to repeat what is found in or projected into the other, thus posing the problem of acting out, working over, and working through that tendency. (Hence transference in this sense refers to self-implication, affective involve-ment, and the *tendency* to repeat.) It is related to (and may help to rethink) what has been termed participant observation, including the more extreme phenomenon of "going native," for example, in a figure such as Frank Ham-ilton Cushing. Transference is also a dimension of a dialogical relation to the past whereby interacting inquirers pose questions to the past and seek answers in ways that require attentive "listening" for responses, including at times significant silences or absent meanings. But it may also involve dubi-ous forms of identification, incorporation, projection, and misconstruction, which are also possible aspects of transference. Transference may also lead to scapegoating in that you may well be prone to victimize or attack with vehemence in the past or present what you refuse to recognize as active or even possible in yourself. (This may be seen as at play in our turn to terror and torture in the at times indiscriminate "war on terror.") Acting out trans-ference with its compulsive repetitions, identifications, and projections may also obviate the attempt to recover and possibly reactivate initiatives of value that may have lost out in the past.

I find that the concept of working through is in general underdeveloped and often ignored in the humanistic uses of psychoanalysis. Its cogent elabo-ration would require discussion and debate among scholars who take it seri-ously. In this respect, I shall simply make a few inadequate points. Working

through involves work on the self and on social processes, but it should not
be taken in a narrow sense to exclude or divert from the role of play, humor,
and laughter (epitomized in Bakhtin's understanding of the carnivalesque).[27]
Still, it involves a critical response to transference enabling remembering in
the best possible way by *activating countervailing forces* to unmediated (projective or incorporative) identification, acting out, the repetition compulsion,
and melancholia (in Freud's sense, involving denial of loss and identification
with the lost other—something at issue in certain apologetic responses to de
Man's early journalism, including, among others, Shoshana Felman's, some
of whose questionable readings may function to keep de Man as ideal object
intact by deflecting critical attention away from him and toward the way
he is being read). It also involves a critical approach to what I have termed
traumatropisms that unguardedly transfigure trauma into the sacred or the
sublime.[28] The open-ended, recurrent process of working through does not
point to the achievement of a total cure or an effort to forget the past and
achieve normalization by "turning the page of history." Nor does it mean
that everything that has happened, everyone who has been lost, may be laid
to rest or transcended. It may rather be seen as an attempt to renew the problem of relating theory and sociopolitical practice and to make different, especially nonvictimizing and other than "traumacentric" and "traumatropic"
options possible.

As Roger Luckhurst observes with reference to my own work, my "insistence on the model of working through suggests that there is a mode
that might renew cultural politics and replace displays of ethical abjection or
the aesthetics of aporia."[29] While recognizing the importance of Luckhurst's
own intervention, I would refer rather to the connection between working
through in a broad sense and the critical investigation of politically pertinent

---

27. In terms that were as much normative and visionary as they were attempts at description of a
past period, Bakhtin wrote: "Both authentic tragedy and authentic ambivalent laughter are killed by
dogmatism in all its forms and manifestations. In antique culture tragedy did not exclude the laugh-
ing aspect of life and coexisted with it. The tragic trilogy was followed by the satiric drama which
complemented it on the comic level. Antique tragedy did not fear laughter and parody and even
demanded it as a corrective and a complement. . . . The comic forms of antiquity . . . fertilized the
Socratic dialogue and freed it from one-sided rhetorical seriousness." *Rabelais and His World*, trans.
Helene Iswolsky (Cambridge, MA: MIT Press, 1968), 121. As in the case of mourning as a mode of
working through, a question that arises is how ambivalent laughter (which implies that there is no
discrete butt of a joke but that in a sense we are all in this together) relates to critical judgment that
is not tantamount to dogmatism or scapegoating and may well in certain ways be empathic, say, with
respect to tyrants Bakhtin portrayed as "people eaters" as well as their supporters.

28. Felman is discussed in *Representing the Holocaust*, chap. 4, and traumatropisms are the subject
of chapter 4 of *History and Its Limits*.

29. Roger Luckhurst, *The Trauma Question* (London: Routledge, 2008), 213.

issues, especially on the level of basic assumptions and frames of reference where thought has implications for practice. In this respect, it is important to expand one's frame of reference from crucial issues of human concern, such as race, class, and gender, to include a nonanthropocentric orientation toward nonhuman beings and the environment in ways that are not simply cultural in any narrow fashion. Whatever one makes of his role in the de Man controversy or his later turn to messianicity and related notions, one might understand Derrida's lifelong project of deconstructing the long tradition of metaphysics as an attempt to work through an important dimension of the past, which for Derrida continued to permeate or haunt the present (including historiography and the social sciences) in often covert yet powerful ways.[30]

Working through the past is a process that may never reach closure or entirely transcend acting out and compulsive repetition but may allow for a reinvestment in the present with openings to the future. This process need not induce affirmations of creation ex nihilo or apocalyptic leaps toward a blank utopia but instead lead one to seek what might be called situational transcendence, informed by a knowledge of past and present constraints and attempting to effect basic social and political as well as personal changes in an unacceptable status quo.[31] On a personal and social level, it may involve relatively modest but very important initiatives such as adopting abandoned animals or assisting in shelters for homeless people. Such ground-level initiatives may mean much for both oneself and the animals or people involved, even at times be a way of helping to overcome the most debilitating effects of trauma and abuse. And it points to activities and creates relationships that need not be stymied by aporias, although it may entail certain sacrifices such as limitations on one's ability to travel or follow proclivities unencumbered by obligations to others.

Effective change would require the articulation of personal and social as well as cultural initiatives with organized political action for structural reform of the economy and major social institutions, such as political parties, banks, and other corporations. Bernie Sanders tried to address this problem in terms of democratic socialism, which was anathema to many Americans. I have indicated that Sanders might have gotten even further if he had

---

30. One finds a valuable understanding of working through both in Adorno's 1957 "The Meaning of Working Through the Past" (in *Critical Models*, where he uses *Ausarbeitung* instead of Freud's *Durcharbeitung*) and in Habermas's commendable intervention in the *Historikerstreit* of the 1980s.

31. On this and related issues, see my "Resisting Apocalypse and Rethinking History," in *Manifestos for History*, ed. Keith Jenkins, Sue Morgan, and Alun Munslow (New York: Routledge, 2007), 160–78.

referred to a new New Deal, which was in effect what he was proposing. One might see this goal as limited but still, especially in the current context, a major progressive step.

On a basic critical-theoretical level, one largely ignored component of an attempt to come to terms with the past and its effects in the present would be to disentangle the sacrificial into its key components of gift-giving and victimization. In sacrifice (even as treated by Derrida in *The Gift of Death*), the victim and the gift are conflated in ways that typically involve violence, notably toward vulnerable scapegoats as victims, with violence experienced or postulated as a source of regeneration or even redemption (including obeying what one takes as the command of God). The point of a critique of sacrifice would be to resist scapegoating and violence while valorizing the gift not identified with the sacrificial victim. I think sacrificial or quasi-sacrificial violence has been a significant dimension of violence against groups and individuals (including the self) that has played an important role in modernity as its denied or repressed (or what Lacan would term its "extimate") other, often mistakenly seen as an atavistic throwback to "barbarism" or "brutality."[32]

The larger goal of working through the past would be the furtherance of an ethos of compassion, justice, and generosity that would extend beyond the human to encompass other animals and the environment. Such an ethos might serve to counteract both the depredations of unregulated, rampant economic exploitation and the typically traumatizing atrocities perpetrated by various regimes in history. In a time often seen as marking the end or emptying out of utopianism, eventuating only in blank utopias or even the upsurge of apocalyptic, trauma-laden dystopias, working through the past in the interest of institutional, practical, and ideological change might be taken as a sobered variant of informed normative practice and utopian aspiration.

---

32. In earlier works, I have argued that sacrificial violence played a significant, often overlooked (but at times exaggerated) role in the Holocaust. The machinery of destruction, industrialized mass murder, and the banality of evil were important. But they were not the only things going on, despite the views of many, even most historians and other commentators.

CHAPTER 2

Humans, Other Animals, and the Humanities

In a frequently quoted assertion, Wittgenstein stated: "If a lion could talk, we could not understand him."[1] This assertion is prototypical of a position I, along with what I hope is an increasing number of others, would like to question. One could even begin by asking how often do "we" understand Wittgenstein? Speaking for myself, I would say that sometimes I do, sometimes I do not, and sometimes I am very uncertain (the latter being perhaps closest to the self-questioning if not skeptical, perhaps wonder-struck state of mind Wittgenstein may have sought to engender in the reader or at least does typically induce in this reader). I think my reaction would be more similar than different with respect to a speaking lion. But I may be close to Wittgenstein's statement in making emphatic, performative remarks, as he often does.[2]

---

1. Ludwig Wittgenstein, *Philosophical Investigations*, trans. G. E. M. Anscombe, rev. trans., 3rd ed. (1953; Malden, MA: Blackwell, 2001), 190. See also my analysis of the problem of humans and other animals in *History and Its Limits: Human, Animal, Violence* (Ithaca: Cornell University Press, 2009), chap. 6.

2. For an attempt to analyze the range and limits of a comprehensive, seemingly totalizing contextual study of Wittgenstein's *Tractatus* as well as to trace the relations between the *Tractatus* and Wittgenstein's later *Philosophical Investigations*, see my *Rethinking Intellectual History: Texts, Contexts, Language* (Ithaca: Cornell University Press, 1983), chap. 3, "Reading Exemplars: *Wittgenstein's Vienna* and Wittgenstein's *Tractatus*". Compare these two comments about Wittgenstein. The first is by Georg Henrik von Wright: "The author of the sentences 'The riddle does not exist' and 'Everything

On one plausible reading, some might even translate what Wittgenstein is saying into an injunction: Whatever you do, do *not* understand what the speaking lion says, at least if you want to keep a safe hold on your putatively secure, separate, and distinct human identity. I would like to confront that injunction with a different one: Do all you can to work through and get over the symptomatic desire for a fundamental opposition between the human and other animals. And try to take critical distance from the compulsively repetitive quest for the essential criterion or set of criteria that underwrites that opposition. Here, somewhat like Wittgenstein, notably with respect to a picture that holds "us" captive, I am pointing to a "therapeutic" transformation, even a kind of conversion experience, in our use of language, our imagination, our emotional responses, and related forms of life. More in line with my counter-injunction, one might even argue that Wittgenstein's assertion about the speaking lion seems plausible to the extent "we" are so removed or alienated from the way of life of lions and other "noncompanion" animals that they are beyond the embrace of empathy, like utterly foreign and typically threatening others (say, terrorists).

I would also like to maintain that the turn to other animals as an integral concern of history and the humanities is not simply the inclusion of another research topic in the agenda of scholars and students. It is a move that implies a reconceptualization of historical studies and the humanities in general. Indeed the humanities become with this turn a field or congeries of fields that is not exclusively centered on the human being, and definitely not an undertaking in which other animals are constituted as the more or less covert "other" or even scapegoat of an idea of the human or the humanities (along with allied fields such as anthropology) that is deceptively understood as universal in its values and adequate in its attempt to make up for or "redeem" traditional exclusions or underemphases. One evident consequence for "posthumanist" research is that the attention to animals and processes affecting them would be a valid question to raise in evaluating work, for example, a study of war and the impact of battle (including bombing) or a

---

that can be said can be said clearly' was himself an enigma, and his sentences have a content that often lies deep beneath the surface of the language. . . . I have sometimes thought that what makes a man's work *classic* is often just this multiplicity, which invites and at the same time resists our craving for understanding." Norman Malcolm, *Ludwig Wittgenstein: A Memoir,* with a biographical sketch by Georg Henrik von Wright (Oxford: Oxford University Press, 1958), 22. The second is the way Malcolm ends his memoir: "When I think of his profound pessimism, the intensity of his mental and moral suffering, the relentless way in which he drove his intellect, his need for love together with the harshness that repelled love, I am inclined to believe that his life was fiercely unhappy. Yet at the end he himself [dying of prostate cancer—DLC] exclaimed that it had been 'wonderful'! To me this seems a mysterious and strangely moving utterance" (100).

study of the thought and writing of figures in various fields, including history and literature. For example, in the extensive literature addressing Joseph Conrad's *Heart of Darkness,* does one typically repeat Kurtz's and even the novel's "blindness" in treating ivory simply as an abstract commodity, with the often traumatic effects of ivory poaching on the elephant and elephant societies themselves ensconced in a heart of darkness? And is "Flaubert's parrot" a stuffed animal we ventriloquize to show our virtuosity as clever readers, perhaps not attending to the way Loulou, the stuffed parrot of Félicité in *Un coeur simple,* is not simply an ironized and objectified simpleton's fetish but a center of devotion in a bereft world, which moved Flaubert to compassion?

A plausible inference from Wittgenstein's or Flaubert's sense of how little we know, as well as an implication of Freud's notion of the unconscious, is that the human is the being that cannot fully know itself. Or, in Heidegger's terms, the human (or what Heidegger replaced with *Dasein*) is the being in question in its being. (Heidegger seemed to "forget," suppress, or repress this view when he asserted with confidence that "the" animal is without or at least poor in world.)[3] Over time and space, human beings have sought, in repeated yet variable ways, a secure identity based on a decisive criterion that opposes the human in binaristic fashion to "the" animal, typically in a manner that enables doing violence to that other. In any case, the implication of my argument is *not* that the (post)humanities may now downplay the importance of such concerns as gender, race, and class (including shocking differences in income and wealth) or that posthumanism implies an antihumanism, even if the passage and practices of humans on the planet have at times been excessive, self-destructive, and devastating for other beings. But it does mean that turning to the issue of the role of other animals in history and sociocultural life, crucially including the varieties of treatment they have been accorded or subjected to by humans, reorients the very way we think about historical research, "humanistic" understanding, and arguably science. It may also accompany skepticism about endlessly repeated yet also contested claims of human uniqueness or exceptionalism. It should raise questions (if not hackles) about dubious or even pointless research (including evolutionary research) ultimately motivated by the repeated desire to

---

3. In his *East West Street* (New York: Alfred A. Knopf, 2016), Philippe Sands quotes one Holocaust survivor he interviews, in his quest to recover lost time, as saying: "I did not forget. I chose not to remember." But can one simply choose not to remember certain things, even if one "chooses" to be an inveterate voluntarist? Choosing not to remember would be at best a continual practice of suppression, which entails the periodic resurfacing and remembering of what one is choosing not to remember.

demonstrate the superiority of the human being, which readily serves to legitimate unjustifiable uses or abuses of other animals, prominently including research that itself requires the capture, imprisonment, and more or less cruel experimentation on other animals.[4]

Two conceptions of the status of the human with respect to other animals have been prevalent both in history and arguably in historical understanding. They have often served to justify the insufficiently regulated, even abusive treatment by humans of other animals in such areas as factory farming, slaughtering, experimentation, captivity in zoos, and hunting for "sport" (at times tantamount to unsportsmanlike, unilateral, risk-free killing at will). I would also note that the interest in the transgeneric combination of the human and the technical or the prosthetic, epitomized in the cyborg, is worth close attention. Of course, the big-screen image of the replicant or the terminator should not be made to obscure the less sci-fi, more pedestrian, and very prevalent factory farm or slaughterhouse. Still, one need not consider attention to different dimensions of the posthuman in terms of a zero-sum game. However important one finds the relation between humans and other animals to be, this does not entail the downplaying of the significance of other issues that have a crucial role in posthumanist approaches, including artificial intelligence (AI), robots, genetic engineering, and the advent of futuristic possibilities (such as a possible takeover of humans by their more inventive inventions).[5]

---

4. A groundbreaking book is of course Peter Singer's *Animal Liberation: New Ethics for Our Treatment of Animals* (New York: Basic Books, 1975). Even if one finds shortfalls in Singer's utilitarian ethics or even in the concept of animal "rights," one must appreciate the force of his descriptions of animal abuse, notably in factory farming and experimentation, as well as of certain of his practical suggestions. In the next chapter, I discuss the positive contribution made by one of his recent essay-reviews.

5. For the role of AI and companies making use of it in disseminating at times misleading or false information on the Web, shaping public opinion, and attempting to influence elections, see the article of Carole Cadwaladr, "Robert Mercer: The Big Data Billionaire Waging a War on Mainstream Media," *The Guardian*, February 26, 2017 (updated February 27), https://www.theguardian.com/politics/2017/feb/26/robert-mercer-breitbart-war-on-media-steve-bannon-donald-trump-nigel-farage (accessed February 28, 2017). The article focuses on Mercer, a billionaire and a noted expert on AI, who is perhaps the principal wealthy supporter of Donald Trump and instrumental in bringing the latter's key adviser Stephen Bannon to Breitbart News. According to Cadwaladr, Mercer contributed millions to Trump's campaign and stressed the importance of flooding the Web with posts that promoted Trump and employed the technique of endless repetition, a technique that might make "fake news" into something believable. On Mercer, see also Jane Mayer, "The Reclusive Hedge-Fund Tycoon behind the Trump Presidency: How Robert Mercer Exploited America's Populist Revolt," *New Yorker*, March 27, 2017, www.newyorker.com/magazine/2017/03/27/the-reclusive-hedge-fund-tycoon-behind-the-trump-presidency (accessed March 22, 2017). An ideologically related development has been the role of the Sinclair Broadcast Group in successfully acquiring local media as sites for disseminating a right-wing agenda.

The first contestable conception of the human/other-animal relation postulates the dominance of the human being over nature, including other animals, which are often simply subsumed as a component of an undifferentiated concept of nature.[6] The great chain of being, on which A. O. Lovejoy and others lavished attention, is generally understood as a vertical series of links in which animals are at the lower end and the human being near the apex (below only divinity and perhaps angels). The implication of this conception is that other animals exist for human use, which is limited at most by notions of human purity or human ethics, notably the concept of cruelty to animals. Yet, even when a subject of legislation, cruelty is typically a very restricted concept that permits a vast range of behavior toward other animals not permitted with respect to humans, including hunting, killing or slaughtering, eating, captivity, forced labor, and subjugation. As is well known, federal and state governments in the United States and elsewhere authorize the killing of thousands of animals, especially birds but of course also deer, coyotes, wolves, and bears, among others, because property owners consider them to be harmful, often demonized pests. (When a deer eats your tulips, it may be fantasized as a big rat that has to be "culled," that is, killed.) An aspect of anthropocentrism and humanism that may remain concealed or repressed is such often lethal human domination. Other animals, perhaps reduced to the homogenizing concept of *the* animal, may be the undisclosed, at times unconscious scapegoat of a restricted humanism, including one that is sensitive to the unacceptable nature of various prejudicial orientations toward other humans, including racism, misogyny, and excessive differences in wealth and income. Indeed certain purportedly global or even universalistic perspectives (including Kant's) may not question the subordination of other animals. Here one may ask whether the prevalent concept of the Anthropocene may function as another version of the dominance and at best the stewardship of humans over all of nature. And, for many, a crucial aspect of

---

6. For the use of an abstract concept of nature that almost obscures the role of animals, see, for example, the otherwise thought-provoking and important book of Siegfried Kracauer (completed after his death by Paul Otto Kristeller), *History: The Last Things before the Last* (New York: Oxford University Press, 1969). Natural law is typically understood as a law that supersedes (or ought to supersede) positive law and convention. Recently a related concept has been extended beyond humans to encompass laws or rights of nature itself that may be argued to limit if not supersede human rights, especially when the latter are invoked in ways destructive of nature and other beings (for example, hunting and killing at least certain animals or practices entailing severe ecological damage). The law or the rights of nature may even be respected or affirmed in courts of law to prevent or inhibit certain human activities, as when sites sacred to indigenous peoples are declared off-limits to human exploitation or when species of animals, such as great apes or killer whales, are recognized as being protected from capture and hunting. See, for example, David R. Boyd, *The Rights of Nature: A Legal Revolution That Could Save the World* (Toronto: ECW Press, 2017).

being a hardheaded realist is the belief that we must use other animals for our purposes if only we do so in as caring and kind a manner as possible. But, while the effects of certain practices may be mitigated, it is difficult to see how you plant electrodes in the brain, train to perform slavish or slapstick tricks, maximize through factory farming the production of meat as foodstuff, or kill in a caring, kind manner. Some animals, such as horses and certain dogs, may genuinely enjoy and benefit from some forms of training and the ensuing activities with humans. But such a situation could hardly be said to be general in human uses and abuses of other animals.[7]

A second orientation may question domination by the human, but its impact on other animals varies. An important religious version of the subdominance of the human is to see humans or "man" as the steward under God of nature, and human treatment of other animals and of nature in general may be governed by divine law. This law, as in the Bible, may, however, allow or at least be prevalently interpreted to allow a great deal of latitude in the treatment, notably including the sacrificial treatment, of other animals. Human judgment or even discretion about how to be a good steward opens the door to many practices that may be questioned from other perspectives. Such practices may allow the exploitation of other animals and of nature in the interest of the human being, who is supposedly guided by a sense of divine direction or the dictates of a sacred text. They may even assume or convey a sense of the fallen nature or abject corruption of the human being through original sin that approximates the human to the lowly animal, even the worm, at least until the promise of redemption raises the human through

---

7. A recent example of possible overreaction is the killing on May 28, 2016, of a young silverback gorilla (Harambe) in a Cincinnati zoo because there was a possibility that the animal might injure a three-year-old child that had fallen into its enclosure. The child escaped the supervision of its mother and was able unnoticed to climb over a low fence and get across a stretch of lawn to fall into the enclosure, provoking some agitation in the gorilla and, even more so, pronounced panic in the mother and the crowd of observers. There apparently was little attempt to calm the crowd. Instead zoo personnel shot the animal, assuming tranquilizers would be "dicey" or take too much time. The child was believed to be in danger, since gorillas are presumably unpredictable, and the gorilla was at times pulling the child across the water by its ankle. No charges were filed against the mother for negligence, since, in the view of the prosecutor, Joseph T. Deters, the mother was not negligent, and three-year-olds do scamper quickly. "It does not equate human life [with the life of the gorilla]," he added. "And they felt that this boy's life was in jeopardy, and they made the painful choice to do what they did." (See the June 6, 2016, account for the *New York Times* by Mike McPhate, http://www.santafenewmexican.com/news/no-charges-for-mother-of-boy-who-fell-into-gorilla/article_709903ed-e51a-53e2-9cab-bba4f862841c.html.) What seems clear is the willingness of many to proceed quickly to conclusions and to speculate about possible animal behavior. (It was pointed out that the normally calm gorilla might have been trying to protect the child in the face of a roiled-up, unpredictable crowd.) The preemptive inference was the need to "sacrifice" the animal because of the possibility of injury to the child. (It turned out that injuries to the child were minor.)

divine grace. Stewardship may itself be understood as entailing some more or less constraining sense of responsibility and compassion—for example, consideration if not respect for the lives of other animals and a use of natural resources (at times seen to include other animals) in a nondestructive, even caring manner that tries to assure their perpetuation for later generations.[8]

A more apocalyptic version of Christianity or a capitalistic evangelicalism, piously dedicated to both divine law and profit maximization, may look to the end of days or otherwise undermine any concern for conservation or preservation of nature and other than human beings (whose lives may be understood to begin with conception). Moreover, a Christian fundamentalism, affirming that the human (or "man") is made in the image and likeness of God, may reject out of hand the animal as constitutive of the human (and, by inference, of divinity or spirituality), reject Darwin and evolution as supportive of a notion of the human animal, and understand human use and possibly abuse of other animals as a God-given human prerogative. Even stewardship may be understood to authorize both limitless exploitation of nature and killing other animals if the practices are believed to serve human interests.

Extremely equivocal is the status of the other-than-human animal as raw material or mere life (what would appear to be the lower limit of reduced secularity) and as quasi-sacrificial victim and scapegoat (which has religious or "postsecular" sides). Even in the slaughterhouse, the perception of the animal as mere life is a consolatory, conscience-saving move that may not hold up both because of quasi-sacrificial motifs, explicit in kosher killing but perhaps not limited to it, and because of the more or less disavowed feeling that an animal is not mere life however much we try to objectify it as such, for example, by giving it a number and not a name. More generally, even

---

8. One finds this orientation in Matthew Scully's plea in *Dominion* (New York: St. Martin's Press, 2002) for mercy toward other animals. His account, while overly restricted and one-dimensional, includes movingly graphic descriptions of animal abuse in such areas as factory farming, biomedical research, game farms, and tax-exempt organizations such as Safari International catering to the very rich, who can afford both trophy spouses and trophy-hunting safaris. The larger issue raised by the killing of the gorilla Harambe at the Cincinnati Zoo is of course the existence of zoos themselves. However modified to ameliorate or disguise their nature, zoos are at some level prisons where animals are on display for the amusement or instruction of human spectators. For a critique of zoos prompted by the incident in the Cincinnati Zoo, see Lori Gruen, "Zoo's Problem Isn't Gorilla Death," *Washington Post,* reprinted in the *Santa Fe New Mexican,* June 6, 2016, A-17. Gruen may pass too quickly over the specifics of this case and what it seems to imply about attitudes toward animals, but well taken is her argument concerning the questionable nature of zoos as well as the contention that a preferable alternative to a carceral system would be the role of sanctuaries for animals who cannot simply be released because of the effects on them of captivity and the human elimination of natural habitat (or "the wild"). See also Éric Baratay and Élisabeth Hardouin-Fugier, *Histoire des jardins zoologiques en Occident, XVIe au XXe siècle* (Paris: La Découverte, 1998).

when animal sacrifice is no longer a practice in a given religion, it may still linger in the form of a "postsecular" religiosity that construes abused or slaughtered animals as sacred or sublime victims or even as saintly beings. For example, in the widely praised 1966 film of Robert Bresson, *Au hasard Balthazar,* a blatantly abused and scapegoated donkey is somehow perceived, both by other characters and apparently by the religiously oriented film-maker, as a saint or martyr with bizarrely redemptive features. Yet such a mystified view in effect serves to justify the unjustifiable. Roger Ebert, who combines misty religiosity with ground-zero secularity, is simply a voice in the choir of uncritical praise in this review of March 19, 2004:

> Robert Bresson is one of the saints of the cinema, and "Au Hasard Balthazar" (1966) is his most heartbreaking prayer. The film follows the life of a donkey from birth to death, while all the time giving it the dignity of being itself—a dumb beast, noble in its acceptance of a life over which it has no control. Balthazar is not one of those cartoon animals that can talk and sing and is a human with four legs. Balthazar is a donkey, and it is as simple as that.[9]

As simple as what? I am tempted to say that the one simple or simplistic thing about this seemingly self-evident, disabused statement is Ebert's apologetic and subcritical understanding of the film and the role of the donkey in it.

A third and different orientation toward other animals is implied by my opening statement concerning a posthumanistic approach that is not antihumanistic but that does situate humans in a broader field of concern in which dominance or its frequent companion, a claim to uniqueness or exceptionality, is not attributed to humans. A posthumanistic approach is both after and beyond humanism in the conception of the scope of compassion, justice, and generosity. It is embedded in a wide-ranging relational or multidimensional perspective not centered on the human being. It is typical in many indigenous cultures for which the human is part of a broader web including all others in the world. A minimal goal from this perspective is that the passage of humans on the planet not be a scorched- or stripped-earth policy of endless consumption and devastation. What the political and ethical implications of a posthumanistic orientation are and might be is an issue that is currently in the process of being worked out, and debates bearing on this process are of the utmost significance.[10] At the very least, the issue should

9. Ebert's review is available at http://www.rogerebert.com/reviews/great-movie-au-hasard-balthazar-1966 (accessed on December 10, 2015).

10. For two significant and forceful contributions to debate on this issue, I would mention Marjorie Spiegel's *The Dreaded Comparison: Human and Animal Slavery* (New York: Mirror Books, 1996),

have a crucial place on not only ethical but also political as well as academic agendas and be the subject of public deliberation, debate, and action. (When is the last or even the first time one heard a politician address the issue of the treatment of animals, other than in passing?) Significant in itself would be the realization that there are no easy or unqualified answers to the question of the legitimate relations between humans and other animals and that any answer is not acceptable if it assumes the domination if not the uniqueness of the human and the quasi-divine (or "natural") right of humans to do what they will with other animals. The minimal insistence of a posthumanistic orientation is that one not fulfill and indeed do everything one can to resist and counteract the further implementation of the assertion that emerges from the conjunction of the titles of three books of the photographer and writer Nick Brandt, whose work on animals is genuinely noteworthy. The combination of these three titles yields the memorable statement "On this earth a shadow falls across the ravaged land." Unfortunately, anthropocentrism, including an anthropocentric humanism as well as religions that privilege the human, may fall within that baneful shadow.

I would like to discuss briefly a very well-received but, I think, dubious book of 2013 that, in the name of science, takes up once again the quest for the distinctive criterion or set of criteria that decisively separates and privileges the human with respect to other animals. The book is entitled, appropriately enough, *The Gap: The Science of What Separates Us from Other Animals*.[11] Its author is Thomas Suddendorf, a German-born Australian psychologist who prides himself on his scientific method in analyzing and evaluating various claims about the similarity or difference between humans and other animals or even the human and the animal in general. Yet science in his conception of it leaves unexamined certain assumptions that assure finding what one is looking for, to wit, conclusions following from the basic assumption of human exceptionality if not uniqueness.

Suddendorf's quest follows a familiar pattern or template that identifies the putative differences by focusing on a couple of features rather than others. Here is how Suddendorf or his copywriter describes the book on its dust jacket, an account repeated in numerous reviews as well as on Amazon:

> In *The Gap*, psychologist Thomas Suddendorf provides a definitive [*sic*] account of the mental qualities that separate humans from other animals, as well as how these differences arose. Drawing on two decades of

---

which has a laudatory foreword by Alice Walker, and Marc Bekoff, *The Animal Manifesto: Six Reasons for Expanding Our Compassion Footprint* (Novato, CA: New World Library, 2010).

    11. Thomas Suddendorf, *The Gap: The Science of What Separates Us from Other Animals* (New York: Basic Books, 2013).

research on apes, children, and human evolution, he surveys the abilities most often cited as uniquely human—language, intelligence, morality, culture, theory of mind, and mental time travel—and finds that two traits account for most of the ways in which our minds appear so distinct: Namely, our open-ended ability to imagine and reflect on scenarios, and our insatiable drive to link our minds together. These two traits explain how our species was able to amplify qualities that we inherited in parallel with our animal counterparts; transforming animal communication into language, memory into mental time travel, sociality into mind reading, problem solving into abstract reasoning, traditions into culture, and empathy into morality. Suddendorf's main idea is that we humans are capable of cognitive feats to which no other animal—not even our impressive cousin the ape—comes close. We are able to imagine endless situations, to create scenarios and narratives about distant places, including the past and future. And, equally important, we have an insatiable drive to share those imaginings with other scenario-building minds. Our uniqueness, the author argues, rests on these two fundamental traits, but plays out in various domains of the human mind.

Suddendorf's own presumably "open-ended ability to imagine and reflect on scenarios" seems rather circumscribed, and his "insatiable drive to link our minds together" to be sated rather quickly. His focus on the imagination, although termed a "cognitive feat," itself appears to fall in the Romantic tradition, and the turn to scenarios and narratives chimes with recent tendencies or trends in cultural studies as well as in historiography. We humans are presumably unique in our ability to spin out endless, varied stories and scenarios, and we also presumably have an irrepressible desire to share our imaginings with others.

In his own scientific mind, Suddendorf is not a Romantic. He in fact sees those who stress commonalities with other animals as Romantic, and those who emphasize only differences as killjoys. Like a typical TV anchor or moderator on a discussion program, he moderately and with seeming reasonableness situates himself in the middle, although his quest is ostensibly for differences that have the added cost/benefit of placing on humans a special, rather familiar moral responsibility: to act as stewards of the world in avoiding destruction and self-destruction. He also sees long-term planning as a feature of our unique imagination and argues that while other animals may show empathy, they fail to develop moral norms and, at a still higher level, to exercise complex moral self-reflexivity in judging self and others.

At this highest level of human exceptionalism, we are close to a rarified and, I think, rarely achieved ideal of human spirituality. Suddendorf has little to say about the stunningly idealistic nature of his criteria of human uniqueness or about the numbers and kinds of humans who do not even come close to satisfying their demands. In fact his own scientific project at times seems quite unimaginative if not downright pedestrian, an endless labor worthy of Dickens's Gradgrind, checking extensively every claim for every trait that is asserted to approximate or distance humans and other animals. And his differentiations among various animals are at times as little elaborated as are his differentiations among groups of humans or humans as individuals. But my basic point, as intimated above, is the very nature and motivation of the kind of quest Suddendorf takes up and the way it, with what I find to be minor and relatively inconsequential variation, repeats and repeats countless earlier quests. These quests, whether religious or presumably secular or scientific, seek some decisive way to locate the identity and uniqueness of the human, to privilege it, and to set it apart as occupying the highest point of evolution to date, indeed the apex of being and history.

Is it simply scientific curiosity that motivates such a quest? And is the anthropocentric quest itself fundamentally flawed, wrongheaded, and inevitably invidious? And why is it a quest that seems to have a recurrent appeal and to strike many as really novel and impressive? Are "we" really all that imaginative, and might we at some point tire of patting ourselves on the back? How many of us are creatures of habit who even enact habits or repeat "talking points" as if they were rigid rituals if not stereotypically instinctive reactions, prompting or even constraining us to resist something imaginative and different? Where does one situate what is even more constraining than habit: the repetition compulsion, notably the repetition of violent scenes and forms of victimization that may arise from or produce traumatic experiences common in abusive practices, genocides, and wars? And where does one situate prejudice and scapegoating, which recently have reared their ugly heads in widespread, captivating ways? These questions might seem especially pertinent at a time in history when the effective role of ethical and political norms and of self-reflexive sensitivity or judgment might be argued to be at one of its low points, while excess or "insatiable drive" comparable to stereotypes of bestial frenzy seems to prevail in economic acquisitiveness and assertions of power not only here but in the globalized economic and political arena. Such questions may also seem pertinent to anyone with a minimal knowledge of modern history and the manner in which human capacities have been used in extremely cruel, destructive, and even genocidal ways. In any case Suddendorf, like many others, is telling us the same old story in at best refurbished vintage garb.[12]

I would like to turn briefly to a discussion of a figure in human and animal studies who has been severely criticized by some but is still taken seriously and quoted by others working in the field: Harry Harlow, who held an important professorial position at the University of Wisconsin. (Alas, Wisconsin, once a bastion of progressivism, has recently become a locus of politicians and their proponents who defend policies that undermine even vestiges of the New Deal, including health care, Social Security, and support of public education, paradoxically enough in a state having, at least until a short while ago, one of the best university systems in the country and the world.)

Harlow is discussed in a number of works, including Deborah Blum's *Monkey Wars*[13] and her *Love at Goon Park: Harry Harlow and the Science of Affection*.[14] Harlow did at best questionable science based on an unempathic behaviorism through which science was invoked to legitimate what amounted to animal abuse and torture in the effort to prove things that should be self-evident. He subjected baby rhesus monkeys to experiments that put them in what he aptly but numbly termed the "Pit of Despair"—a stainless-steel isolation chamber to which the monkeys, separated from their mothers, were confined for long periods of time without contact with other monkeys or humans. The only objects that the monkeys had were a surrogate mother made of metal wire and a terry cloth to which they typically clung with hopeless abandon. Harlow "discovered" that the deprived monkeys became disoriented and lacked animation. They were not recognized by others of their species, who, among other responses, tried to gouge out their eyes. The inventive Harlow added to the "Pit of Despair" a "Rape Rack"

---

12. For a very different approach, see Frans de Waal's *Are We Smart Enough to Know How Smart Animals Are?* (New York: W. W. Norton, 2016). De Waal strives for a nonanthropocentric perspective that opens onto an array of similarities and differences that resist reduction to simple oppositions subordinated to the quest for decisively differential criteria separating the human from other animals and leading to a putative demonstration of human superiority or even uniqueness. (There may of course be specializations, such as the octopus's incredible capacity for disguise, including the capacity to change the color of its skin in response to various challenges.) While defending nonintrusive experiments with animals, De Waal brings out often hidden biases in experiments on animals and stresses evidence for the role of empathy and even a sense of fairness in other species. For De Waal the great chain of being and its displaced hierarchies give way to complex networks embedding humans in an ecology of linkages and articulations that bind humans, animals, and all of nature.

13. Deborah Blum, *Monkey Wars* (New York: Oxford University Press, 1994).

14. Deborah Blum, *Love at Goon Park: Harry Harlow and the Science of Affection* (New York: Berkley Books, 2002).

where adult females raised in conditions of isolation were tied and raped.[15] The offspring of these unions received no maternal care from their alienated mothers, who instead mistreated them, for example, by eating their fingers or crushing their heads.

Harlow was not a throwback to a fantasized Stone Age or a scientific tough guy who got a little too "medieval." For Blum, Harlow's approach was "mainstream" or even progressive for his time—the 1980s! And she often strives for ameliorative, upbeat messages, even ascribing later improvements to the impact of, or reaction to, Harlow's experiments. (I would observe that, with some notable exceptions, such as the use of artificial insemination instead of rape racks, procedures similar to Harlow's are still standard practice on factory farms. Too often the latter might more appropriately be termed cramped, inhumane confinement camps, for example, in the production of pigs, veal, and chickens, where comparisons with punitive prisons or even with concentration camps seem irresistible, including the offensively euphemistic language used by interested parties to describe what goes on under their auspices.) Blum provides much important information and attempts, in however strained a manner, to be balanced in showing both sides

---

15. The issue of rape among other animals is an important and, to the best of my knowledge, underinvestigated issue. (I thank Mahinder Kingra for bringing it to my attention.) The contrast is pronounced with respect to the prevalent, justifiable concern about human rape, which feminist criticism brought to the forefront of attention. The temptation is great to take an anthropocentric approach to the problem of rape in other species, and the topic opens a large field for comparative study and critical thought. How to determine "consent" or willing participation in other species presents some obvious difficulties, but the issue is crucial when inquiring into rape. A rape rack where females are immobilized and males can penetrate them at will is a clear-cut case where consent is absent and force is dominant. Humans who enforce or enable rape in other species should incur liability, arguably criminal liability. (The common use of artificial insemination introduces an added level of complexity.) One question is how widespread rape or forced penetration is in breeding practices and whether this is even an issue addressed in regulations and regulatory practices. Scenes showing the use of rape racks in the breeding of pigs may be found in Victor Schoenfeld and Myriam Alaux's documentary, *The Animals Film*, which contains footage of uses and abuses of animals in factory farming, experimental (including military) research, hunting, and breeding. It even includes secret government footage along with other material such as newsreels and propaganda films, and it brings out the prevalence of abusive practices as well as the role of the international animal rights movement in opposing them. The important, controversial documentary, released in 1981 and narrated by Julie Christie, is an important achievement. On a somewhat hopeful note, some zoos have been implementing a process for orangutans, a species threatened by extinction in the wild through destruction of their habitat. In a manner analogous to procedures at the human dating service Tinder, female orangutans are able to use computers to see photos of potential mates and to choose those they find appealing. The result brings together animals on the basis of what appears to be their preferences. See Amy B. Wang, "An Orangutan Will Have a Chance to Find Her Mate—Through Tinder," *Washington Post*, January 31, 2016, https://www.washingtonpost.com/news/animalia/wp/2017/01/31/an-orangutan-will-have-a-chance-to-find-her-mate-through-tinder/?utm_term=.fd656dc8504e (accessed March 20, 2017).

of every issue, an approach that can be questioned in cases where the issues involve extreme imbalance, for example, in the power and prerogatives of the human experimenter (or keeper) and his or her defenseless objects of experimentation (or production). She nonetheless notes that the passage of a revised Federal Animal Welfare Act in 1985 was largely due to the pressure of animal protection groups and achieved over the often staunch resistance of major pro-research-and-experimentation institutions such as the National Institutes of Health, the American Psychological Association, and the National Association for Biomedical Research, as well as many individual scientists experimenting on animals, including primates. She observes that the National Center for Research Resources, through which federal primate centers were being run, was dedicated to "one theme": "to supply scientists with the tools that they need. In this case [AIDS research], the tools happen to be monkeys" (252). A special provision for monkeys included in the 1985 law was the need for attention to their "psychological well-being," although the determination of that condition was left to individual institutions undertaking experimentation, subject to review of federal inspectors, of which there were very few provided. Before the passage of the law in 1985, animal experimenters could treat animals largely as they saw fit.[16] Those handling farm animals, to which statutes on cruelty do not apply, still typically have this license for abuse and excess with minimal regulation, often by legislators or (when provided) inspectors in basic accord with their runaway capitalistic ethos.

---

16. See Blum, *The Monkey Wars*, especially 24ff., 113ff., 121ff., and 184ff. The United States Department of Agriculture (USDA) is responsible for enforcement of the 1966 Animal Welfare Act. In February 2017, the USDA decided to remove from public view all of the agency's information on its regulation of animal welfare laws, including all records about animal research laboratories. The decision was presumably related to a case under litigation concerning the alleged use of caustic chemicals on the legs of Tennessee walking horses to make them acquire their distinctive gait. An important reason was that disclosure of records might infringe attorney-client privilege, a reason that was seen by critics as an insufficient, even diversionary, rationale. A February 7 Freedom of Information Act (FOIA) request by BuzzFeed News, asking for all emails and other records regarding the decision to remove the database and documents from the Web, was met by the reception from the USDA of 1,771 pages of records, all of which were blacked out. Meeting with objections and suits, the USDA started to restore some of the censored documents online. But the removal of databases made it much more difficult for interested parties to find information they sought, including material pertinent to USDA prosecution of institutions that violate animal welfare laws. See Peter Aldous, "The USDA Won't Say Why It Hid Animal Welfare Records from the Public," *BuzzFeed News*, April 29, 2017, https://www.buzzfeed.com/peteraldhous/usda-animal-welfare-redacted-documents?utm_term=.vnk66WZZ2#.wv1WW0bbe (accessed April 30, 2017). One concern is that the number of monkeys used in experiments has doubled since 2002, mostly because of efforts to develop drugs and vaccines against biological weapons along with treatments for radiation exposure and chemical attacks. To some significant extent, this turn of events might be seen as another traumatic, terroristic effect of both deregulation and the "war on terror." Animals can of course be traumatized, and the effects of abusive behavior can be devastating on them and extremely unsettling for compassionate humans who come in contact with or care for them.

Harlow's abusive treatment was supposed to provide proof that monkeys and by inference baby humans required love and nurturing, or what Harlow with robotic lyricism called "contact comfort," in order to grow without becoming extremely unbalanced and even psychotic. I think that what he proved, aside from the obvious, was that he himself might be seen as professionally deformed if not crazed and that what he did in the name of science brought out the severe deficiencies of laws and practices protecting animals from abuse not only in experimentation but in factory farms, slaughterhouses, "sport" hunting (especially on game farms or for trophies), and various activities in which humans assume the right to use and abuse other beings for their own curiosity, amusement, self-interest, sadism, or hubristic sense of power and dominion. The look on the faces of some of the utterly disoriented baby monkeys that Harlow made the objects of his wayward curiosity and conception of scientific research hauntingly remains with you. That look, reminiscent in certain ways of photographs of Franz Kafka, testifies that animals can speak through facial and other gestures even if they do not have the words to say what they mean. Here even baby monkeys seem like lions that roar in an intelligible way. Figures such as Kafka, and more recently J. M. Coetzee, come close to finding such words, notably in Kafka's memorable story "Report to an Academy" about an ape named Red Peter who was traumatized into becoming almost human. (The technique of trying to make animals human through traumatization and terror is also critically explored in H. G. Wells's remarkable 1896 novel, *The Island of Doctor Moreau*.) But the look of an animal, even beyond the important question of the nature of various animal languages or symbolisms, may be enough to bring out the inadmissible if not demented nature of certain human activities and the need for a basic reconceptualization of the place of the human in nature and the dire need for ethical, legal, and political limits—limits on what humans can inflict on other beings when they have the power and the technology to do so. What Harlow did not that long ago may not be quite acceptable in research on animals today, although it is echoed by certain practices in factory farming. Institutions such as universities generally have oversight over experimentation through largely internal boards of researchers. But the question remains whether the laws and practices that now prevail are in fact sufficient to prevent abusive forms of treatment and whether a basic reconceptualization of the place of humans and animals is necessary in creating a world that is fit and just for all its inhabitants.

There is an addendum to the story of Harry Harlow that indicates its continued relevance. In other words, Harlow is not simply the disavowed Hitler of animal research, making "playing the Harlow card" a dubious rhetorical strategy. In early October 2014, Dr. Ruth Decker via Change.org circulated a petition protesting testing on baby monkeys at the University of Wisconsin that seemed eerily similar to Harlow's experiments, although the university issued a statement trying to counter this charge.[17] Decker, by the way, finds these experiments to be pointless and unjustifiable, and she has provided updates on her activities and related legal processes. In her initial letter of protest (emphases are in the original), Decker observes:

As an alumna of the University of Wisconsin-Madison's School of Medicine, I am horrified to learn that my alma mater plans to conduct highly controversial and cruel experiments that will torture and kill baby monkeys.

The experiments, led by Dr. Ned Kalin, will take newborn rhesus macaque monkeys away from their mothers (who have been restrained or drugged against their will while their baby is removed). The defenseless baby monkeys are then sent to solitary confinement [one point contested by the University of Wisconsin—DLC]—**where they are terrorized and exposed to anxiety-inducing stressors including live snakes, painful skin-punch biopsies, and stressful brain scans. After this relentless torture, they are killed before the age of two.**

Decker continues:

The university gained notoriety in the 1960s when Harry Harlow first isolated infant primates from their mothers in the now infamous maternal deprivation studies. The effects were devastating. **The babies went into shock, huddling in the corners of their cages, clutching themselves, rocking, and self-mutilating.** Today, such methods are considered extreme and unethical yet are being revived in Kalin's proposed research. I am shocked that this great university, which holds itself as a premier institution, is regressing to engage in these barbaric studies.

Painless methods of research that do not involve animal suffering and that better assess the cognitive aspects of anxiety disorders are already available. The maternal deprivation method, which one

---

17. Dr. Decker's petition may be found at https://www.change.org/p/university-of-wisconsin-cancel-the-unethical-torture-and-killing-of-baby-monkeys (accessed January 3, 2015). On the University of Wisconsin's response, see "Primate Freedom," October 26, 2014, http://primateresearch.blogspot.com/2014/10/responding-to-university-of-wisconsin.html (accessed November 20, 2014). This article quotes and attempts to refute the university's response, which apparently was taken down from the Web.

researcher calls "hopelessly crude and antiquated," traumatizes baby monkeys in the worst ways imaginable.

By early October 2014, the petition had received well over 300,000 signatures. On the Jane Velez-Mitchell show of October 3, 2014, Decker's position was supported by Wayne Pacelle, president of the Humane Society of the United States, as well as by Velez-Mitchell herself. I shall quote from the University of Wisconsin's attempted rebuttal of Dr. Decker's letter in which the sole significant point, in my judgment, is that the type of maternal deprivation in the post-Harlow experiment was less drastic in that it involved "peer-rearing" and the inducement of only mild depression, although how you could control for depression was not explained, especially given the conditions of capture, methods of causing depression, and subsequent treatment of the monkeys. And, as Velez-Mitchell indicated, it seemed absurd to seek a cure for depression by increasing depression and, I would add, by doing so in helpless animal victims who generally are not depressed other than at the hands of humans who are cruelly curious, venal, or seeking to satisfy publication requirements for tenure even when the scientific value of experiments is highly contestable if not patently pointless. In any event, here are some key sections of the University of Wisconsin's response:

> It's gratifying to see so much interest in basic research—especially research at the University of Wisconsin–Madison aimed at a better understanding of the anxiety and depression disorders that trouble millions of Americans and result in suicides in some of them. [Note that no evidence is given of the way experiments on monkeys help understand or alleviate "anxiety and depression disorders" in Americans or any other humans.—DLC] But it is tremendously disappointing that what it takes to draw that interest is a well-worn set of falsehoods and exaggerations deliberately pitched by activists [in some quarters a pejorative term or even a synonym for terrorists—DLC].
>
> Like nearly all criticism of this research, the petition invokes the fifty-year-old work of UW–Madison psychologist Harry Harlow. [One might question the university's math here on work that went on at least into the 1980s.—DLC] But UW–Madison's recently approved work on early life stress bears no meaningful resemblance to Harlow's controversial methods.
>
> Instead of solitary confinement, as the petition irresponsibly reports, UW–Madison researchers selected a method of peer-rearing in which young monkeys are raised by human caretakers and alongside monkeys of a similar age. Peer-rearing was chosen because it has

reliably produced mild symptoms of anxiety in young monkeys. [One might ask here how precisely do babies "rear" other babies and how one would react to a practice that took human babies from their mothers and had them reared by peer infants or toddlers under the unspecified supervision of humans.—DLC]

The reader can judge for her- or himself, but I find these statements to be a rhetorical masterpiece of euphemistic, evasive glossing such as one might expect in recent political campaign rhetoric but not from a major university. I shall refrain from going into the efforts of Dr. Decker to refute the claims of the University of Wisconsin or her further efforts on behalf of the monkeys. The reader may look this up online. I would wager that the university statement was written not by more or less independent observers but by faculty or staff with an interest in the research and/or the university's understandable concern for the tarnishing of its reputation. In any case, the university's statement shows little if any genuine concern for the effects of the experiment on the infant monkeys, seeks only to state rather minimal ways in which practices such as so-called peer-rearing supposedly alleviate conditions, and refers to undocumented and unsubstantiated claims about how the research will benefit humans even if it entails severe harm to the experimental animals. In the experiments in question, the monkeys are "euthanized" after a year to allow operating on their brains.

It is difficult for a nonexpert to propose ground rules for acceptable research on animals. But one possibly less intrusive kind is observation in a natural habitat, which massive destruction (a prominent feature of the Anthropocene) has sometimes rendered impossible. An alternative is observation and nonharmful, even mutually beneficial interaction in sanctuaries, for example, in the work of Frans de Waal at the Yerkes Research Center at Emory University. In such facilities, one may have work with and not simply on other animals, work that affects humans as well as other animals. It may also take forms that are not narrowly instrumental or anthropocentric in nature. It is nonetheless noteworthy that experimental procedures are regulated internally by institutions such as universities, and the federal or state supervision of such regulation is minimal and, like other supervision or government regulation, is opposed adamantly by agribusiness and producers of animals for experimentation whose lobbyists often have the campaign-attuned ear of representatives in Congress and in state legislatures.

Other than experimental animals may be at risk, at times high risk (which will be briefly treated in chapter 3). Perhaps the most widespread danger is in factory farms where animals do not range freely but are kept in often

cramped conditions and subjected to harsh treatment at times close to torture. Conditions in slaughterhouses, which typically service a number of factory farms, may be comparable to those in factory farms themselves. In the
United States, the fact that state statutes on cruelty to animals do not apply
to farm animals opens the door to abuse, and of general concern is the recent attempt to "roll back" regulations across the board. Animals in the wild
may have some protection by statutes concerning endangered species or by
the work of game wardens. The effectiveness of such tenuous protection is
debatable. But two types of animal have little or no protection.

One type is composed of those considered pests who may simply be killed
at will by whoever considers them to be a danger or a nuisance. These include
mice, rats, squirrels, and skunks. In some places also included are coyotes,
and one profit-making phenomenon is the organized coyote hunt, where
there is a prize for the "winner" who kills the most coyotes. The one-sided
rationale for such hunts is of course the danger posed to livestock, but the
animus and the avid passion for the hunt may well be in excess of any plausible danger to livestock.[18]

A second form of unprotected animal killing may be even less defensible.
It is the trophy hunt, primarily in reserves where large animals, including
elephants, are subject to killing by "hunters" wealthy enough to pay the required fees. These reserves are to some extent like large barrels in which
captive fish are shot. Trophy hunts become tantamount to outright slaughter
when the shooting is automated, and one simply presses a button that trig-
gers the weapon that shoots and kills to provide a trophy. Even in an open
field, it is difficult to see how trophy hunting can be considered a sport, since
the animal has little chance of defending itself or even of escaping. Trophy
hunting may be the height of anthropocentric, narcissistic arrogance in the
relation of humans to other animals, not altogether dissimilar to hunting for
trophy spouses or partners. It may be worth noting that the latter practice
has been seen as a characteristic of Donald Trump, while the former is the
avowed "sport" of his sons.[19]

---

18. See, for example, Dan Flores, *Coyote America: A Natural and Supernatural History* (New York:
Basic Books, 2016). Flores traces the remarkable range and adaptability of coyotes, even going to the
point of asking whether differences are at times so great as to suggest different species. His compassionate account of the lives of coyotes and of various human views of them, including their key role
in many indigenous myths, combines careful science and engrossing storytelling.

19. With the support of Donald Trump and in line with the Republican policy of extreme deregulation, the Republican-dominated Senate voted, on strict party lines (52–47), to abolish a federal
rule restricting specific "hunting" practices in national wildlife refuges in Alaska, including trapping,
baiting, and aerial shooting. In my judgment, these practices of risk-free slaughter and maiming,
whose regulation even on federal land would now be up to the state of Alaska, should not be seen

How animals live or are made to live before they die or are killed, notably for human consumption, self-interest, curiosity, or amusement, is what may be termed the ethical minimum in the human treatment of other animals. More generally, one may perhaps anticipate the time when the issue of other-than-human animals, understood in nonanthropocentric, broadly relational and ecological terms, will be conjoined in a non-zero-sum manner with such crucial questions as race, class, and gender in critical and theoretical inquiry. Other animals are a massive category of beings that have been underprotected and subject to human use and abuse, something that becomes intensified under capitalism, particularly when it is deregulated and left to the workings of privatization and an unabashed profit motive. Bringing into question the existence of, or even the repeated quest for, decisive criteria separating the human from other animals has widespread ramifications, indicating the need for a marked paradigm shift in the relations of humans, animals, and nature in general. Such a shift would not only mark a turn away from anthropocentrism but also point to the limitations (but not the simple irrelevance) of "rights" discourse, both human and animal. Without simply taking one back to traditional ideas of natural law, it would underscore a need for legitimate limits regulating relations, along with a demand for justice applicable to all beings in an interactive network that places sovereignty in question, whether human or divine. And it would require complex, mutual negotiations among claims, a conception of duties toward other animals as well as fellow humans, and normative as well as legal regulation of various forms of human assertiveness.

---

as hunting even on a very broad definition of the practice. Allowable with the repeal of the federal regulation would be the killing of mother bears and cubs as well as wolves and their pups. Senator Martin Heinrich, Democrat from New Mexico, commented that allowing such killing would put the "federal stamp" on methods that "the public views as unethical." *Santa Fe New Mexican,* March 22, 2017, A-2.

CHAPTER 3

Trauma, History, Memory, Identity

What Remains?

Despite the considerable amount of work already devoted to the topic, the nexus of trauma, history, memory, and identity is still of widespread interest, and much remains to be investigated on both empirical and theoretical levels.[1] The ongoing challenge is to approach the topic without opposing history and memory in a binary fashion but instead by inquiring into more complex and challenging relations between them as well as into what may not be encompassed by the binary. This account attempts to set out a research agenda that is multifaceted but with components that are conceptually interrelated and that call for further research and thought.

Historical research based on written and related documentary sources may contest or correct individual or collective memory, but the opposite may also be the case. The former has generally been the often cogent emphasis of

---

1. See, for example, Pierre Nora, ed., *Les lieux de mémoire*, 3 vols. (Paris: Gallimard, 1984); Jeffrey K. Olick et al., eds., *The Collective Memory Reader* (Oxford: Oxford University Press, 2011); Susannah Radstone and Bill Schwarz, eds., *Memory, History, Debates* (New York: Fordham University Press, 2010); Paul Ricoeur, *Memory, History, Forgetting,* trans. Kathleen Blamey and David Pellauer (Chicago: University of Chicago Press, 2004); Dan Stone, ed., *The Holocaust & Historical Methodology* (New York: Berghahn, 2012); Wulf Kansteiner, "Finding Meaning in Memory: A Methodological Critique of Collective Memory Studies," *History and Theory* 41 (May 2002); 179–97; Kansteiner, "Genealogy of a Category Mistake: A Critical Intellectual History of the Cultural Trauma Metaphor," *Rethinking History* 8 (2004): 193–221. See also my *History and Memory after Auschwitz* (Ithaca: Cornell University Press, 1998), esp. chap. 1.

historians. In this account, without downplaying the value and importance of archival research, I shall focus on the latter possibility, that is, memory posing questions to history (or historiography). In a necessarily selective manner, I shall indicate where histories based on standard written archives as well as works claiming historical status may, like memory itself, be problematic and usefully supplemented and even contested or corrected by an appeal to memory. Indeed what conceptually ties together the various case histories I address is the issue of the role of memory in them, traumatic memory (or post-traumatic effects) and memory (or memory work) that counteracts post-traumatic effects and supplements, at times serving as a corrective to, written sources. Of course written archives themselves are often repositories of testimonies and various accounts that are based on memory, further indication of the dubiousness of a dichotomy between the written and the remembered or the oral. What is generative of anxiety and open to question in written history may be projected exclusively onto memory as a scapegoat of sorts.[2] In any case, it is misleading to see memory only or even distinctively as the locus of an attempt to absorb history or as a misguided quest for heritage, a more real or "present" past, or unproblematic identity (or "identity politics").[3] Certain memorial endeavors may be open to criticism, but that does not entail either a disregard for all approaches to memory or

---

2. One may detect here an inversion of the process Jacques Derrida addresses in one dimension of his *Of Grammatology* (trans. with a preface Gayatri Chakravorty Spivak, 1967; Baltimore: Johns Hopkins University Press, 1974; 40th anniversary edition in 2016). As noted in chapter 1, one may privilege written documents over orality and memory while still scapegoating the subordinated "other" by projecting onto it whatever causes anxiety in the self or the dominant entity. One general point I would draw from Derrida is that writing and orality (or memory) are inscription systems of instituted traces that may operate differently in various historical and social contexts but should not be construed in terms of a decisive binary opposition that functions as a scapegoat mechanism.

3. By the 1990s important historians in France expressed strong reservations if not outright hostility to memory studies as inimical to genuine history, including even historians who had been prominent in the study of memory, such as Pierre Nora and Henry Rousso. Rousso, in his 1994 *Vichy un passé qui ne passe pas* (coauthored with Eric Conant), singled out Jewish memory as excessive, and Nora in an interview in 2006 went so far as to reference his earlier mention of a "tyranny" while adding to it a charge of the "terrorism" of an "aggressive" and "pathological" memory in French public discourse. (See Michael Rothberg, *Multidirectional Memory: Remembering the Holocaust in the Age of Decolonization* [Stanford: Stanford University Press, 2009], 269.) On these and related issues, see also the insightful account of Carolyn J. Dean, *Aversion and Erasure: The Fate of the Victim after the Holocaust* [Ithaca: Cornell University Press, 2010].) The suspicion or even dismissal of memory studies as well as the postulation of a decisive opposition between history and memory has continued in certain approaches to history. See, for example, François Hartog, "Time and Heritage," *Museum* 57 (2005): 7–17; Kerwin Lee Klein, "On the Emergence of Memory in Historical Discourse," *Representations* 69 (2000): 127–50; and Gabrielle Spiegel, "Memory and History: Liturgical Time and Historical Time," *History and Theory* 41 (May 2002): 149–62 (where Spiegel arrives at the questionable conclusion that modern historiography postulates a sharp divide between past and present and keeps the past in the past).

downplaying the at times traumatic pressure of the past and its involvement with, or intrusion into, the present. I argue for the relevance to history of a critical but nondismissive approach to the study of memory, trauma, and identity formation and discuss significant new work as well as indicating the continued pertinence of somewhat older work in the field.

In recent work, trauma has, often with good reason, come to hold an important place in memory studies.[4] Trauma brings out in a striking way the importance of affect and its impact on memory, pointing both to traumatic memory in the form of post-traumatic effects (repetition compulsions, startle reactions, overreactions, severe sleep disorders, including recurrent nightmares, and so forth) and to the challenge to work through them in a viable but perhaps never totally successful fashion. Still, it is important to inquire into trauma and post-traumatic effects in a manner that does not isolate but instead links them to the investigation of other significant problems, including the more general relations between history and memory, involving the role of testimony and oral history.

Trauma and traumatic events, experiences, or processes, such as genocides and other forms of violence and abuse, may involve double binds and limit what may be represented with any degree of adequacy. But there are dimensions of the traumatic that can be represented, and should be as lucidly and accurately as possible. One familiar double bind, which has to be negotiated by anyone addressing the traumatic, is well expressed in the subtitle of a book by two French psychoanalysts who play a variation on the final sentence of Wittgenstein's *Tractatus*: *Whereof One Cannot Speak, Thereof One Cannot Stay Silent.*[5] Yet silences may also speak in their own way, having a performative dimension that is not devoid of objective significance and moral force. The very breaks or gaps in an account such as a testimony may attest to disruptive experiences and relate to a reliving of trauma that collapses the past into the present, making it seem or feel as if it were more "real" and "present" than contemporary circumstances. With respect to trauma, a simple postulation does not suffice to distinguish between past and present, and it may function to occlude the role of trauma and post-traumatic effects.

---

4. See the perceptive overview in Roger Luckhurst, *The Trauma Question* (London: Routledge, 2008). See also the cautionary ethnographic inquiry into the political uses and abuses of an appeal to trauma and victimhood in Didier Fassin and Richard Rechtman, *The Empire of Trauma: An Inquiry into the Condition of Victimhood,* trans. Rachel Gomme (2007; Princeton: Princeton University Press, 2009).

5. See Françoise Davoine and Jean-Max Gaudillière, *History and Trauma,* trans. Susan Fairfield (New York: Other Press, 2004). See also Naomi Mandel, *Against the Unspeakable: Complicity, the Holocaust, and Slavery in America* (Charlottesville: University of Virginia Press, 2006).

The ability to make an effective, nondeceptive distinction depends on working through traumatic and post-traumatic experience in a way that requires, inter alia, memory work that situates the trauma in a past related to, even in a sense still bound up with live issues in, but not repeatedly relived or conflated with the present.

Only in the relatively recent past has trauma become a concern in historiography, even with respect to events and processes in which its role should be apparent. Still, the style of a prevalent approach to historiography, in its quest for objectified facts, ready readability, entertaining anecdotes, free-flowing narrative, and classical balance, threatens to take the trauma out of trauma. Such a narrative may be like a screen memory that conceals troubling, perhaps traumatic phenomena or, more generally, problems that would call for a different but culturally variable, noncodifiable approach. Notably in certain areas of literary criticism and related forms of critical theory, the reaction to an ameliorative orientation may go to the opposite extreme of construing trauma as an incomprehensible affront to understanding.[6] In this vein trauma sometimes assumes the form of utterly unspeakable experience, blank unreadability, the unsymbolizable Lacanian "real," or even the sublime object of endless melancholia and impossible mourning.[7]

---

6. See Cathy Caruth's *Unclaimed Experience: Trauma, Narrative, and History* (Baltimore: Johns Hopkins University Press, 1996). An influential (but not the only) line of thought in her work stresses the way "trauma thus seems to evoke the difficult truth of a history that is constituted by the very incomprehensibility of its occurrence." In contrast to traumatic memory such as "the flashback or traumatic reenactment," which for the survivor presumably conveys "both *the truth of an event,* and *the truth of its incomprehensibility,*" narrative and integration into memory bring a loss of precision and beyond that "another, more profound disappearance: the loss, precisely, of the [traumatic] event's essential incomprehensibility, the force of its *affront to understanding.*" Caruth, "Recapturing the Past: Introduction," in *Trauma: Explorations in Memory,* ed. Caruth (Baltimore: Johns Hopkins University Press, 1995), 153–54. The traumatic event, bringing an incomprehensible "experience of shock," seems to assume, at least via its aftereffects, a valorized or even sublime status that stymies both historical understanding and perhaps even processes of working through.

7. On this and related issues, see especially my *Writing History, Writing Trauma* (2001; Baltimore: Johns Hopkins University Press, 2014 [with a new preface]) as well as *History in Transit: Experience, Identity, Critical Theory* (Ithaca: Cornell University Press, 2004), esp. chap. 3, "Trauma Studies: Its Critics and Vicissitudes." See also Karyn Ball, *Disciplining the Holocaust* (Albany: State University of New York Press, 2009), which brings up the vexed issue of affect in scholarship, including sadomasochism and rage. What I term empathic unsettlement (which resists unmediated identification) might include, at least in scholarship, not rage but outrage, which is tempered and tested by critical judgment. At points it may also bring a sense of vulnerability and disempowerment. In his important book treating diaries written *during* the Holocaust, Amos Goldberg calls for a rectification or even a shift in much previous historiography by "directing attention to dimensions and aspects of the topic that have largely been ignored: radical disintegration, narrative gaps and ruptures, the penetration of the Nazi 'other' into the Jewish story [including into the very voices of victims—DLC] and, above all, the extreme helplessness of Jews during the Holocaust." See Amos Goldberg, *Trauma in First Person: Diary Writing during the Holocaust* (Bloomington: Indiana University Press, 2017), 258. An

Trauma and its causes are indeed a prominent feature of history that should not be airbrushed or denied. But to construe trauma as evoking essential incomprehensibility is to obscure dimensions of traumatic events and experiences that are amenable to at least limited understanding, which may help to avert the incidence of trauma or to mitigate and counteract its effects. These dimensions include efforts to work on and through compulsive post-traumatic effects in enabling critical judgment, opening possible futures, and diminishing or eliminating the causes of historical traumas such as prejudice, scapegoating, and extreme differences of wealth, status, and power.[8]

In *Haunting Legacies: Violent Histories and Transgenerational Trauma*, a significant book that takes account of much earlier work, Gabriele Schwab stresses the value of situating trauma in larger contexts and histories of violence. She especially emphasizes the study of inter- or transgenerational transmission of trauma and its effects or symptoms for the descendants of both victims and perpetrators. In the latter respect, very important for Schwab and more generally is the work based on interviews and testimonies by Dan Bar-On on Jews and Germans, Israelis and Palestinians.[9] Also very significant are

---

especially interesting section of the book compares and contrasts the diaries of the Dresden, secular-oriented Jew Victor Klemperer, who converted to Protestantism, married a gentile, and survived the Holocaust, and Chaim Kaplan, an Orthodox Jew who was killed in Warsaw yet whose diary indicates ways the discourse of the Nazis at times penetrated him to create a kind of gray zone in his identity.

8. Without having the expertise to offer critical commentary, I shall simply make cautious mention of a recent study by a research team at New York's Mount Sinai Hospital led by Rachel Yehuda. It claims that genetic changes stemming from the trauma suffered by Holocaust survivors are capable of being passed on to their children. This claim refers to so-called epigenetic inheritance, earlier associated with Lamarck and termed the inheritance of acquired characteristics. Here what I think is the plausible but insufficiently validated assumption seems to be that traumas bringing profoundly disruptive psychosomatic changes may have genetic consequences. This controversial argument concerning the genetic transmission of effects of trauma would provide a biological correlate of the argument concerning psychic and social intergenerational transmission, but it should be stressed that it would not be necessary for the latter. See Helen Thompson, "Study of Holocaust Survivors Finds Trauma Passed On to Children's Genes," *The Guardian*, August 21, 2015, http://www.theguardian.com/science/2015/aug/21/study-of-holocaust-survivors-finds-trauma-passed-on-to-childrens-genes (accessed August 22, 2015). The original article, "Holocaust Exposure Induced Effects on FKPBS Methylation," by Rachel Yehuda et al., is in press as of 2015 in *Biological Psychiatry: A Journal of Psychiatric Neuroscience and Therapeutics* and is available online at http://dx.doi.org/10.1016/j.biopsych.2015.08.005.

9. See Gabriele Schwab, *Haunting Legacies: Violent Histories and Transgenerational Trauma* (New York: Columbia University Press, 2010). See also Dan Bar-On, *Legacy of Silence: Encounters with Children of the Third Reich* (Cambridge, MA: Harvard University Press, 1989) and *Tell Your Life-Story: Creating Dialogue among Jews and Germans, Israelis and Palestinians* (Budapest: Central European University Press, 2006). Someone interviewed and discussed by Bar-On is Martin Bormann, who bore his father's infamous name, felt the burden of his legacy, led a difficult life, but emerged in time as a person who steadfastly bore witness to the past. See as well Clara Mucci, *Beyond Individual and*

the classic, at times quite difficult texts of psychoanalysts Nicolas Abraham and Maria Torok, who often draw on their clinical practice.[10] This work was very important for Derrida in his critique of ontology and turn to what he famously termed "hauntology" in which the past and its "ghosts" haunt the present, often in elusive and uncanny ways. Abraham elaborated the idea of the transgenerational "phantom" that returns to unsettle the present with respect to crimes or transgressions that have not been worked through (or in his preferred concept, "introjected," in contrast to incorporated as a kind of unrepressed unconscious that does not exert pressure for release but whose "crypts" must be opened and decrypted). A famous example Abraham explores is the ghost of Hamlet's father, who, he speculates, has committed a secret, unavowed crime, which constrains his restless return to haunt his melancholic son. One elementary implication of this line of thought is that a phantom or ghost, whether as metaphor or as hallucination, is a form of traumatic memory or post-traumatic effect.

Schwab is herself a scholar who was raised in postwar Germany and who interweaves into her account the memory of some of her own experiences as a child growing up in a so-called perpetrator nation. She notes the importance of phenomena that may never make it into a written archive: "Children of a traumatized parental generation . . . become avid readers of silences and memory traces hidden in a face that is frozen in grief, a forced smile that does not feel quite right, an apparently unmotivated flare-up of rage, or chronic depression. . . . The second generation [and, she also argues, possibly later generations—DLC] thus receives violent histories not only through the actual memories or stories of parents (postmemory) but also through the traces of affect, particularly affect that remains unintegrated and inassimilable." (*Haunting Legacies*, 14).

Schwab also writes:

Is it not plausible that the children of perpetrators would be haunted by the crimes committed by the generation of their parents? . . . This

---

Collective Trauma: Intergenerational Transmission, Psychoanalytic Treatment, and the Dynamics of Forgiveness (London: Karnac Books, 2013). See also Roger Frie, *Not in My Family: German Memory and Responsibility after the Holocaust* (New York: Oxford University Press, 2017), which provides a careful cross-disciplinary interweaving of historical narrative, psychoanalytic commentary, and personal memory concerning the involvement of relatives in the Nazi regime on the level of "ordinary" Germans. And see Roger Frie, ed., *History Flows through Us: Germany, the Holocaust, and the Importance of Empathy* (New York: Oxford University Press, 2017), which contains a collection of essays offering informative material on transgenerational trauma and explores interacting ways of attempting to understand the past as accurately and empathically as possible.

10. These texts are in part collected in *The Shell and the Kernel* vol. 1, ed. and trans. with commentary Nicholas Rand (1987; Chicago: University of Chicago Press, 1994).

acknowledgment of the effects of transgenerational haunting in no way exculpates or absolves these descendants of perpetrators from assuming responsibility for their legacy. On the contrary, such a systemic perspective suggests that people have no choice but to be responsive to and take responsibility for the history they inherit, no matter on which side of the divide they were born. It is in this sense that the controversial term *Kollectivschuld,* that is, a transgenerational transmission of guilt and shame, can be used in productive ways. (26)

I would rather refer to descendants' *feelings* of guilt and shame related to a transgenerational transmission of symptoms or effects of trauma—a process that for Schwab should not be denied, melancholically affirmed, or rendered sublime but arduously worked through. Here the descendants of victims and of perpetrators may possibly share something significant, for they inherit a burden for which they are not but may feel guilty and for which they are within limits answerable and may assume responsibility. I would also note that, despite the Nazi cult of hardness that might serve to avert traumatization of perpetrators, cases of perpetrator trauma along with the transmission of traumatic effects to descendants of perpetrators would contradict Himmler's well-known assertion in his Posen speech (or speeches) of October 1943 that the Nazi killing of Jews had caused "no defect [or damage] within us, in our soul, in our character" (keinen Schaden in unserem Innern, in unserer Seele, in unserem Charakter).[11] This was not quite the case for some, perhaps many, perpetrators, at least in relation to their descendants and intimates.

Evident in Claude Lanzmann's 1985 film *Shoah* is the difficulty in getting perpetrators to give testimony without the interviewer resorting to trickery and even lies, as in the exchange with the guard at Treblinka, Franz Suchomel. In Adam Benzine's 2015 documentary, *Spectres of the Shoah,* Lanzmann (in terms hauntingly recalling the testimony of Abraham Bomba in *Shoah*) addresses the very severe beating he received when discovered with a camera by another former SS man. The reluctance of perpetrators to discuss their actions, especially regarding genocidal practices, is one reason one might be inclined to take very seriously and give special prominence to certain portions of Himmler's Posen speeches of October 1943, for in them one has a major protagonist in the Holocaust in a sense testifying not to outsiders,

---

11. For one translation of this section of Himmler's speech, see *A Holocaust Reader,* ed. and trans. Lucy Dawidowicz (West Orange, NJ: Behrman House, 1976), 133.

where one might expect evasion and prevarication, but to high-ranking insiders, who one may assume are attuned to what Himmler is saying.

At times the children of even major perpetrators may be more willing to be interviewed. Pertinent here is Philippe Sands's 2015 documentary film, *A Nazi Legacy: What Our Fathers Did*, which contains extended interviews with the children of two important perpetrators, Niklas, son of Hans Frank (*Gauleiter* [provincial head] of the Generalgouvernement [the Nazi-occupied portion of Poland]) and Horst, son of Otto von Wächter (*Gauleiter* of Galicia). Although friends since childhood and burdened with apparently similar pasts, Niklas and Horst have sharply divergent (and no doubt overdetermined) responses. Niklas Frank severely criticizes and heatedly repudiates his father and his crimes, whereas Horst von Wächter remains a devoted son and defends his father's actions as he sees them. Hans Frank was tried and hanged at Nuremberg as a major war criminal, whereas Otto von Wächter was indicted but fled and never came to trial. Near the end of the film, on a trip to Lviv (Lemberg under the Nazis), where they visit a burnt-out synagogue and nearby killing fields, Niklas, increasingly upset by Horst's unwillingness to come to terms with the crimes of his father, realizes he can no longer compartmentalize his friendship with Horst or divorce the man from his unacceptable views and attachments.[12]

There are signs that Niklas Frank was disturbingly haunted by his relation to his father, who showed him virtually no affection in his childhood and strongly (and in all probability mistakenly) suspected that he was not Niklas's biological father. Sands reports Niklas's words to him: "'I am opposed to the death penalty,' he said without emotion, 'except for my father.'" Niklas carries in his "wallet a small black-and-white photograph. . . . An image of his father's body, laid out on a cot, lifeless, taken a few minutes after the hanging, a label across his chest." Of this bizarre memento mori, Niklas says: "Every day I look at this . . . to remind me, to make sure, that he is dead."[13]

Like perhaps many other children of perpetrators (even the more exemplary son of Martin Bormann), Horst von Wächter tries to dissociate or split the father into good and bad personas so that he can hold onto and affirm the good while, however indecisively, rejecting the bad. The good father is typically the private family man whom the child can still love, while the bad

---

12. See also Sands's more comprehensive book, based on memory, oral testimony, and archival documents, *East West Street: On the Origins of Genocide and Crimes against Humanity* (New York: Alfred A. Knopf, 2016). One of the epigraphs of this book, which stylistically often resembles a text of W. G. Sebald, is from Nicolas Abraham's 1975 "Notes on the Phantom": "What haunts are not the dead, but the gaps left within us by the secrets of others."

13. Sands, *East West Street*, 350.

father is the political man involved in and perhaps committed to Nazi ideology and even related crimes. Horst, however, makes a further dissociation in splitting the political man, who, he implausibly believes, remained good and "liberal," from the Nazi regime in which the father presumably was implicated only as a cog not responsible for the regime's quasi-autonomous momentum.[14] More decisive and arguably more ideologically damaged than Horst von Wächter, in her blind dedication to the memory of her father, is the neo-Nazi Gudrun Burwitz, daughter of Heinrich Himmler. Gudrun, born in 1929, has throughout her life defended (perhaps identified with) her father, sought however unconvincingly to redeem his image, and helped other Nazis either escape or have as good a legal defense as possible in facing prosecution. She blames Allied propaganda for besmirching Himmler's good name and has adamantly supported Nazi ideology in the postwar period. She is often known (and by neo-Nazis admired) as "the princess of Nazism."[15] In a more positive light, one may, in certain respects, see the writings of W. G. Sebald (whose father served in Poland but refused to discuss his war experiences) as an attempt to come to terms with a manifestly haunting past.[16]

Especially during the most recent generation, testimonies have come into special prominence, forming a genre that cuts across the oral and the written.[17] Their recording in videos raises the question of the digital and its status

---

14. One should not ascribe logical consistency to Horst von Wächter's casting about for ways to justify his father. Sands observes that Horst "had somehow constructed a distinction between his father and the system, between the individual and the group of which he was a leader." But he also comments that Horst, "unable to condemn," nonetheless thought "it was the fault of Frank's General Government, of the SS, of Himmler. Everyone else in the group was responsible, but not Otto. Finally, he said, 'I agree with you that he was completely in the system'" (*East West Street,* 245).

15. On Gudrun Burwitz (who refused to be interviewed) and some other children of major perpetrators (including Niklas Frank and Martin Bormann), see Stephan Lebert and Norbert Lebert, *My Father's Keeper: Children of Nazi Leaders; An Intimate History of Damage and Denial,* trans. Julian Evans (2000; London: Little, Brown, 2002).

16. See Mark O'Connell, "Why You Should Read W. G. Sebald," *New Yorker,* December 14, 2011, http://www.newyorker.com/books/page-turner/why-you-should-read-w-g-sebald (accessed May 28, 2016). See also my discussion of Sebald in *History, Literature, Critical Theory* (Ithaca: Cornell University Press, 2013), chap. 3.

17. See, for example, my discussion in *Writing History, Writing Trauma,* chap. 3. Geoffrey Hartman's role at the Yale Fortunoff archive has been especially prominent, but many other video archives now exist. See Hartman's *The Longest Shadow* (Bloomington: Indiana University Press, 1996). See also Annette Wieviorka, *The Era of the Witness,* trans. Jared Stark (1998; Ithaca: Cornell University Press, 2006). The traumatic legacies of slavery and the treatment of African Americans in the United States form a vast subject on which much has been written. I shall simply mention two well-known texts. Toni Morrison's *Beloved* (New York: Alfred A. Knopf, 1987) has been perceptively read as an exploration of the post-traumatic aftermath of slavery and the attempt to work through its disconcerting legacy and haunting "ghosts." (See, for example, Satya Mohanty, *Literary Theory and the Claims of History* [Ithaca: Cornell University Press, 1997] and James Berger, *After the End: Representations of Post-apocalypse* [Minneapolis: University of Minnesota Press, 1999]). In the context of the novel, *Beloved*

as a source in which the oral and the written enter into sustained interaction, exemplified in the online article, video, or blog that elicits numerous more or less impromptu comments often having the feel of oral responses. Besides its possible evidentiary value, giving testimony may itself be crucial to working through trauma and its symptoms, and a reason for survival may be the desire (in an oft-repeated phrase) to tell one's story. Testimony also raises in acute form the role of memory, for it is typically memory that allows witnesses to access their experience of events, and it is significant that testimony has a distinctive dimension with respect to experience with its important but problematic relation to events. A witness gives testimony or bears witness to the way he or she experienced events, and it is this experience, which has a prima facie "authenticity," that at times cannot be accessed in other ways. Oral testimonies are of course supplemented by written accounts, such as diaries and memoirs, with possible discrepancies between the two posing a special object of critical analysis. Oral testimony plays no significant role in the work of many historians, notably of the Holocaust, in part because of the plausible fear that the "tricks" memory plays may jeopardize the credibility of other accounts that may be subjected to doubt or denial, especially by negationists. Still, along with the way memory may accurately supplement or even correct written history and its standard archival bases, even memory's "tricks" and the reasons for their occurrence are themselves valid and valuable objects of historical and critical scrutiny.

It has become evident that one must carefully and at times critically attend to the voices of victims as well as those in other subject positions, such as perpetrators, collaborators, bystanders, and commentators. Although significant studies using testimonies have appeared (for example, those I later mention by Christopher Browning and Jan Gross), one may ask whether historians have made sufficient use of the many testimonies now available or whether they still show a marked preference for written documents in conventional archives. Oral and video testimonies and their own specific archives are, however, worthy of sustained attention for a variety of reasons: their distinctive relation to experience or the way events are

---

should not be seen simply as post-traumatic effect or symptom. As Morisson herself puts it, "For me the author, Beloved the girl, the haunter, is the ultimate Other. Clamoring, forever clamoring for a kiss." See Toni Morrison, *The Origin of Others*, foreword by Ta-Nehisi Coates (Cambridge, MA: Harvard University Press, 2017), 91. In the form of a testimonial letter to his son, Ta-Nehisi Coates, in *Between the World and Me* (New York: Penguin Random House, 2015), explores at times traumatic problems of racism facing contemporary African Americans, epitomized in the largely unexplained shooting of his young friend, Prince Jones, for Coates a manifestation of racism and police violence against blacks, even in the case of an unpunished officer who himself was black.

lived; their role in the reconstruction of events and experience, both when corroborated by other sources and in their absence or relative paucity; the manner in which they enable one to hear the grain of the embodied voice in relation to facial expressions and bodily gestures, making "voice" more than a metaphor; and the way they bring up the issue of the "tricks" memory plays, at times related to post-traumatic effects and the interplay of conscious and unconscious forces involved in the movements and vagaries of memory.[18]

The still controversial gray zone is one area in which testimonies may enable development and qualification of Primo Levi's fine-grained analysis.[19] In other words, there are shades of gray, running from implication to degrees of complicity and culpability, that require discriminating analysis, and testimonies often may enable that kind of analysis. Here the judgments of survivors themselves are of particular importance, especially since the commentator may hesitate to assume a subject position that authorizes such judgments. It is noteworthy that, in chapter 2 of *The Drowned and the Saved*,[20] where he treats the problem of the gray zone, Levi makes a tensely nuanced argument indicating that the gray zone of often troubled or even forced complicity of victims was most significant in groups such as the Sonderkommandos and certain members of Jewish councils (on whom he

---

18. Saul Friedländer, in his monumental two-volume *Nazi Germany and the Jews, 1939–1945* (New York: HarperCollins 1997, 2007), intentionally tries to punctuate or even disrupt his own narrative with the "voices" of victims and survivors (Victor Klemperer, for example), at least with respect to their written accounts in diaries and memoirs but not their oral testimonies or videos. A noteworthy use of testimony based on memory is that of Christopher Browning in his microhistorical study *Remembering Survival: Inside a Nazi Slave Labor Camp* (New York: W.W. Norton, 2010), which is devoted to reconstructing the history of a small complex of Nazi slave-labor camps in occupied Poland—Wierzbnik-Starachowice. Browning relies primarily on 292 testimonies of Jewish survivors, collected between 1945 and 2008. Despite his awareness of the fallibility of memory, he argues that in this case the oral testimonies, when examined critically, are by and large the most reliable available evidence for reconstructing forms of life and especially the ways victims suffered and struggled to survive in the harsh conditions of life in this work camp. See also Jan T. Gross, *Neighbors: The Destruction of the Jewish Community in Jedwabne, Poland* (Princeton: Princeton University Press, 2001). Gross brings out the role of Poles attacking Jews without the constraint of the few German soldiers or officials in attendance. On a single day (July 10, 1941) in a town of some 2,500 of which two-thirds of the residents were Jewish, Jews were humiliated, beaten, and massacred, with some 1,600 Jewish men, women, and children forced into a barn and killed in the fire that Polish neighbors set to it. Gross draws on concordant accounts of other commentators, memoirs of relatives of victims, and testimonies given in the course of trials of some of the perpetrators in 1949 and 1953 as well as (inter alia) memories and memorabilia (such as photographs) of others, including a rabbi and a survivor hidden by a Polish family.

19. The gray zone of course poses problems of comparative interest, for example, with respect to Vietnamese who cooperated or fought with Americans or *harkis* who assisted the French in Algeria.

20. Primo Levi, *The Drowned and the Saved* (1986; New York: Vintage Books, 1988).

nonetheless suspends judgment [60]).[21] He also argues that victims should not be confounded with perpetrators (which would be for him "a moral disease or an aesthetic affectation or a sinister sign of complicity" [48–49]) and that he and most other survivors might not be proud of everything they did in surviving or lend themselves to sacralization as saints or martyrs. In a sometimes dubiously appropriated hyperbole acceptable for someone in his position but not I think for others (such as commentators), Levi proposes that not survivors like himself but rather the "drowned"—the killed, the struck speechless, the utterly abject such as *Muselmänner*—were the true "witnesses."[22] With respect to prisoners "who occupied commanding positions," such as Kapos, Levi asserts that "judgment becomes more tentative and varied." Some might be "members of secret defense organizations," but "the greater part . . . ranged from the mediocre to the execrable," and "it was not unusual for a prisoner to be beaten to death by a *Kapo* without the latter having to fear any sanctions," even when limitations were introduced after 1943 as the need for labor became acute.[23] Additional close studies of survivor testimonies and commentaries might well reveal a gamut of differential

---

21. Christopher Browning, in *Collected Memories: Holocaust History and Postwar Testimony* (Madison: University of Wisconsin Press, 2003), recounts the killing on a deportation train to Auschwitz of privileged members of the Starachowice Jewish council by Sonderkommandos from Majdanek (79–82). In *Eichmann in Jerusalem: A Report on the Banality of Evil* (New York: Viking, 1963), Hannah Arendt notes that there was an outburst, in both Hungarian and Yiddish, during the Eichmann trial directed at a witness who was a member of the Budapest Jewish council, Pinchas Freudiger, ostensibly seen by survivors as having betrayed them in his own self-interest (124). See also Saul Friedländer's critique of Arendt's carte-blanche condemnation of Jewish councils and his own useful summary of their differing roles in *Nazi Germany and the Jews*, vol. 2, *1939–1945: The Years of Extermination* (New York: HarperCollins, 2007), xxiii–xxiv. See as well the classic work of Isaiah Trunk, *Judenrat: The Jewish Councils in Eastern Europe under Nazi Occupation* (Lincoln: University of Nebraska Press, 1972).

22. One may also recall that Levi took a respectful but perplexed distance from Paul Celan who for him was to be "meditated upon and mourned rather than imitated" (piuttosto meditato e compianto che imitato), and an attempt was to be made not to remain within suffocated language on the edge of silence that "attracts us as chasms attract us" but to say with humility and as lucidly as possible what could indeed be said and had to be said in the interest of saving the past from falsifiers. See Primo Levi, *Other People's Trades* (New York: Summit, 1989), 173–74. (The translation of "compianto" has been changed from "pitied" to "mourned." For the Italian, see Primo Levi, *L'altrui mestiere* [1985; Turin: Einaudi, 1998], 53.) At other times Levi recognized the legitimate differences between poetry and expository prose and never fully resolved the tension between his desire for lucidity even in literature and his sense that one could only in limited ways express lucidly the role of obscurity and the dark regions within experience that were at times prominent in the Shoah. On the issue, see Sam Magavern, *Primo Levi's Universe: A Writer's Journey* (New York: Palgrave Macmillan, 2009), esp. 148–52.

23. Levi, *The Drowned and the Saved*, 45–46. See also Levi's *Se questo è un uomo*, translated by Stuart Woolf as *Survival in Auschwitz* (1958; New York: Macmillan, 1961); and René Wolf, "Judgment in the Gray Zone: The Third Auschwitz (Kapo) Trial in Frankfurt (1968)," *Journal of Genocide Research* 9, no. 4 (2007): 617–35. Wolf focuses on the difficulties of prosecution for state-sponsored crimes, but his overall assessment of Kapos is close to Levi's (see esp. p. 619).

critical judgments or actions with respect to different shades of gray, from degrees of resistance to collaboration and complicity and, on the part of commentators, from decisiveness to qualifications and even irresolvable uncertainty or gaps in understanding.[24]

Special mention should be made of oral history, itself based in large part on testimony. Especially in relation to certain indigenous cultures, oral history is crucial in the reconstruction of the past, and archaeology is its vital supplement. Certain sites, such as petroglyphs, may well be living, even sacred parts of a culture, not simply in the past but in the contemporary world as well. Indigenous societies, where religion is not centered on a belief in God or some transcendent, "totally other" being, tend to see the sacred and its spirits in relation to the land or the earth.[25] This is one factor that makes land-based sovereignty so important and renders extremely disorienting, even traumatic, the forced displacement of groups onto typically inhospitable reservations, along with the extraction of minerals, often in exploitative ways by extratribal agents and at times involving the desecration or even looting of sacred places. An important book discussing the National Museum of the American Indian, located on the National Mall in Washington,

24. See Samuel Moyn, *A Holocaust Controversy: The Treblinka Affair in Postwar France* (Waltham: Brandeis University Press, 2005) for a discussion of the heated responses of survivors as well as others (including prominent intellectuals) to the controversial 1966 book of Jean-François Steiner concerning the August 2, 1943, uprising of inmates at Treblinka. See also the long, scathing comment, taking the form of a testimonial letter to Steiner in 1968, by Richard Glazer, one of the survivors of the uprising at Treblinka. (Glazer was a key witness interviewed in Lanzmann's *Shoah*.) His comment on Steiner is available at http://holocaustcontroversies.blogspot.com/2006/10/richard-glazar-on-jean-francois.html (accessed on December 15, 2015). Steiner's father died in a subcamp of Auschwitz. Steiner himself had served for a year (1959) as a parachutist in the French military in Algeria and, still in his twenties, wrote his fictionalized, seemingly historical account (what he termed a "stage-produced or staged narration") apparently to compensate for what he felt as shame over Jews in the Holocaust putatively "going like sheep to the slaughter." For him this image might be countered by a version of the uprising at Treblinka—one that nonetheless seemed to present certain heroic resisters as exceptional in contrast to the complicity of many inmates, including Sonderkommandos. Moved by a sense of solidarity with fellow inmates and of memorial duty to get at the truth as faithfully as possible, Glazer was outraged by Steiner's book and recounted its many distortions, including its self-serving, uninformed, tunnel-vision glorification of the uprising. He was especially upset by its misrepresentation of Kapo Kurland, who, among the prisoners, was highly respected and served as a senior member of the revolutionary committee. Glazer concludes: "You should not have written such sensation-mongering, cruel concoctions about real people, using their real names, which really existed not so long ago and are remembered, so that their nearest and dearest would have the right to bring you to bear witness before the public—if any of them had lived or had had sufficient money to do so." On Glazer, see also Moyn, *A Holocaust Controversy*, 137–40.

25. See, for example, John (Fire) Lame Deer and Richard Erdoes, *Lame Deer Seeker of Visions: The Life of a Sioux Medicine Man* (New York: Simon & Schuster, 1972) and *Spirit & Reason: The Vine Deloria, Jr., Reader*, foreword by Wilma P. Mankiller, ed. Barbara Deloria et al. (Golden, CO: Fulcrum Publishing, 1999).

DC, is entitled *The Land Has Memory.*[26] The way land has memory may be more infused with the sacred than what Pierre Nora has famously termed *lieux de mémoire,* although the latter may also at times be sacralized, especially when they are also trauma sites.

I have intimated that the turn to experience and testimony necessarily entails a concern with memory. An important consideration is that in certain cases oral history drawing from memories, despite its problematic dimensions, is especially important, since there may be no written documents or at least few if any such documents left by the less powerful and the oppressed. This is notoriously the case with American Indians and their disastrously beleaguered treatment at the hands of the U.S. government and its "westward-ho" citizens. Note that the binary opposition between history and memory obscures the ways written history and not only memory may be affected by ideology, emotion, self-interest, and manipulation as well as by problematic archival sources, hence at times open to question as an accurate account of the past. It is a commonplace that modern historiography, notably (but not only) in Germany with a key figure such as Leopold von Ranke, arose in a symbiotic relation with pronounced, emotionally laden nationalism. And Frederick Jackson Turner influentially postulated an open frontier in the western United States, even presenting it as a basis of American democracy—a frontier that could be perceived as open or generative of democracy only by vaporizing American Indians inhabiting the land and the country.[27] Archives themselves, rather than being seen as the bedrock of certainty in history or even as the invariably more reliable source of documentary evidence, might arguably be understood more critically as an inscription system whose contents and processes may, to a greater or lesser extent, be worked over by forces, including affective and ideological forces, comparable to those at play in memory with its suppressions, repressions, and selective inclusions, exclusions, and distortions.

---

26. Duane Blue Spruce and Tanya Thrasher, eds., *The Land Has Memory* (Washington, DC: Smithsonian Institution, 2008). On indigenous and especially American Indian societies, see Gregory Cajete, *Native Science: Natural Laws of Interdependence,* foreword by Leroy Little Bear, JD (Santa Fe, NM: Clear Light Publishers, 2000).

27. With the political resurgence of fact-free assertion and even the big-lie technique (tell a big prejudicial lie and stand your ground), such views are far from a thing of the past. A self-proclaimed Christian Tea Party member and supporter of Donald Trump, one William Strong of Pennsylvania, stated to a reporter after a visit to New Mexico: "They call themselves Native Americans, but anybody that's right-minded knows that America was an uninhabited country and some of the Indians moved in there and now that they want their land, they're calling themselves native, meaning first in time [and] first in right and that therefore they're entitled to it." Reported by Daniel J. Chacón, *Santa Fe New Mexican,* June 16, 2016, A-4.

A recent book offers a view of the archive as a problematic "source": Ann Laura Stoler's widely praised *Along the Archival Grain: Epistemic Anxieties and Colonial Common Sense.*[28] While seeking as accurate an account of the past as possible, Stoler treats the archive of the Dutch East India Company from the 1830s to the 1930s not simply as a repository of facts but as a process shaped in good part by the affective investments of midlevel administrators in charge of dealing with the mixed population of the Dutch East Indies, notably in the case of the nineteenth-century administrator Frans Carl Valck. As Stoler puts it, the archive harbors "unsure and hesitant sorts of documentation and sensibilities. . . . Grids of intelligibility were fashioned from uncertain knowledge; disquiet and anxieties registered the uncommon sense of events and things; epistemic uncertainties repeatedly unsettled the imperial conceit that all was in order. . . . Against the sober formulaics of officialese, these archives register the febrile movements of persons off balance—of thoughts and feeling in and out of place. In tone and temper they convey the rough interior ridges of governance and disruptions to the deceptive clarity of its mandates" (1–2). To the extent this evocation of the affectively charged, sometimes problematic written archive accounts for a significant dimension of its nature, it renders at least that dimension in a manner that makes it as reliable or unreliable as memory and provides little purchase for a decisive opposition between the two.

In her acclaimed *Allure of the Archive*, Arlette Farge, who works on judicial archives (including police reports), makes an argument that parallels Stoler's.[29] The suggestive French title is *Le goût de l'archive*, with *goût* (usually translated as "taste") having a more sensually aesthetic range of connotations than "allure," especially given its proximity to *dégoût* (disgust), not so much its opposite as its dangerous supplement, which at times threatens to surface as Farge evokes the quirks and exasperations of her experience in archives. While avowing her passion for archives and her quest for ways of translating them into convincing, nondistortive, self-questioning narratives, Farge sees the archive as "a gap-riddled puzzle of obscure events" marked by "ruptures and dispersion . . . stutters and silences. It is like a kaleidoscope revolving before your eyes" (94). Like Stoler, Farge makes frequent reference to Michel Foucault, but one might also refer to Jacques Derrida's *Archive Fever: A Freudian Impression*, where he relates the archival to an intricate, even

28. Ann Laura Stoler, *Along the Archival Grain: Epistemic Anxieties and Colonial Common Sense* (Princeton: Princeton University Press, 2008).

29. Arlette Farge, *Allure of the Archive*, foreword by Natalie Zemon Davis, trans. Thomas Scott-Railton (1989; New Haven: Yale University Press, 2013).

vertiginous series of problems, including memory, messianicity, virtuality, haunting, and the political.[30] After an allusion to the ghost of Hamlet's father, one even has an enigmatic, seemingly Nietzschean reference to "the coming of a *scholar of the future*, a scholar who, in the future and so as to conceive of the future, would dare to speak to the phantom" (39). Without daring to speak to the phantom and restricting my account to a delimited interpretation of haunting revenants as post-traumatic effects, I would note that another translation of the French title *Mal d'archive*, on the analogy of *mal de mer* (seasickness), would be "archive sickness," of which fever would be only one possible symptom, the other and perhaps more pressing one being vertigo, even or perhaps especially in the historian with a passion for archives. Vertigo may be induced in archives when one is overwhelmed by an excess or unsettled by a paucity of information, both of which may render dizzyingly problematic or contestable assertions and narratives that one bases on what is present (or at times absent, interpolated, or hypothesized) with respect to an archive. The status of the archive is of course further complicated by the play of forces that go into the creation and composition over time of what is (or is not) placed and preserved in it.[31]

---

30. Jacques Derrida, *Archive Fever: A Freudian Impression*, trans. Eric Panowitz (1995; Chicago: University of Chicago Press, 1996).

31. See, for example, the account in Edward T. Linenthal, *Preserving Memory: The Struggle to Create America's Holocaust Museum* (New York: Columbia University Press, 2001). See also Antoinette Burton, ed., *Archive Stories: Facts, Fictions, and the Writing of History* (Durham: Duke University Press, 2005). Expanding the notion of the archive to include various nonconventional sources, notably oral accounts, Burton in her introduction asserts that, "by foregrounding a variety of archive stories," her collection aims "to begin to diffuse the aura which now more than ever surrounds the notion of the 'real' archives, especially those which historians have dealt with" (6). It also attempts to counteract "historians' comparative silence about the personal, structural, and political pressures which the archive places on the histories they end up writing—as well as those they do not" (90). Among the many significant essays in the book, Ann Curthoys's "The History of Killing and the Killing of History," raises the question of the reliability of archives and their political uses and abuses by examining the debate surrounding Keith Windschuttle's claims (notably in his 2002 *Fabrication of Aboriginal History*) that certain historians fabricated evidence to exaggerate the existence and prevalence of violence against Aborigines in Tasmania. The debate also brought up the issues of the conflict between Western and indigenous understandings of law, the dismissal of indigenous oral tradition along with the exclusive validation of written documentation, the appeal to extreme positivism as a pretext for negationism (as in the case of Robert Faurisson in France), and the role of the pernicious legal fiction in the Australian legal system (often referred to as the doctrine of *terra nullius*) that denied legal standing to Aborigines on the grounds that preconquest Australia lacked a sovereign power and hence was a no-man's-land in which Aborigines, who had been there for some 50,000 years, were not persons with legal standing able to sue over land rights, a doctrine rescinded only as late as the 1992 Mabo case. In her contribution, "The Colonial Archive on Trial," Adele Perry gives a similar account concerning the procolonialist delegitimation of indigenous oral history, title to land, and understanding of law in the 1991 case *Delgamuukw v. British Columbia*, which was overturned by the Supreme Court of Canada in 1997 with the finding that the earlier decision "had not paid sufficient

In an expanded sense, the archive can be taken to include published texts and available artifacts. This is especially the case when they are read or interpreted with an attentiveness to their less manifest or secret, even hidden or cryptic dimensions that may connect with related dimensions of society and culture.[32] Here deserving of special notice are texts that are marginalized, less read, perhaps even frequently read but not well understood or rendered thought provoking. An important initiative of recent movements in critical theory, such as deconstruction notably in its interaction with psychoanalysis, has been to inquire into what might be termed the more archival dimensions of even seemingly well-known texts that resist ready understanding. One provocative insight into the aporia or double bind is that it marks a textual trauma, possibly related to an existential trauma, that has not been worked through and may resist closure as well as the latter's mistaken conflation with the process of working through. To offer but one example, the Holocaust and the Algerian War have been at times coupled as interacting or linked phenomena with traumatic dimensions, notably in French writing and sociopolitical life, as in the work of Charlotte Delbo.[33] Here a series of traumatic events or experiences may function variably both to conceal and to point to one another in intricate and contestable ways, for example, in the writings of Camus, Foucault, and Derrida. What are the positioning and role of the Holocaust in Camus's *The Fall* of 1956 compared with the at most obscure role of the Algerian War in that text as well as the war's more explicit status in other of Camus's texts, including his political and social writings around the same time?[34] Does Derrida's assertion that "cinder" or "ash" may be the best way to render "trace" in his understanding of it provide a belated recognition of the more covert effects of the Holocaust in his earlier writings,

---

attention to the oral archive" (344). The general point touched on in various contributions is that the colonial archive has often been read in the past, notably in cases at law, as a bulwark of colonialism, and the reading has typically relied on the validation of the written and the denigration or dismissal of the oral as well as memory, an invidious orientation that is unfortunately common in conventional historiography. In *Dust: The Archive and Cultural History* (New Brunswick: Rutgers University Press, 2001), Carolyn Steedman takes what she puts forth as a critique of Derrida into a materialization of the archive as a source of infectious dust that literally causes fever in the dedicated historian with a *goût de l'archive*. She also goes into the rather disgusting conditions of her research trips in England with stays in hotels where the bedding itself might claim archival status and make the skin crawl even in the absence of ghosts.

32. In E. A. Poe's "The Purloined Letter," the object of interest and desire is concealed because, or in spite, of its manifest location in a manner reminiscent of the open secret.

33. On this and related issues, see Rothberg, *Multidirectional Memory*.

34. For my view, see *History and Memory after Auschwitz*, chap. 3. For an opposing interpretation, see Debarati Sanyal, *Memory and Complicity: Migrations of Holocaust Remembrance* (New York: Fordham University Press, 2015).

which often seem, at least on one level, to resemble a survivor's discourse alluding to a disruption or catastrophe that is not or cannot be named? Where if anywhere are the Nazi genocide and its perpetrators and victims in Foucault's 1961 book on madness, a book published the year of the Eichmann trial?[35] And why is Foucault so insistently critical of Freud and prone (like Gilles Deleuze) to read him in a very restricted manner even when Foucault addresses problems, such as the archaeological, the genealogical, and the related role of displacements (rather than simple epistemological breaks) over time, in ways that arguably parallel Freud's thinking on these issues? A more general point with respect to such questions is that an interest in the archival need not exclude and may instead invite a renewed interest in what is published, even though its pressure may give the latter a distinctive swerve.

Deserving much more than brief mention is the role of testimony, memory, and trauma, as well as the status of archives, with respect to the highly charged problem of child abuse, including in institutions where children are under the supervision and control of often respected or even revered authority figures. Attention has been focused on "pedophile priests" in the Catholic Church in a manner that should be more comparative but not diversionary or prone to homophobic appropriation.[36] The problem in the Catholic Church has nonetheless been systemic and worldwide, not simply a question of random individuals or a few "bad apples" in the clergy. A researcher restricted to available written documents would not have gotten very far in the investigation of this problem. What seems evident is the protection of offending clergy not only by police or judges but also by the church hierarchy up to the highest levels, including the episcopate and the Vatican. From their avoidance or suppression of the issue as well as many of their guarded statements, the concern of the hierarchy has seemed to be more the status and reputation of the church than the fate of the victims or arriving at the truth. One key factor making it difficult to determine the precise extent of the problem is the secret and closed status of the centralized archives in the Vatican where information on abuse has presumably been stored for a very

---

35. See *Folie et déraison: Histoire de la folie à l'âge classique* (Paris: Librairie Plon, 1961), translated by Jonathan Murphy and Jean Kalpha as *History of Madness* (New York: Routledge, 2006) with a foreword by Ian Hacking and an introduction by Jean Khalfa. See also my discussion of the book in *History and Reading: Tocqueville, Foucault, French Studies* (Toronto: University of Toronto Press, 2000), chap. 3.

36. For example, Amy Berg's 2015 documentary, *Prophet's Prey*, brings out the extent of sexual and spiritual abuse, prominently including that of minors, in the Fundamentalist Latter-day Saints whose leader, Warren Steed Jeffs, received a life sentence. Arguably pertinent would also be a comparison with rapes in the military, or for that matter in academic institutions, and the defensive, self-protective response of the institution, its hierarchy, and its "faithful."

long time. Marco Polito, the Vatican correspondent for *Fatto Quotidiano*, in a statement in Alex Gibney's 2012 film, *Mea Maxima Culpa*, claims that such information has been archived since the fourth century.

In *Sex, Priests, and Secret Codes*, Thomas P. Doyle, A. W. Richard Sipe, and Patrick J. Wall assert that secrecy about the most severe sexual crimes has been especially pronounced in the church since the issuance to hierarchy of a little known 1962 papal document: "The tribunal and other church personnel who were involved in processing cases were bound by the church's highest degree of confidentiality—the Secret of the Holy Office—to maintain total and perpetual secrecy" under pain of automatic excommunication. While automatic excommunication was not imposed on accusers and witnesses, they were nonetheless obliged to take the oath of secrecy and could be threatened with excommunication for breaking silence.[37] A later papal document of 2001 imposed further restrictions, for example, the obligation of the bishop or other superior to send results of a preliminary investigation to the Vatican, where officials would decide whether the case would be processed in the Vatican or returned to the local diocese for prosecution. Doyle, Sipe, and Wall further note: "Because the archives of the Holy Office, now known as the CDF [Congregation for the Doctrine of the Faith], are closed to outside scrutiny, it is impossible to determine the number of cases referred to it between 1962 and the present" (51). On the basis of interviews between 1960 and 1985 with 1,500 priests or their sexual partners, Sipe estimated that 6 percent of priests were sexually involved with minors, 20–25 percent with adult women, and 15 percent with adult men (58)—findings largely confirmed by later studies (68, 212). With respect to the harm done to victims, Sipe and his coauthors take note of the incidence of trauma and post-traumatic symptoms and refer to an "open wound," observing: "There is an incredible helplessness on the part of the abused child—most abused minors either feel responsible for the abuse occurring, or so powerless that they feel they cannot disclose the abuse to their parents or, often, anyone else" (79). What seems clear is the importance, in the disclosure of abuse, of the testimony and memory of both victims and others, such as investigative journalists and lawyers.[38]

---

37. Thomas P. Doyle, A. W. Richard Sipe, and Patrick J. Wall, *Sex, Priests, and Secret Codes: The Catholic Church's 2,000 Year Paper Trail of Sexual Abuse* (Los Angeles: Volt Press, 2006), 49. Among many other works, see also the relatively early and extremely judicious account of Philip Jenkins, *Pedophilia and Priests: Anatomy of a Contemporary Crisis* (1996; New York: Oxford University Press, 2001).

38. Largely nonsensationalistic but hard-hitting accounts are provided in Alex Gibney's 2012 film, *Mea Maxima Culpa: Silence in the House of God*, and Tom McCarthy's 2015 Academy Award–winning film, *Spotlight*, which focuses on Boston. In *Mea Maxima Culpa*, a particularly disorienting

In a different register, the Pulitzer Prize–winning *New York Times* journalist Timothy Egan, in his book of 2012, *Short Nights of the Shadow Catcher: The Epic Life and Immortal Photographs of Edward Curtis,* gives one prominent example of the importance of memory and oral history in checking, contesting, and possibly changing a dominant narrative.[39] (Here, despite the traumatizing dimensions of conflict between colonists and American Indians, key witnesses do not seem to have been confronted with the difficulty of working through immediate traumatic or post-traumatic experience to be able to remember and give testimony.) Custer's famous last stand at Little Bighorn in June 1876 soon became the occasion for a national story of tragic heroism and military prowess attaining an almost mythical status that has recently undergone significant demystification. Edward S. Curtis, Egan's "Shadow Catcher," is or should be well known for his twenty volumes containing over 2,200 photographs of numerous Indian tribes as well as for his ethnographic knowledge and his role in the preservation of native languages. His vision was not only justifiably sharpened by increasing sensitivity to the injustice to which American Indians were subjected but at times shaped by the then widespread idea that Indians were a vanishing race (the theme of one of his most famous photos of Navajos, who of course did not vanish and are the largest tribe of American Indians with some 300,000 members). Curtis became a staunch, even outraged defender of the rights of indigenous peoples, including their right to continue practicing their religions and other customs, at a time when such practices were not only excoriated by many but actually made illegal, with prosecution for offenses that might even be applied to students of native cultures who took part in or represented their ceremonies and way of life.[40] Curtis, always threatened by prosecution and

rationale is offered by perhaps the most notorious offender at St. John's School for the Deaf in St. Francis, WI, Father Lawrence Murphy—predatory, protected, praised, and unpunished through retirement, despite the abuse of some 200 children. One of Murphy's contentions is that by victimizing defenseless children, he was taking their sins upon himself, seemingly construing his behavior as some perverse *imitatio Christi.* A. W. Richard Sipe's earlier work was important for the *Spotlight* reporters, and Thomas P. Doyle appears in *Mea Maxima Culpa.*

39. Timothy Egan, *Short Nights of the Shadow Catcher* (New York: Houghton Mifflin Harcourt, 2012); see esp. pp. 164–75. Almost every aspect of Custer's career, and nothing more than the battle of the Little Bighorn, remain hotly contested, and in treating Custer one is on unsettled ground. For a good sense of the problems in the historiography on Custer, see the review by Thomas Powers, "Custer's Trials: A Life on the Frontier of a New America, by T. J. Stiles," *New York Review of Books,* December 17, 2015, 78–80. Powers stresses the strongly positive affective investment of many historians (including Stiles) in Custer and his representation.

40. Curtis is not uncontroversial. While he attempted to increase recognition of the adverse conditions and mistreatment of Indians and to counteract negative stereotypes of them, his photographs have been seen as romanticizing Indians and, despite his own financial sacrifices in undertaking his massive project, became increasingly high-priced, iconic prizes sought by collectors. A recent

at times incarcerated, interviewed (with the assistance of his close friend and associate the Crow Alexander Upshaw) three Crow (or Apsaroke) scouts (Goes Ahead, Hairy Moccasins, and White Man Runs Him—a name that seems ironic). The three had served with Custer against the Sioux, the Cheyenne, and the Arapaho, and observed Custer's behavior at Little Bighorn. Their memories converged on a counternarrative of Custer as a coward if not a traitor who allowed his officer, Major Marcus Reno, an object of extreme mutual dislike, to engage the Indians gathered at Little Bighorn, without Custer's assistance and support. Custer waited on the sidelines until the American military forces under Reno underwent significant losses and retreated. Then Custer, expecting glorious victory, entered into battle himself and led his troops to their destruction. This behavior seemed strange to the Crow Indians observing it, one of whom (White Man Runs Him) "said he begged Custer to intercede, scolding him for letting soldiers die," but to no avail (165). Curtis believed that "had Custer charged, at a time when the Indians had yet to fully assemble, the battle might have ended in victory for the Americans, or in a draw" (quoted, ibid.).

Curtis's attempt to make public this oral history–based version of the Battle of the Little Bighorn was opposed or suppressed from a variety of directions, including Custer's dedicated and determined wife, Libby, and her allies in more or less high places. Even Curtis's friend and supporter, Teddy Roosevelt, expressed what was no doubt the face-saving and nationalistic view of many in urging if not demanding that Curtis not shake the ship of state by revealing an account presumably damaging to its interests—an account, in TR's words, that "makes Custer out to be both a traitor and a fool" (quoted, p. 173). Curtis restricted himself to observing in volume 3 of his monumental work, *The North American Indian*: "Custer made no attack, the whole movement being a retreat" (quoted, p. 175). Egan clearly finds credible the account Curtis got at through oral history based on the testimony of Indian survivors of the battle who were allied with Custer. In any event, this episode brings out the importance of oral history and the way it may challenge prevalent narratives or even become integrated into the prevalent if not dominant narrative, especially when there is an absence or paucity of credible written accounts and testimony from witnesses with other perspectives.

It is widely recognized but still worth emphasizing that memory, including traumatic memory, has a crucial role in the formation of individual and

---

exhibition of some of his work and that of indigenous artists at the Portland Art Museum is entitled "Contemporary Native American Photographers and the Edward Curtis Legacy" (see http://portlandartmuseum.org/exhibitions/contemporary-native-photographers/ [accessed May 12, 2016]).

collective identities (a principal reason why Alzheimer's is such a dreaded condition). And the tense relation of memory and history is particularly fraught with respect to identity formation. The problematic nature of both memory and historical representation is bound up with the problematic nature of identity itself. History, memory, and identity may be marked both by a desire for unification or integration and by processes of decentering, pluralization, and splitting. Trauma is paradigmatic of the latter processes. Traumatic experience has dimensions that may threaten or even shatter identity and may not be "captured" by history, recorded in written archives, or contained by conscious recall. Yet it may paradoxically become the center or vortex-like hole of identity formation, especially in the founding or foundational trauma, an issue to which I shall return. More generally, there is a complex relation between identity and processes such as repression, dissociation, and denial that resist conscious recollection, especially with respect to a self or community seeking unity through identity-forming memory. Repression, dissociation, and denial are typically related to disconcerting events or experiences one resists acknowledging as unsettling aspects of the problematic identity of oneself or one's group. And the line between at times interacting processes of conscious suppression and unconscious repression or denial may in certain cases not be altogether clear-cut. Still, in an apparent paradox, the extremely disconcerting or traumatic may also be affirmed or embraced as the foundation of identity.

Without discounting manipulative interests that may well have a role in shaping concepts or deploying memory, one may maintain that historical repetitions may go beyond an instrumental frame of reference and have a compulsive, even post-traumatic dimension when patterns or templates from the past are regenerated, at times in self-defeating ways, to prefigure contemporary situations that may in fact significantly differ from them. The struggle in the 1970s between the German government and the Baader-Meinhof Group (or Red Army Faction) tended to be patterned, at times compulsively, on the opposition between the Nazis and their opponents, especially resisters, or rather their relative absence or limitations that had to be compensated for by contemporary activists, with both the government and Baader-Meinhof seeing their opponent as the resurgent Nazi menace.[41]

---

41. This dynamic is investigated carefully and with extensive use of oral history in Jeremy Varon, *Bringing the War Home: The Weather Underground, the Red Army Faction, and Revolutionary Violence in the Sixties and Seventies* (Berkeley: University of California Press, 2004). Varon's book is itself an excellent example of critical comparative history in treating together, while being alert to the differences between, Baader-Meinhof in Germany and the Weather Underground in the United States.

In *The Seventh Million* (1993), Tom Segev has traced the nature and effects of the resurgent Nazi scenario in Israeli policy in the postwar generation.[42] For example, he quotes David Ben-Gurion on December 13, 1951, addressing members of his party with particular reference to its Holocaust survivors: "We don't want to reach again the situation you were in. We do not want the Arab Nazis to come and slaughter us" (369). For Ben-Gurion, as for prosecutor Gideon Hausner, the import of the Eichmann trial in 1961 transcended the individual Adolf Eichmann. Notably through witnesses whose testimony might have only an indirect or tangential relation to Eichmann, the trial broke the silence in Israel itself about the Holocaust and its victims as well as serving to unify the nation. Moreover, Segev is quoted as saying that Ben-Gurion wanted everyone to recognize that "whatever the world owes to the victims, they now owe to Israel."[43]

In *The Seventh Million* itself Segev presents Menachem Begin as prepossessed by the memory of the Holocaust, attempting to make it part of the culture of all Israelis whatever their origins, and prone to repeat its scenarios in current political situations. Segev refers to a letter to President Ronald Reagan in which Begin "wrote that the destruction of Arafat's headquarters in Beirut had given him the feeling that he had sent the Israeli army into Berlin to destroy Hitler in his bunker" (399–400). With apparent agreement, Segev quotes the noted writer Amos Oz, writing in an Israeli newspaper (*Yediot Aharonot*) on July 2, 1982: "Hitler is already dead, Mr. Prime Minister. . . . Again and again, Mr. Begin, you reveal to the public eye a strange urge to resuscitate Hitler in order to kill him every day anew in the guise of terrorists. . . . This urge to revive and obliterate Hitler over and over again is the result of a melancholy that poets must express, but among statesmen it is a hazard that is liable to lead them along a path of mortal danger" (quoted p. 400).

Benjamin Netanyahu often appears to operate in terms of a combination of instrumental rationality and *Realpolitik*. But, in the address he gave at the Yad Vashem Holocaust History Museum in Jerusalem on April 27, 2014, commemorating Holocaust Remembrance Day, his approach was at least somewhat different. In deriving supposed lessons from the past, Netanyahu relied on a "today-just-like-then" trope in drawing a direct parallel between the threat posed by Nazis to Jews in the period leading up to the Holocaust and the contemporary threat posed by Iran to Israel. He asserted:

---

42. Tom Segev, *The Seventh Million: The Israelis and the Holocaust* (New York: Hill & Wang, 1993).

43. See Gavin Esler, "How Nazi Adolf Eichmann's Holocaust Trial Unified Israel," *BBC World News*, April 6, 2011, http://www.bbc.com/news/world-12912527 (accessed June 1, 2016).

I have said many times in this place that we must identify an existential threat in time and take action in time. . . . Iran is calling for our destruction. . . . Today, just like then, there are those who dismiss Iran's extreme rhetoric as one that serves domestic purposes. Today, just like then, there are those who view Iran's nuclear ambitions as the result of the natural will of a proud nation—a will that should be accepted. And just like then, those who make such claims are deluding themselves. They are making an historic mistake.[44]

With the existence of the State of Israel and its military power (its allies, notably the United States, remained unmentioned), there was for Netanyahu one decisive difference between then and now: "Unlike our situation during the Holocaust, when we were like leaves on the wind, defenseless, now we have great power to defend ourselves, and it is ready for any mission." To the extent one may take these statements at face value or perhaps see them as recognizing the force of traumatic memory by making ideological and political use of it, Netanyahu would seem to be within the same frame of reference as predecessors such as Begin. Moreover, in inaccurate, incendiary comments made at the 37th Zionist Congress, in 2015, Netanyahu in effect blamed the Palestinians for initiating genocide during the Holocaust by asserting that "Hitler didn't want to exterminate the Jews at the time, he wanted to expel the Jews," and pointing to the Grand Mufti of Jerusalem, Haj Amin al-Husseini, as convincing Hitler to turn from expulsion to genocide.[45]

44. See the "Full Transcript of Netanyahu Speech for Holocaust Remembrance Day," http://www.timesofisrael.com/full-transcript-of-netanyahu-speech-for-holocaust-remembrance-day/ (accessed December 4, 2015).

45. See, for example, the story of Greg Botelho for CNN on October 22, 2015, http://www.cnn.com/2015/10/21/middleeast/netanyahu-hitler-grand-mufti-holocaust/ (accessed October 23, 2015). In the face of widespread criticism, including that of Israeli historians, Netanyahu retracted his statement within ten days. See Jodi Rudoren, "Netanyahu Retracts Assertion That Palestinians Inspired Holocaust," New York Times, October 30, 2015, http://www.nytimes.com/2015/10/31/world/middleeast/netanyahu-retracts-assertion-that-palestinian-inspired-holocaust.html?_r=0 (accessed December 8, 2015). Nonetheless, the fact that Netanyahu was initially inclined to make such an extreme, even outlandish statement is significant as an indication of his state of mind. The political assassination of Yitzhak Rabin on November 4, 1995, was undertaken by Yigal Amir, an Orthodox Jew opposed to Rabin's sustained peace initiative on the grounds that withdrawal from the West Bank would deny Jews their biblical heritage presumably reclaimed by establishing settlements. Rabin's assassination had a disastrously chilling effect on the peace process, furthered the appointment of right-wing prime ministers, and abetted the building of settlements in the occupied territories, often illegally financed with state funds and housing some 400,000 "settlers" whose numbers continue to grow. See Shimon Dotan's documentary The Settlers, released in January 2016 at the Sundance Film Festival, as well as Dotan's on-site interview with Amy Goodman on January 28, 2016, available at http://www.democracynow.org/2016/1/28/the_settlers_new_film_reveals_history (accessed January 29, 2016).

For many Israelis the 1948 war has been seen and celebrated in terms of the achievement of an independent state. For many Palestinians and their sympathizers, it is the *Nakba* ("catastrophe" or "disaster"—the Hebrew word would be *Shoah*). During it almost three-quarters of a million Palestinian Arabs fled or were driven from their homes, which created a massive refugee problem for themselves, their descendants, and Israel and the Middle East in general. A planned launch of a Hebrew-language book (with the translated title *The Holocaust and the Nakba: Memory, National Identity, and Jewish-Arab Partnership*) at the Van Leer institute in Jerusalem, focusing on a multidimensional and relational instead of an invidiously comparative or competitive approach to the Holocaust and the Nakba, drew criticism from those who nonetheless took the event as involving not merely competitive memory but what they saw as an inadmissible (if not sacrilegious) comparison with the Holocaust. The director of the Van Leer, Professor Emeritus at the Hebrew University Gabriel Motzkin, who asserted he was "a Zionist through and through," defended the event and is quoted as saying that the book "has many different views," including several "right-wing" articles, and that "the real issue about the Nakba is that Israeli society is 'unwilling to understand the trauma that constitutes the identity of this other people.' "[46]

It would be misguided to ignore the actual threats posed to Israel by its declared enemies, including Iran, or to leave unmentioned the severe treatment of Palestinian refugees in other countries.[47] Still, the Israeli government has treated the occupied territories in harsh and violent ways that have been opposed by a segment of the Israeli population, including Refuseniks in the army who, while devoted to Israel and to its military, have found certain policies unacceptable and have refused to implement them. But the scenario may be reversed, with the Jew or the Israeli seen as the neo-Nazi, and the

---

46. See Ariel Ben Solomon, "Israel Unwilling to Understand Nakba, the Trauma That Constitutes Palestinian Identity," *Jerusalem Post*, August 28, 2015, http://www.jpost.com/Arab-Israeli-Conflict/Israel-unwilling-to-understand-Nakba-the-trauma-that-constitutes-Palestinian-identity-413486 (accessed December 3, 2015). Of course Motzkin himself and other Israelis, such as Dan Bar-On and Amos Goldberg, are trying to foster an active appreciation of the plight and suffering of Palestinians and, in spite of seemingly intractable problems, to further the peace process. For a collaborative effort between a Palestinian and an Israeli, see Bashir Bashir and Amos Goldberg, "Deliberating the Holocaust and the Nakba: Disruptive Empathy and Binationalism in Israel and Palestine," *Journal of Genocide Research* 16, no. 1 (2004): 77–99. See also the compassionate, informative account in Jo Roberts, *Contested Land, Contested Memory: Israel's Jews and Arabs and the Ghosts of Catastrophe* (Toronto: Dundurn, 2013).

47. Among the many commentaries on the issue, see, for example, Olga Khazan, "Refugee: Palestinians in Arab Countries Have It Bad, Too," *Washington Post*, November 30, 2012, https://www.washingtonpost.com/news/worldviews/wp/2012/11/30/palestinians-israel-settlements-arab-countries-refugees/ (accessed December 2, 2015).

Arab or, more specifically, the Palestinian as the victim. Without being able to do justice to the intricacies of the situation in the Middle East or American reactions to it, including the role of extremism and terrorism in segments of Islam, recently reaching a high point in ISIS, I would simply point out what should be apparent: without attributing excessive causal weight to trauma and its aftereffects, one may nonetheless insist that an unfortunate feature of more or less compulsive repetition is to obscure the significance of other factors and to severely limit political and social options in the present that would require among other things a careful analysis of the at times manipulative role of present forces as well as an attempt to work through the past rather than to displace and repeat it under the influence (or making use) of compulsive, traumatic memories.[48]

Already invoked is a notion that warrants more reflection and research: the founding or foundational trauma, the trauma that carries a powerful affective charge and may be transformed or transvalued in ideological ways.[49] Here a crisis or catastrophe that disorients and may devastate the collectivity or the individual may uncannily become the basis of an origin or renewed origin myth that authorizes acts or policies that appeal to it for justification. A foundational trauma and a related myth of origins may be operative both in written histories and in collective (or individual) memory. (For example, witness the role until recently of the French Revolution in French history, memory, and politics, a phenomenon given an explicitly religious, indeed sacrificial significance by Joseph de Maistre on the far right and imbued with a more secular religiosity by Jules Michelet and others in the Republican tradition. A somewhat analogous point might be made about the Civil War in the United States and its legacy of divided loyalties and fervid commitments if not a perceived "clash of civilizations." I have alluded to the role of the Holocaust as a contested foundational trauma experienced by some as a religious *tremendum* or as the basis of an identity-forming civil religion. These examples could be multiplied.) Unworked-through trauma, especially when it is foundational or structural, can become invidious and self-centered,

---

48. Relevant in this respect are discussions in the journal *Tikkun* as well as Avraham Burg's *The Holocaust Is Over, We Must Rise from Its Ashes* (New York: Palgrave Macmillan, 2008). See also the review of this book in *Tikkun* 26, no. 2 (2011): 37–39 by Jonathan Friedman. Friedman writes that, for Burg (a former member as well as speaker of the Knesset), "Holocaust memory, identity politics, and the Israel-Palestine conflict are indelibly linked by trauma, and the inability to resolve the lingering effects of this trauma has crippled all efforts at peace. In the years that have passed since the publication of Burg's book in 2008, Israel has moved further away from the place of healing and reconciliation he calls for and instead toward a place of greater fear and anger" (37). Unfortunately, a significant segment of the population in the United States has recently been very close to that fearful place.

49. Compare my discussion in *Writing History, Writing Trauma*, chap. 2, esp. xii–xiv and 80–85.

lending itself to some very dubious uses and abuses. It can even assume an ambivalently sacred or sublime status, both terrifying and awe inspiring in nature.

The so-called Western tradition and societies that appeal to it have had founding traumas as myths of origin. The construction of modern societies as having too much memory or exceptional "trauma cultures" may be short-sighted and at times exaggerated. The fall of Adam and Eve, as interpreted in much of Christianity, plays the role of a foundational trauma, leaving a legacy of exile, distance from the divine presence, and "original sin." It may also be construed as an ambivalent felix culpa linked to redemption and hope for a reborn, higher spirituality. Original sin has had quite a future under Christianity as well as in secular analogues (such as Freud's primal crime and "archaic heritage" of guilt, the Lacanian "real," or the melancholic and/or traumatic sublime). With reference to the New Testament, along with the Fall and original sin, the new founding trauma is, of course, the agonized crucifixion of Christ, which redeems believers from the heritage of guilt stemming from original sin. Along with their irreducible religious significance as signs of sanctity, stigmata have as one perhaps obvious but still pertinent interpretation their status as post-traumatic effects in one who identifies with and incorporates the life of Christ to the point of reliving psychosomatically and psychically what one did not in fact live: Christ's suffering and crucifixion leading to his death and resurrection.[50]

In the United States, the devastating terrorist attacks on September 11, 2001, were immediately perceived in terms of a new founding trauma, supplementing and perhaps displacing earlier myths of origin. September 11, or 9/11, also quickly achieved a quasi-sacral quality, giving rise to commemorative events and making almost taboo certain kinds of critical analysis, for example, into causes of such an event, both shockingly unexpected and all-too-expectable, with respect to animosity toward the United States and certain of its policies. In the aftermath of the Cold War, 9/11 provided a new enemy that could unite the country in solidarity against the terrorists or even the more abstract notion of terror itself. Repeated invocation of the war on terror has functioned to screen or divert attention from other problems, including the destructive, traumatizing nature of American bombing of the Middle East. It has also served to justify intensified surveillance and data collection and to legitimate the suspension of constitutional rights for

---

50. Already alluded to in chapter 1 is Alan Jacobs, *Original Sin: A Cultural History* (New York: HarperCollins, 2008), an episodic yet far-reaching account of original sin, including the importance of Paul and Augustine in its elaboration.

those accused of terrorism, at times enabling or even authorizing the use of terror and traumatization in handling those suspects.[51] How to pursue other than militaristic and repressive policies in the aftermath of 9/11, with their effect on the national (self-)image and troubled sense of identity, has become a dilemma for the United States.[52]

I shall close by returning briefly to an ethically, politically, and affectively charged issue that is fundamental to the problem of identity and "identity formation" and concerning which a great deal remains to be done: the issue of critical animal studies. This issue is quite pertinent to a discussion of history, memory, and trauma, and it warrants attention, even though obvious constraints enable only the raising of certain questions, the making of some more or less controversial claims, and the attempt to prompt further discussion.

As Éric Baratay writes in introducing his ambitious study, *Le point de vue animal: Une autre version de l'histoire*, "History, constructed by human societies, is always recounted as an adventure that only concerns humans (*l'homme*). However, animals have participated or still participate abundantly in the great events or in the slow phenomena of civilization."[53] One may reinforce Baratay's assertion by pointing out that even references to the universal and the global are generally restricted to humans. (As noted earlier, genocide, even when extended to other than national or ethnic groups, remains confined to humans while excluding animal species, and the related notion of crimes against humanity is not crimes against humanity or other animals.)

---

51. For the illegal use of torture during the administration of George W. Bush, see the Senate summary report released in October 2015 at http://www.nytimes.com/interactive/2014/12/09/world/cia-torture-report-document.html?_r=1 (accessed on December 4, 2015).

52. Noteworthy is Judith Butler's argument in favor of transforming self-mourning in the United States after 9/11, which lent itself to violence and war, into a form of grief that recognizes and respects mutual injury and vulnerability based on the self's own dispossession and "the unconscious imprint of my primary sociality"—a view that resonates with notions of transference and alterity (including alterity within the self, notably unconscious processes). See Judith Butler, *Precarious Life: The Powers of Mourning and Violence* (London: Verso, 2004), 28. I have intimated that transference is related to one's "primary sociality" in that it involves implication in others, including, I think, other animals and affectively charged "objects" of study. A key problem is how to understand the possibilities and limits of agency as well as responsibility with respect to vulnerability, receptivity, and mutual implication of self and other.

53. Éric Baratay, *Le point de vue animal: Une autre version de l'histoire* (Paris: Éditions du Seuil, 2012), 11 (my translation). However, Baratay's work along with that of others indicates that changes have been under way. See also Éric Baratay and Elizabeth Hardouin-Fugier, *Zoo: A History of Zoological Gardens in the West*, trans. Oliver Welsh (London: Reaktion Books, 2004). An important instance of the increased interest of historians in such questions is the special issue of *History and Theory* 52 (December 2013) edited and introduced by Gary David Shaw. In his insightful introductory essay, Shaw elucidates the rise of the historical interest in other animals and their relations with humans as well as the theoretical, conceptual, and methodological problems that accompany this turn.

Engaging the problem Baratay raises would require extending research be-yond humans and stressing the importance of decentering and situating hu-mans in a larger network of relations. It would involve a careful, comparative study of memory, trauma, affect, and identity with respect to other animals, along with a noninvidious comparison of humans and other animals with an emphasis on their interactions and coevolution. And it would bring out mutual dependency in a larger ecological setting, at times in a cooperative rapport but at other times under the hegemonic and self-interested control of humans.[54]

I have already pointed to the obvious issue concerning whether the mul-tiplicity of differences, specificities, and similarities both between and within humans and other animals can be totalized into a binary opposition justify-ing the postulation of a gap or decisive break between "the" human and "the" animal—a break itself at times construed as a foundational trauma taking the human away from animality and instinct into the "higher" realm of culture.[55] Perhaps more basically, one may question the very motivation that induces time and again in history the desire to locate the decisive (but recurrently shifting, contestable, and recalibrated) criteria that presumably separate or create a gap between humans and other animals. In an impor-tant sense, a transformative recognition would be that the very symptom to be worked through—psychically, ethically, and politically—is that repeti-tive, seemingly compulsive desire issuing from anthropocentric fixation and the drive to have secure, essential knowledge of precisely what it is to be human. (A more or less displaced religious quest for "redemption" from ani-mality and embodiment may also be at play.) This recognition might serve to further an other than anthropocentric orientation geared to demonstrat-ing supposed human self-identity and superiority if not exceptionalism and too easily serving to justify questionable human uses and abuses of other animals.

As noted in chapter 2, Frans de Waal, in his wittily entitled *Are We Smart Enough to Know How Smart Animals Are?* stresses the various types of intel-ligence and ability in different animals, including remarkable cognitive

---

54. In this account, given the attention to trauma and its effects, I focus on the latter eventuality while in no sense denying more positive and mutually beneficial relations between humans and other animals that both may remember quite well. Such relations are crucial in averting, or counteracting the effects of, trauma, as is evidenced in the role of certain animals in therapy for humans as well as the possible success of caring for traumatized animals.

55. This so-called passage from nature to culture has been discussed by many, including Sigmund Freud and Claude Lévi-Strauss. It is arguably at issue in the Fall and original sin, where the snake is made the "heavy" and humans separate themselves from the rest of nature.

achievements and feats of memory.[56] Like Darwin, he argues for differences of degree not kind between humans and other animals and observes that "uniqueness claims typically cycle through four stages: they are repeated over and over, they are challenged by new findings, they hobble toward retirement, and then they are dumped into an ignominious grave" (126). However one eventually constructs the complex configuration of similarities and differences bearing on any putative differentiating criterion, the question remains whether and in what manner it would validate human uses and abuses of other animals—a question that would have to be addressed not on narrowly scientific but on ethical and political grounds. An initial consideration is that insofar as animals are under human supervision and control, a minimal ethical condition in their treatment is how they are allowed or made to live as well as die, notably when they are killed for human consumption. (This has of course been an important concern in the work of Temple Grandin, who addressed ways of averting or at least mitigating the traumatization of animals in slaughterhouses.) This condition is far from acceptably met in many agribusiness firms and factory farms.[57]

A nuanced appraisal of the possibilities and limits of reform under capitalism is offered by Peter Singer in "Open the Cages!," a review of Wayne Pacelle's *The Humane Economy: How Innovators and Enlightened Consumers Are Transforming the Lives of Animals*.[58] Singer argues that capitalism did not cause "speciesism," which has existed in many cultures and political regimes, and, I would add, whose history over time and space itself offers a vast field for comparative research. But, less optimistic than Pacelle about the possibilities of basic change under capitalism, Singer indicates how the unregulated profit motive may pose barriers to a humane or moral economy and aggravate the exploitation of other animals (and, it should be obvious, human beings as well). Without seeing them as structural changes with respect to the relation between humans and other animals, he notes with approval certain reforms,

---

56. Frans de Waal, *Are We Smart Enough to Know How Smart Animals Are?* (New York: W. W. Norton, 2016). De Waal offers a general survey of recent research and an extensive bibliography. His work also shows the possible extent of bonding, respect, and affection between humans and the animals with whom they interact.

57. One need not appeal to invidious distinctions between dogs and other animals or specious oppositions between Western and Chinese culture to find unacceptable the "dog meat festival" in Yulin that involves practices such as mutilating, torturing, and boiling dogs alive, apparently in the misguided belief that trauma and stress enhance the taste of meat.

58. Wayne Pacelle, *The Humane Economy: How Innovators and Enlightened Consumers Are Transforming the Lives of Animals* (New York: HarperCollins, 2016). Singer's review is in the *New York Review of Books*, May 12, 2016, 22–26. Pacelle took office on June 1, 2004, as president and CEO of the Humane Society of the United States.

such as the prohibition in California and the European Union of crates for veal calves and gestating sows and of battery cages for egg-laying chickens, enclosures that are extremely confining and prohibit basic movements such as getting up, lying down, or turning around.[59] But Singer also notes how much is still permitted, notably in the United States with its business-friendly federal and state governments, even in the face of significant public advocacy of "animal rights," which often fails to register in government action and major political parties. He observes that "the overwhelming majority of calves, pigs, and laying hens will . . . still be kept indoors, in large crowded sheds, and the reforms do nothing to change the ways they are transported or slaughtered. Nor do any of these reforms touch the industrial production of chickens for meat, which John Webster, professor of animal husbandry at the University of Bristol's School of Veterinary Science . . . has described as 'in magnitude and severity, the single most severe, systematic example of man's inhumanity to another sentient animal.' "[60] Singer adds: "The problems of chicken production are not simply due to the fact that the birds are raised in vast crowded sheds in air reeking of ammonia from their accumulated droppings. The more fundamental problem is that today's chickens have been bred to grow three times as fast as chickens raised in the 1950s. Now they are ready for market when they are just six weeks old and their immature legs cannot handle the weight they gain" (26). Given that there are 8 billion chickens raised annually for meat in the United States, the result is that 2.6 billion birds live in chronic pain for the last third of their short lives. With respect to the wretched conditions of these animals, the discourse of trauma might seem euphemistic.[61]

What I think arises from the questioning of a radical divide between the human and other animals is not a simple, dogmatic, and possibly self-righteous

---

59. Such confinement of movement was a key feature of the "little ease" torture chamber, for example, in the Tower of London.

60. John Webster, *Animal Welfare: A Cool Eye towards Eden* (Malden, MA: Blackwell Science, 1994), 156, quoted in Singer's review of Pacelle, *The Humane Economy*, in the *New York Review of Books*, 26.

61. Despite the availability of much information, certain ways animals are treated may still be subject to the operation of the open secret, that is, one knows enough to know that, at least at a certain point and for a variety of reasons (including apprehension about unsettling effects on oneself), one does not want to know more. It should nonetheless be noted that humans who handle animals in arguably abusive ways, at times under the constraint of finding underpaid and unwanted work, are liable to undergo post-traumatic effects. On workers in slaughterhouses, see, for example, Donald D. Still and Michael J. Broadway, *Slaughterhouse Blues: The Meat and Poultry Industry in North America*, foreword by Eric Schlosser (Belmont, CA: Wordsworth/Thompson Learning, 2004). Moreover, "hunting" with a misnamed "sports" rifle, such as the AR-15 assault weapon (easily converted to a fully automatic gun and also a blatant threat to humans), is not a sport but a form of slaughter, although conventional hunting for food by knowledgeable people may be less harmful to both animals and the environment than certain forms of factory "farming."

orientation, for example, in defense of vegetarianism or in opposition to any form of experimentation, however noninvasive. Vegetarianism or even veganism is on many grounds defensible. But without far-reaching changes in existing structures and practices, neither may be feasible as an option for everyone, especially the poor. The more general point is that the treatment of other animals is not simply a free choice or a matter of taste. It is an ethical and political issue whose problematic nature requires an attempt to come to terms with a complex network of similarities and differences linking humans and other animals with different modes of being. In certain areas, decisions seem more readily apparent than in others. I have intimated that one major consideration is that the way other animals are treated or made to live before they die, insofar as this comes under human control, is a crucial enabling condition of further decisions that presuppose it. Many if not most aspects of factory farming and important components of experimentation on other animals for the putative benefit of humans are unjustifiable and tend to be directed by commodification, the conception of other beings as "human resources," and their reduction to objects of manipulative control underwritten by a lack of respect for their forms of life. One may well argue that there is an obligation to be as informed as possible about the conditions under which other animals are raised, treated, and subjected to a regime that is questionably seen as under the sovereign dominion of the human who plays God or seeks the authorization of such a divinity.

A crucial question here is whether a different orientation would involve getting beyond the frame of reference in which "the" animal is the paradoxical "other" that is both mere life or foodstuff and a sacrificial object to be killed or otherwise rendered a victim for the material or spiritual benefit of some "higher" being (including human beings). In any event, how humans and animals relate to one another is part and parcel of their complex, far-from-certain "identities," and a comparative study of the variations in this relationship over time and space is a crucial concern of history in its interaction with memory.[62] I have also indicated that there is a nontrivial, metaphoric—but not "simply" metaphoric—sense in which the land or the earth may be said to have memory and perhaps even to be wounded and desecrated by invasive, destructive, exploitative procedures such as drilling and fracking, not to mention bombing, with its often unnoticed, disastrous effects on animals in zoos, homes, the streets, and the wild.[63]

62. For one thought-provoking study, see Boria Sax, *Animals in the Third Reich: Pets, Scapegoats, and the Holocaust*, foreword by Klaus P. Fischer (New York: Continuum, 2000). For a discussion of relations to other animals in American Indian societies, see Cajete, *Native Science*, chap. 5.

63. But see Hilda Kean, *The Great Cat and Dog Massacre: The Real Story of World War Two's Unknown Tragedy* (Chicago: University of Chicago Press, 2017) for the largely repressed or suppressed story of the panicked killing of companion animals by the people of London during the first four

Changing the frame of reference to include other animals need not be taken as a panacea or indentured to a golden-age mythology. Nor need it obliterate distinctions, denigrate humans, or reject everything that has been done under the rubric of humanism. As I have intimated, it should be seen as interwoven with the entire network of problems earlier raised with respect to history, memory, trauma, and identity. Moreover, one may criticize anthropocentrism along with human exceptionalism and still acknowledge the at times beneficial or even inevitable role of a critically tested anthropomorphism, which involves processes similar to those operative in empathy.[64] Empathy or compassion, not unmediated (projective or incorporative) identification, enables attentive listening (or reading, including of animals' body language) and responsive yet possibly critical and self-critical understanding. Empathy may be understood as involving an affective rapport that may in some sense include yet also limit identification, engage the imagination, problematize identity, and allow for recognition of alterity with respect to both self and others, including possible limits to communication, self-knowledge, and "feeling one's way into" another being. Moreover, it should be evident that empathy or compassion is not sufficient for understanding or action, and contextualization, theorization, and critical judgment are significant checks on the tendency toward unmediated identification (and possible secondary traumatization).[65]

---

days of World War II. Over 400,000 animals were killed, a number six times that of civilian deaths from bombing during the entire course of the war. Two contrasting reasons offered by Kean are the concern of "owners" for loved animals "sacrificed" to avoid their suffering the harsh effects of war, and absence of provision by the government for companion animals seen as useless "luxury" goods taking scarce resources from humans.

64. See Lorraine Daston and Greg Mitman, eds., *Thinking with Animals: New Perspectives on Anthropomorphism* (New York: Columbia University Press, 2005). See also De Waal, *Are We Smart Enough?* esp. 24–26, and on empathy, 132–33.

65. I have tried to explore these issues in other works, notably *Writing History, Writing Trauma.* For a tunnel-vision and truncated approach to empathy, which unsurprisingly rejects its pertinence for understanding and responding to significant problems, see Paul Bloom, *Against Empathy: The Case for Rational Compassion* (New York: HarperCollins, 2016). Bloom simply conflates empathy and identification, separates emotion from reason, and defends what he oxymoronically terms "rational compassion." In the growing literature on the relations between humans and animals, see, for example, Kari Weil, *Thinking Animals: Why Animal Studies Now?* (New York: Columbia University Press, 2012) and Cary Wolfe, *Animal Rites: American Culture, the Discourse of Species, and Posthumanist Theory* (Chicago: University of Chicago Press, 2003) as well as Wolfe, *What Is Posthumanism?* (Minneapolis: University of Minnesota Press, 2010). In the latter book, Wolfe asserts, with respect to relations with other animals, the basis of justice is not rights or even capabilities but (quoting Derrida) "the finitude that we share with animals, the mortality that belongs to the very finitude of life, to the experience of compassion" (81). See also Jacques Derrida, *L'animal que donc je suis*, ed. Marie-Louise Mallet (Paris: Éditions Galilée, 2006), translated by David Wills as *The Animal That Therefore I Am* (New York: Fordham University Press, 2008), as well as Derrida's *The Beast & the Sovereign*, trans. Geoff Bennington, 2 vols., The Seminars of Jacques Derrida (Chicago: University of Chicago Press, 2009, 2011). See as well my *History and Its Limits: Human, Animal, Violence* (Ithaca: Cornell University Press, 2009) and *History, Literature, Critical Theory* (Ithaca: Cornell University Press, 2013).

I would stress that the overall point of the foregoing discussion has not been to reverse fixated binaries and attendant hierarchies, whether between humans and other animals or between history based on standard archives and the role of memory work, especially in its recognition of and attempt to work through pervasive traumatic legacies. The point has rather been to further a different frame of reference with enhanced complexity and flexibility. In the process, I have questioned the overly general rejection of memory and memory studies, which is based on a rigid binary orientation. I have also tried to further ways in which historiography and critically tested memory, understood as having a supplementary relationship, can converge in the interest of a self-questioning but more accurate representation of the past and a more desirable bearing on the present and future. The only historiography making a difference in the present and future may well be one that conjoins critically tested memory and comparably tested document-and-text-based knowledge in furthering collective projects seeking truth, compassion, and justice. Of course the examples or case studies I address could well be re-oriented or multiplied to include many others. And in pursuing the global initiatives of recent historiography, the problems become more not less difficult, and the chances of misdirection (for example, through "humanitarian" interventions) increase alarmingly. Here the best directive may still be a variant of Gramsci's truly memorable injunction "Pessimism of the intellect, optimism of the will"—a determined will, I would add, not driven by apocalyptic desire for some unknown, "totally other" state of affairs but tempered and informed by critical judgment and knowledge of the past.

CHAPTER 4

Frank Hamilton Cushing and His "Adventures" at Zuni

Frank Hamilton Cushing, even more so than Edward S. Curtis, remains a contested figure, especially among American Indians. This contested status was evident during Cushing's stay at Zuni and has continued to this day. One issue centers around the role of participant observation, which Cushing personifies and of which he may well have been the initiator, at least with respect to the discipline of anthropology. A question arising from the way he at times pushed the limits of the "method" is whether or to what extent it allowed him to see and share aspects of Zuni life otherwise inaccessible to him or induced him to disclose dubiously if not betray that way of life and its more secret, even sacred sides.[1]

Cushing lived from 1857 to 1900 and was at Zuni from 1879 until 1884. Thus he was a very young, largely self-educated man of twenty-two upon his arrival and still quite young when he left. (His formal education, if it can be called that, was limited to one month at Cornell University, where he visited

---

1. The 1994 book of some forty-three cartoons or sketches by the Zuni artist Phil Hughte (thirty-nine years old at the time the book was published) may be read as a not entirely unsympathetic critique of Cushing in the form of an intentionally humorous but often pointed commentary on mutual perceptions or misperceptions of the "other" on the part of Cushing and his various, at times strongly divided interlocutors at Zuni. See *A Zuni Artist Looks at Frank Hamilton Cushing: Cartoons by Phil Hughte,* captions by Phil Hughte, foreword by Triloki Nath Pandey (Zuni, NM: Pueblo of Zuni Arts & Crafts, 1994).

an anthropology professor who told him that his desire to find artifacts in the region around Ithaca, New York, would produce no results. Cushing returned in an hour with a large sack full of artifacts and perhaps with the impression that further work at a university or college was not quite what he was looking for.) Cushing's life and work at Zuni, as well as his activity elsewhere (for example, at Key Marco in Florida) pose challenging questions for both anthropologists and Zunis as well as for other indigenous peoples. They also raise questions for all those interested in the problem of relations between groups marked by very significant differentials in power and ways of life. These questions of course arise as well in the case of one's own group, especially insofar as it has a colonial or neocolonial form of power over significantly different others. Such power amounts at times to domination stemming from conquest or unilateral imposition that to a greater or lesser extent exploits or abuses others whose own status, voice, and subjectivity may be denied, systematically misconstrued, or manipulated in self-serving, instrumental ways. This was structurally the case with Cushing at Zuni and to a greater or lesser extent has remained the case with anthropologists and the discipline of anthropology (as well as with clergy as their frequent religious accompaniments) whatever may be the subjective attitude of given individuals. Cushing's own relation to the Zuni was, as we shall see, both extremely empathic and at times intrusively domineering.[2]

A structural imbalance can be effectively challenged only by structural, including institutional, changes in the nature of the relationship. Anthropologists themselves rarely have the power to effect such changes. Typically, they are (like members of the clergy) directly or indirectly agents of dominant powers—political, social, and religious. They have at times been complicit with those powers as willing agents of control, even sharing a prejudiced view of "native" populations or at least participating in an objectifying, scientistic ideology that takes others simply as objects of inquiry. It may by now be commonplace but still important to observe that the results of such inquiry may be used by political, social, or religious powers to exert or reinforce processes of domination and exploitation. Even when they do not take the people with whom they work simply as "native informants," anthropologists themselves are willy-nilly informants with respect to the powers they serve. Even a map, constructed as objectively as can be, may be a device for exerting control, and cartography is not simply an "innocent" form of purely

---

2. Despite important contextual differences, one might perhaps see a limited similarity between Cushing and Claude Lanzmann insofar as identification at times went beyond compassion and enabled intrusiveness that overrode respectful consideration for the other.

scientific inquiry. Perhaps even more subject to manipulation is the disclosure of folkways, including religious beliefs and practices, that have not only
been taken as privy or secret by tribal members but guarded as parts of a
heritage that may be appropriated if not plundered, commodified, or turned
against its rightful heirs. Even the best-intentioned anthropologists have
been "code breakers" whose interpretation and explanation of other ways of
life have been used for purposes the anthropologists themselves may oppose
and regret. Structurally, anthropologists are what Jean-Paul Sartre termed,
in a telling turn of phrase, subaltern functionaries of the superstructure—a
category he would also apply to historians, literary critics, or philosophers
such as himself, however much he tried to subvert that role and its functions.

At the time of Cushing, who lived and worked at Zuni under the auspices
of John Wesley Powell of the Smithsonian Institution, such intended or unintended consequences of the anthropological quest to know the other were
generally not explicitly and thematically made a part of the practice and
self-consciousness of the anthropologist. The commonplace saying "Knowledge is power," even when a constitutive element of science in general, was
rarely given a self-reflexive twist. Yet scientific or rather scientistic ideology
was prevalent and more or less constitutive of anthropology at its formative
moments. It was expressly avowed by such figures as Matilda Coxe Stevenson, Cushing's constant bête noire and the formidable "trailing spouse" of
James Stevenson, the head of Cushing's "expedition" to Zuni. In significant
ways, a more or less insistently objectifying understanding of anthropology
as science was also prominent in such important figures as A. L. Kroeber and
Franz Boas, who tended to share a largely negative estimation of Cushing,
as well as in Cushing's own hostile brother-in-law Frederick Webb Hodge.
It may be observed that Kroeber and Boas had a comparable view of Edgar
Lee Hewett (1865–1946), an important figure in anthropology as well as in
the very act of defining Santa Fe's institutions and practices, such as its now
famous (or infamous) "style," the anthropology department and museum at
the University of New Mexico, and what are now the School for Advanced
Research and Indian Market.[3] Like Cushing, Hewett believed that the "native" was not simply an "informant" but a subject with knowledge, although
Hewett had an entrepreneurial and impresario-like bent that was different
from Cushing's manner of knowing by mimetically doing what the other
had done, a view that sometimes got Cushing into trouble when he redid and

---

3. On these and related issues, see, for example, Chris Wilson, *The Myth of Santa Fe: Creating a
Modern Regional Tradition* (Albuquerque: University of New Mexico Press, 1997).

embellished an artifact in ways that invited charges of forgery or passing off his own handiwork as the original.

Jesse Green, a professor of English (not anthropology), has compiled an excellent edition of Cushing's letters and coedited a collection of Cushing's writings. Green observes that, for Hodge, Cushing "was a prima donna who never took field notes and relied instead on his memory and intuition." Yet, as Green adds, "it is now clear that Cushing did have the habit of scrupulously recording his activities and observations each day."[4] Still, a negative view of Cushing has, to a greater or lesser extent, persisted among later commentators, who drew back from Cushing's own critical response to an objectifying anthropology or at least from the extremes to which it sometimes led. One finds a significantly negative coloration in the approach of, say, Curtis Hinsley Jr. in his important book, *Savages and Scientists*. Hinsley, for example, writes:

> [Cushing] lived for the great moments of discovery; they were a necessity for him. Cushing had no time for the deadening chores of scientific

---

4. Jesse Green, ed., *Cushing at Zuni: The Correspondence and Journals of Frank Hamilton Cushing, 1879–1884* (Albuquerque: University of New Mexico Press, 1990), 348n1. Green also edited with an introduction (and a foreword by Fred Eggan) an excellent volume, *Selected Writings of Frank Hamilton Cushing* (Lincoln: University of Nebraska Press, 1979), which includes Cushing's tour de force "My Adventures in Zuni" (46–144). Cushing's most prominent scholarly work is probably *Zuni Breadstuff* (New York: Museum of the American Indian Heye Foundation, 1920), which seems prescient in its focus on food as crucial to the nature and understanding of culture and society. I have earlier referred to what is probably his best-known text, which addresses the relation between humans, animals, and gods in Zuni culture, *Zuni Fetishes*, intro. Tom Bahti (1883; Las Vegas: KC Publications, 1990). Fetishes of animals, considered originally to be calcifications or concretions of the animals, are helpers and protectors of humans. In his introduction, Bahti observes that "the purposes for which fetishes may be used are varied: hunting, diagnosing and curing diseases, initiations, war, gambling, propagation, witchcraft, and detection and protection against witchcraft" (n.p.). In Zuni as in many indigenous cultures, animals are placed on a higher level of being than humans and considered to be more mysterious and difficult to understand. In *Zuni Fetishes*, Cushing writes: "In this system of life the starting point is man, the most finished, yet the lowest organism; at least, the lowest because most dependent and least mysterious. In just so far as an organism, actual or imaginary, resembles him, is it believed to be related to him and correspondingly mortal; in just so far as it is mysterious, is it considered removed from him, further advanced, powerful, and immortal. It thus happens that the animals, because alike mortal and endowed with similar physical functions and organs, are considered more nearly related to man than are the gods; more nearly related to the gods than is man, because more mysterious, and characterized by specific instincts and powers which man does not of himself possess" (9). See also Gregory Cajete, *Native Science: Natural Laws of Interdependence,* foreword by Leroy Little Bear, JD (Santa Fe, NM: Clear Light Publishers, 2000), esp. chap. 5. Cajete writes: "Participating in ceremonies in their honor created empathy for an animal or animals, as well as a context for relationship. The various animal dances of Native cultures provide an understanding of the relationships with animals. Relational psychology (ecology) must be 'worked,' or constantly renewed. Another way of working this relational psychology was to create a clan totem, a symbol that commemorated a people's links with an animal. Each totem had a story and emerged as a way to entreat the animal spirits for their protection and intercession with other worlds" (165). Needless to add, the understanding of the relation between various indigenous peoples and animals is still subject to variation and debate.

polish and proof. The flash of brilliance, promising insight, far-reaching theory—then Cushing was moving on, leaving the litter of his research strewn across the Southwest and elsewhere for others to pick up, if they could. Here was genius of a sort, but its credentials came increasingly under question. . . . Brilliant intuition alone went only so far.[5]

In her *Four Anthropologists: An American Science in Its Early Years*,[6] Joan Mark echoes these comments (119) and goes on to reinforce Hinsley's analysis of the shift in generations from Cushing to Boas and others:

Cushing saw himself in the same way that Alice Fletcher saw herself, as an interpreter of Indian life to those outside it. A dramatic shift in tone and method took place between their kind of ethnographic work and that done by Franz Boas and his students. Cushing gloried in the cleverness of the Zuni people, and implicitly in his own cleverness, in being able to follow along and trace the interconnections in their culture. He was an insider telling the rest of the world something it did not know. For later anthropologists the approach was more often that of scientists telling one another things about a group of people which the people did not know about themselves. (121)

One should, however, recall (as Mark herself does on pp. 122–23) that Claude Lévi-Strauss, himself someone with a virtuoso if not inspired touch who described himself (notably in his masterful *Tristes Tropiques*) as having an impatient groundbreaking and moving-on approach to problems, praised Cushing, and did so not for his presumably "insider" ethnography but for an ability to elaborate models of Zuni culture that were not empirical but analytically structural in nature. And a more recent generation of anthropologists has distanced itself from a perhaps hubristic idea of anthropology as a science that transcends a people's self-understanding in its own objective perspective on them, finding more of value in Cushing's empathic approach and even in the self-questioning prompted by the difficulties and binds Cushing arrived at. From a somewhat distinctive perspective, I also have doubts about a one-dimensionally objectifying, narrowly professionalized approach to the study of others, but shall nonetheless indicate points at which I think Cushing went too far in his own combination of a scientific ethos (which he

---

5. Curtis Hinsley Jr., *Savages and Scientists: The Smithsonian Institution and the Development of American Anthropology, 1846–1910* (Washington, DC: Smithsonian Institution Press, 1981), 205.

6. Joan Mark, *Four Anthropologists: An American Science in Its Early Years* (New York: Science History Publications, 1980).

did not reject) and a tendency to relate to his objects or subjects to the point of identifying with them and "going native," as the saying goes.

Cushing was perhaps the first "live-in" anthropologist, and one who took living with the other to the point of almost becoming that other. But I would also like to contend that the latter tendency is inevitable at least as a temptation for someone with an orientation that resists full objectification and instead has a marked critical distance (if not a strong dose of alienation) vis-à-vis his or her own society and profession. Indeed someone who recognizes the other as a subject not only having a voice but a dialogic position encounters an other who should have (but rarely does have) power comparable to his observers, with things to say that include knowledge about his or her way of life and arguably about the desirable way life in general should be lived. Objectification in this sense is itself a dubious extreme and an abusive version of the attempt to know while maintaining some critical distance both from others and from oneself. From the perspective I am suggesting, one-sided objectification might be seen as a disavowal of transference and of participant observation that may, however, backfire when it induces self-certainty, even unmediated projective identification, and unacknowledged, at times uncontrolled judgments, evaluations, or affective reactions. Moreover, insofar as transference is an inevitable but possibly denied or obstructed mode of co-implication, and participant observation is one form of it, the latter is not a simple choice of one methodology among others. It is as difficult to understand and to control as transference in general. And it is a propensity or a condition that has to be confronted in some viable way. Its dismissal or denigration is a manner of denying or avoiding it, which is to be distinguished from criticizing the manner it is used or abused.

As already intimated, Cushing is frequently seen as an early proponent of participant observation—one who took questionable liberties with both observation and participation. His most notorious abuse of observation, which at some points almost caused him injury or even threatened his life, was to sketch and take notes during Zuni religious ceremonies to the manifest dismay or even outrage of his Zuni hosts. His sense of participation went to the extreme of identification, inducing him to become a member of the Zuni tribe, a priest of the Bow in the Zunis' most important religious society, and a warrior—indeed, as he indicated in ending certain letters, "1st War Chief," who underwent a process of initiation, including taking the scalp of a member of another tribe (the Apache). Participant observation has become a "methodology" in which the two extremes of overobjectification and overidentification may be explicitly recognized, the tension and anxiety they cause engaged, and a self-conscious intersubjective or dialogic disciplinary effort made to control responses in ways that engender compassionate or empathic knowledge that in certain respects is objective without being one-dimensionally objectifying.

I would like to make a few more comments about participant observation and then turn to the often critical observations of the "Anglo" Jim Ostler whose "discourse" (as it is labeled) is included in the book *A Zuni Artist Looks at Frank Hamilton Cushing: Cartoons by Phil Hughte.* Aside from Hughte's sketches, the book also contains briefer observations of another commentator, the curator of collections at the University of New Mexico's Maxwell Museum of Anthropology, Krisztina Kosse. I shall quote only one of Kosse's observations that is particularly memorable: "What we would hate above all else is a perfect human being. Phil Hughte's Cushing—curious, insensitive, bright, courageous, greedy, and vain—escapes such an undesirable fate" (122). (Who could wish for a better epitaph?) I shall also mention one point about the sketches that serves as their leitmotif and perhaps epitomizes Hughte's appreciation of the nature of the relations between Cushing and the Zunis: Anglos including Cushing are portrayed with no eyes, and the Zunis either share this fate or have their headbands covering their eyes. The seemingly obvious implication is that for Hughte the relations in question took place in mutual blindness.

Hortense Powdermaker writes: "We know less about participant observation than about almost any other method in the social sciences."[7] I have contended that one fruitful way to see participant observation is as a form of what in psychoanalysis is addressed with reference to transference. I would immediately add that this suggestion should not obscure the asymmetrical structural and power relations that frame transference. Such asymmetrical relations in different ways also frame and constrain the psychoanalytic relation itself. The patient comes to the analyst in a position of lesser power that may involve extreme vulnerability, suffering, and self-doubt, while the analyst, even if not assuming the position that Jacques Lacan critically termed that of the "subject-supposed-to-know," is still in a position of greater power and authority. This power takes an institutional form when the analyst is in a position to report to state or other agencies, with the authorization to institutionalize or incarcerate, what the analyst takes to be the patient's mental and psychological competence and ability to function in society. The very distinction between transference and countertransference underscores the contestable assumption that the analyst is initially in control of self and situation

---

7. Hortense Powdermaker, *Stranger and Friend: The Way of an Anthropologist* (New York: W. W. Norton, 1966), 9.

and that the transference onto him or her by the analysand or patient may help to engender a countertransference wherein the analyst's putative "neutrality" may be jeopardized. In view of what I see as the dubiousness of this assumption, I prefer to refer to the analyst and analysand as implicated in a transferential relation that poses problems, some similar, some different, for both—problems that may be acted out and worked over and through to various degrees. I would also make a similar argument in the case of anthropologists and indigenous peoples (as well as historians and their peoples of the past), although here the power differentials may at times be more marked and even more subject to abuse than in the one-on-one or small-group clinical relation.

Transference in psychoanalysis applies primarily to the transference of the parent-child relation onto the psychoanalytic situation in ways that enhance the power of the analyst but may also induce the analysand's inappropriate acting out of earlier childhood scenes in the analytic situation itself. J. Laplanche and J.-B. Pontalis write that "classically, the transference is acknowledged to be the terrain on which all the basic problems of a given analysis play themselves out: the establishment, modalities, interpretation, and resolution of the transference are in fact what define the cure."[8] Not all the basic problems of an anthropological (or historical) relation are played out in transference, although the form they take may well be affected by it. And for "the cure," which I think is misapplied in cultural studies and perhaps is a deceptive goal in general, I would substitute "the attempt to work over and possibly through problems." Freud believed that transference affected all human relations (I would add even relations with other than human beings). Psychoanalysis highlighted and foregrounded transference, which was both the strongest aid in an analysis and could also be a forceful hindrance—what Derrida termed a *pharmakon* where the antidote, depending on the dosage, is both poison and cure. Simply put, transference is a basic mode of affective investment or involvement in the other, which may go to the point of love or hate (or both).

I have argued that transference is a form of self-implication in the other with the tendency to repeat as well as projectively reprocess or incorporate the processes active in the other or in the object of inquiry. Objectivity may itself be redefined in a nonscientistic manner as the attempt to work over and through rather than simply act out or compulsively repeat affectively charged forms of implication in the other or object of inquiry. Yet some of

---

8. J. Laplanche and J.-B. Pontalis, *The Language of Psychoanalysis* (1967; New York: W. W. Norton, 1973), 455.

the most compelling and consuming types of transference may be found in obsession, compulsion, traumatic and post-traumatic symptoms, and phenomena such as possession, haunting, and preoccupation with specters and ghosts. A post-traumatic symptom, such as identifying with a lost loved one and even reliving what they have lived (including states of extreme abjection and suffering), may even be experienced by an intimate not as a symptom but as a bond with the dead that one is loath to give up or even work through. I would suggest that witchcraft is one way a group may try to control transference and localize anxiety by resisting the possibility of possession by opaque, uncanny forces and projecting the possibly undecidable or perhaps uncontrollable source of such anxiety onto a definite other, often a scapegoated, vulnerable (yet possibly feared as too powerful and threatening) member of one's own or another group.

The Zuni believed in witchcraft and punished witches harshly, possibly by torture and death. This is an aspect of their life concerning which Cushing touched on only at times. An amusing aside here is that when Cushing in the spring of 1882 took a group of five Zunis and one Hopi to the East Coast, one of the Zunis addressing an audience in Salem, Massachusetts, congratulated the people of Salem because they too apparently took witchcraft quite seriously and made efforts to wipe it out. Cushing himself had a very prepossessing if not possessive form of transference with respect to the Zuni and was taken to be both a member of the tribe and someone at times close to a major transgressor if not a witch in its midst. Zuni was of course divided concerning Cushing, with one faction being largely hostile to him, notably the important figure Luna, and another that was strongly devoted to him, perhaps most importantly the "Governor" Palowahtiwa. The latter at first was upset by the young man's brash intrusiveness (Cushing simply moved into his house uninvited and benefited by the code of hospitality) but came in time to consider him a younger brother. (It would also seem that given individuals, both at Cushing's time and afterward, have been internally divided concerning how to understand and respond to Cushing and his role in Zuni.) An indication of Cushing's importance in Zuni is that, in addition to his status as one of the Priests of the Bow, he was given the exceptional name Tenatsali (Medicine Flower), ascribed to only one member of the tribe at a given time.

Transference involving self-implication with respect to the other or the object of inquiry may induce identification. Empathy is often conflated with identification. I think this is a misidentification. Empathy is better seen as form of compassion involving both proximity to and distance from the other. In other words, empathy requires the recognition of the difference of the other as well as mutual closeness or proximity (skewed, needless to say, by differences of power, status, and wealth as well as tempered or modified by judgment—positive, negative, and mixed). But recognizing the difference or "alterity" of the other helps to counteract identification with the attendant tendencies to project or simply incorporate the other in ways that may obliterate differences or at least to ride roughshod over (at times warranted) resistances to one's own desires, initiatives, interpretations, and explanations, including the desire to make the other an object of as total a "scientific" knowledge as possible. I would relate empathy or compassion to the attempt to work through transference while counteracting but never simply transcending tendencies to act out, compulsively repeat, incorporate, or projectively reprocess that in which one is affectively invested or implicated.

Like many if not most of us, Cushing was suspended between acting out and working through, with a pronounced propensity to identify with the Zuni and to take empathy to the extreme point of identification by becoming one of them while not quite relinquishing his identity as a "Westerner," a citizen of the United States, and an anthropologist for the Smithsonian Institution. He adopted Zuni customs, ate Zuni food (despite his initial extreme dislike of it), underwent initiation, took Zuni opponents as his opponents and friends as his friends, and in so many ways seems to have gone just about as far as one could go. He even ostentatiously and notoriously dressed like a Zuni (or, in full regalia, perhaps less like a Zuni than like an almost parodic exponent of Santa-Fe style avant la lettre), despite the jibes and ridicule of some of his associates (notably Matilda Stevenson). But one line he would never bring himself to cross, despite the urging of his closest Zuni friends and supporters, was the sexual together with the marriage line. He was more than encouraged to marry a Zuni, but he went back east to marry a white woman (Emily Magill) and bring her to Zuni. Cushing never comments on this ostensibly important chapter in his life, and I have not found significant commentary on it, much less an interpretation, even speculative, concerning why it occurred. You would think that a person so fully identified with the other would take marriage as a crucial component of what it is to be bound up, even at one with the other. Perhaps at some level Cushing resisted full identification at least in the sensitive area of sexuality and marriage. But here, as on the question of Cushing's sexuality in general, one can only speculate in ways that may lead in the direction of questionably wild analysis, especially in the absence of evidence on which one might at least base speculation. Cushing was quite thin, had a fragile constitution, and was frequently ill. Yet he endured hardships, including very cold weather and long trips on horseback, that might subdue a burly hulk of a man.

Jim Ostler's "discourse" is included toward the end of *A Zuni Artist Looks at Frank Hamilton Cushing: Cartoons by Phil Hughte*.[9] At the publication of the book, Ostler had worked for ten years as a financial middleman for the Zuni. He understood his role in a carefully delimited manner as based on mutual self-interest. As he puts it, "My role has been less that of a trader and more that of an entrepreneur who works for the tribe and is charged with making as much money as possible in a way that is acceptable to the tribal council and all of its 7,000-plus constituents" (107). He had many friends yet sees even friendship in Zuni as "almost like a business relationship in Anglo-American society where each party feigns a real depth to the relationship while knowing that if 'business' turns down or a better offer is made by a competing firm the relationship may end with barely a murmur" (114). Despite this narrowly instrumental, "economic-man" idea of friendship, Ostler apparently was Hughte's good friend and played a key role in encouraging his work as an artist and in compiling the sketches included in the book.

Ostler is disparaging if not dismissive about participant observation and differentiates sharply between participation in a community and "external" observation of it, especially as a social scientist: "In my view participant observation is an armchair conceit: it tries to place a framework for getting 'inside' information, but fails to recognize how the act of recording, and then divulging what is recorded, can undermine the society being investigated. It is a matter (certainly it was for the Zunis) of divulging 'secrets' of participants in religious societies by one who was a participant; it is also the telling of 'secrets' to an outsider by anyone who is Zuni. Such acts are by their nature disloyal" (110). Ostler certainly points to very significant issues. The presence and activity of anthropologists do pose problems, but so does the role of anyone in a society who is not entirely embedded in a habitus or way of life but rather posing sometimes difficult or embarrassing questions that may unsettle, or at least point out the ways unsettlement has already taken place, in a society. I think that if one is not acutely aware of these problems, indeed these tensions and possible contradictions, and does not attempt to engage them and counteract adverse consequences as effectively as possible, one is not undertaking participant observation but rather engaging in fairly unambiguous spying or disloyalty. Ostler has little tolerance for ambiguity or appreciation of tense complexities, especially in hybridized roles. For him it is best to have one thing or the other, and the categorical boxes containing

---

9. Together with Marian Rodee, Ostler coauthored a book I mentioned earlier on a subject also treated by Cushing (whom they often approvingly quote), entitled *The Fetish Carvers of Zuni*, rev. ed. (Albuquerque: Maxwell Museum of Anthropology, University of New Mexico, 1995).

things are to be kept separate. Cushing did at times go too far, but is the viable alternative refusing to go any significant distance by remaining within a binary logic whereby "you're in-or-you're out," an external observer (or perhaps a business associate) or a member of the tribe for whom strict secrecy is the hallmark of loyalty and tribal (or national) security?

Ostler at points has a purely instrumental, business-oriented mentality even when it comes to Cushing at Zuni, seeing both him and Zunis as doing things because it served self-interest. For example, he says of Governor Palowahtiwa, who obviously had a very strong affective bond with Cushing, "Palowahtiwa was familiar with Americans, and may well have thought Cushing might be one American whom the Zunis could use, and the governor himself might use in some as yet undetermined way to work for the interests of his own political faction" (114).

Ostler interestingly speculates that "the greatest threat to the Zuni system is the indigenous anarchists—namely the witches. Strong efforts are made to remove the anarchists. In fact, an important role of witches is to contrast the disorder of non-Zuni life with the order of life that is Zuni" (116). As Ostler understands him, Cushing, at least in his disruptive role in Zuni, seems close to being a witch. Ostler's own response, affective and judgmental, toward Cushing, to whom he early on refers as "THE Whiteman in Zuni" (107), is at points quite negative, approximating the hostility of the most "traditional" Zuni (such as Luna). Evoking echoes of some of our own recent "witch hunts," Ostler even writes that "perhaps [Cushing] was a cultural spy in the sense that he sought to take that which was secretly held by the Zunis to outsiders and that which was secretly held by one religious society of Zuni and render it public. This sense of spying has less to do with undermining that which is spied upon as indifference to the undermining . . . as in the case of the *paparazzi* sneaking photos of the British Royal Family or of a reporter publishing the private life of his political subject." In the case of Cushing and other anthropologists, the analogue of the newspaper for the paparazzi is the anthropological or ethnographic institution in quest of information and artifacts, and "Cushing's loyalties were pre-eminently to the Smithsonian Institution and to the 'science' of ethnology." But, in the very next sentence, Ostler qualifies this conclusion, which seems to overlook tensions between Cushing and his institutional affiliations along with the depth of his involvement in Zuni life. He notes that, "as with any maturing person, Cushing appears to have experienced a shifting of loyalties—a strengthening of his loyalty to the Zuni people (and their institutions), a strengthening of his loyalty to personal ambition, and a weakening of his loyalty to the institution of the Smithsonian and the Bureau of Ethnology." He further observes:

As evidence of his growing loyalty to the social institutions of the Zunis I would cite the newspaper interview Cushing gave to the *Washington Evening News* in 1892 . . . wherein he describes the occurrences of witches in Zuni, the extraction of confessions, and the punishments. Even though a newspaper had reported that two Zuni women had been executed for practicing sorcery he made the case that "there is no truth to the report," that the U.S. Government made a grave error in sending troops to Zuni, and that the troops should be recalled immediately. He went on to state that "sorcery in Zuni does not wholly depend upon superstitious beliefs" and that he had known several sorcerers who were better characterized as "anarchists of primitive life." He continued, "it is their endeavor to overcome the sacred assemblies [and in so doing] they resort to violence and very frequently to actual poisoning." (112)

Here Ostler quotes Cushing on witches as anarchists in terms he himself adopts, yet he also at times pictures Cushing as disordering Zuni life if not as tantamount to a witch. Despite his manifest desire for clear-cut binaries, Ostler seems to leave the reader with a Cushing who remains a riddle composed of a multitude of conflicting forces that resist disentanglement, somewhat like the impenetrable "navel" of the dream that marks the limit of understanding and interpretation for Freud.[10] Near the end of his account, Ostler defers to the Zuni and pointedly states that when he asked an elderly Zuni he had known for years what he thought of Cushing, the Zuni said:

He was a good man. I was told that although he was a Whiteman he behaved like a Zuni. I was told that he lived with other pious men [Zuni religious leaders] and when that happens one begins to believe in things like Zuni religion. I was told that that happened to him. I heard that when there was raiding by Navajos in the West, they would steal livestock and sometimes kill the sheep herders. I heard that Cushing went with a group of Zunis and he killed one of the raiders. I think it was that reason that he became a Bow priest . . . for when you do something like that or kill a bear, then the clan takes immediate steps—does not wait a day —to initiate. (117–18)

---

10. "There is often a passage in even the most thoroughly interpreted dream which has to be left obscure; this is because we become aware during the work of interpretation that at that point there is a tangle of dream-thoughts which cannot be unraveled and which moreover adds nothing to our knowledge of the content of the dream. This is the dream's navel, the spot where it reaches down into the unknown." Sigmund Freud, *The Interpretation of Dreams* (1900), ed. and trans. James Strachey with Anna Freud, vol. 5 (London: Hogarth Press, 1981), 525.

But then Ostler immediately adds: "On the other hand, for many Zunis, Cushing's initiation was an anomalous act and one can still find older Zunis who when under attack by their kinsmen will say, 'Well, whatever it is alleged that we have done, at least we did not initiate an outsider'" (118).

It may be that there is still ambivalence both in individual Zuni and in the tribe about the role of Cushing in their life and history, an ambivalence that may attest to a continuing unsettlement that might not have been effectively resolved. One key aspect of such a resolution could well be the realization that it is not a bad thing to initiate into one's tribe or society an outsider, even when he or she poses problems for you, as Cushing did even for the Zuni governor and others who came to accept him. Of course the difficult problem is how precisely an anthropologist (or anyone relating to a group) addresses aspects of the practice or belief of the group without going to the extremes of either objectification that avoids co-implication, compassionate interpretation, and even careful reconstruction, on the one hand, or intrusive disclosure that is invasive and disrespectful, on the other. There is no formula or algorithm that "solves" this problem, which engages transferential co-implication in general and is constitutive of writing or representing "culture," a problem that is particularly knotty when the group in question maintains, for what may well be legitimate reasons, a code of secrecy about certain ways of life, which is not to be equated with paranoia about national security.

CHAPTER 5

What Is History? What Is Literature?

The nature of history and of literature as well as the relations between them has been an issue discussed and debated for centuries, becoming most contentious with the professionalization of history in the nineteenth century. Often each area or field has been discussed in its own terms with restricted comparison to others, and the vis-à-vis of history and literature has frequently not been one another but, for example, the social sciences for history or the fine arts for literature. In the recent past, historians in general have been more concerned about the interaction of history with social science or economics than with literature. For some historians of a social-scientific bent, literature and, more decidedly, fiction have been the other tout court. And literary critics and scholars have shown varying degrees of interest in history, with one of the more prominent exemplars of a decided turn to history being of course the New Historicism.[1] Historians'

---

1. There have, however, been many critical accounts of the understanding and use of history in the New Historicism. For one extended account, focusing on the work of Stephen Greenblatt, see Sara Maza, "Stephen Greenblatt, the New Historicism, and Cultural History, or, What We Talk about When We Talk about Interdisciplinarity," *Modern Intellectual History* 1 (2004): 249–65. With respect to the standard new-historical practice of juxtaposing anecdotes drawn from historical events and from literary texts, Maza observes in perhaps too binary and generalizing a manner: "The anecdote in cultural history is always an opening to a wider cultural pattern, not, as Greenblatt would have it, an object of 'wonder' or the means to an 'effect' or 'touch' of the real" (263). And with respect to

recent (re)turn to an interest in narrative has provided some renewed regard for literature and the similarities or differences between the role of narrative in history and in literature (or in fiction), along with some familiarity with literary theory. But this turn has been limited and not constitutive of the so-called linguistic or cultural turn more generally. For most historians, a strong interest in literature has been more the exception than the rule. Hence the appearance of a book focused on the relations not only of history and literature but also of history and social science is a significant event.

In his intellectually ambitious and highly readable *L'histoire est une littérature contemporaine: Manifeste pour les sciences sociales,*[2] Ivan Jablonka seeks something other than a mere combination of history, social science, and literature. He would like history, itself understood as a social science, to be a literature of the real world. He is also interested in literature informed not only by the results but, more importantly, by the forms of reasoning and inquiry of history and related social sciences (notably anthropology and sociology). He explores some very significant issues concerning the complex relations between history and literature, and the success of his book is a function of the degree to which he explicates, defends, and accomplishes his ambitious goal.

For Jablonka, history is both a social science and a literary undertaking, and history is not confined to its status as an academic discipline. His focus is historical thinking and writing, which he argues are interrelated attempts to tell the truth (*dire le vrai*—a rather problematic and difficult-to-translate turn of phrase) about reality (or the real—*le réel*). Hence a key focus is what are generally termed truth claims. He expands on this view by construing historical thinking as a form of cognition, a manner of reasoning, a set of methods, a mode of posing and pursuing answers to questions, and a way of formulating and testing hypotheses, even when history writing is open to a multiplicity of styles and takes a narrative form, the latter being his own emphasis.

---

the talismanic "touch of the real," she further contends that "lurking around the edges of Catherine Gallagher and Greenblatt's manifesto [*Practicing the New Historicism* of 2000] is the suggestion that the literary text is, in the end, the great beneficiary, with 'the real' as the medium of enchantment: 'We wanted the touch of the real in the way that in an earlier period people wanted the touch of the transcendent'" (256). One might infer that, in its construction of "the touch of the real" as a displacement of a desire for transcendence, the New Historicism is not so much a historicism as a variant of the prevalent postsecular turn as well as a movement from hypotaxis and certain forms of argument to parataxis, epiphany, juxtaposition, montage, bricolage, and segues. From this constellation, it is a short step to esteem for Walter Benjamin and intense interest in W. G. Sebald.

2. Ivan Jablonka, *L'histoire est une littérature contemporaine: Manifeste pour les sciences sociales* (Paris: Éditions du Seuil, Librairie du XXIe siècle, 2012); translations from the French are my own.

A crucial distinction for Jablonka is between literature and fiction, for history is literature addressing the real, and it makes use of fictions only in controlled and restricted ways—what he terms "fictions of method" and what others have treated in terms of heuristic fictions. In this respect, especially interesting are his discussions (and endorsement) of counterfactual history and of hybridized texts (he refers in passing to those of W. G. Sebald). But he also at least briefly touches on various kinds of "literature of the real": objectivism (*Neue Sachlichkeit*), testimony, the new journalism, the nonfictional novel, creative nonfiction, and "memoirs, essays, autobiographies, commentaries, journals" (244) as well as collages assembled from the Internet whose importance he emphasizes (273–74).

I shall return to the question of how one may extend Jablonka's line of thought concerning history and fiction. Here I shall simply observe that fiction itself may not be purely fictive but rather offer an imaginative perspective on, or even reading of, historical events and processes, which may both be compared with and offer suggestions or even hypotheses for historical research. One instance already touched on is the role of trauma and post-traumatic effects over generations, explored, for example, in the novels of Toni Morrison or William Faulkner, notably with respect to slavery and its aftermath. The Holocaust and colonialism, along with their consequences, present another forceful series of examples to which Jablonka himself is sensitive. The list could of course be extended and is not confined to the case of the historical novel.[3]

I think that the essay deserves more than mere mention as a form of historical thought, for its experimental and critical impetus are very significant in a manner that need not be narrative and goes beyond a narrowly ancillary status as a "think piece." Much historical and social-scientific thought, especially in discussion and argument among scholars about controversial issues, takes the form of the essay, and it is significant that one unreflected aspect of the work of those who emphasize the role of narrative, including Jablonka (as well as figures such as Arthur Danto, Fredric Jameson, Paul Ricoeur, and

---

3. On these issues, see also the thoughtful book of Jeffrey Andrew Baresh, *Collective Memory & the Historical Past* (Chicago: University of Chicago Press, 2016). Baresh does not treat the role of displacements over time or of trauma and post-traumatic effects with respect to memory. The latter would usefully supplement his informative account of collective memory and the way what he finds to be its distinctively modern form is shaped by the role of the media and the sense of immediacy or imagined community they at times attempt to engender. A still very useful reference point, which Jablonka's book may be seen as in certain ways updating, is Philippe Carrard, *Poetics of the New History: French Historical Discourse from Braudel to Chartier* (Baltimore: Johns Hopkins University Press, 1992).

Hayden White), comes in essays rather than narratives. More insistently essayistic is the work of such important figures as Theodor Adorno, Jacques
Derrida, Georg Lukács, and Michel de Montaigne, and even certain novelists,
such as Robert Musil, incorporate the essay in their hybridized narratives.
Jablonka's *L'histoire est une littérature contemporaine* itself takes the form of
an extended essay, and it is intended as a kind of theoretical accompaniment
or discourse on method with respect to his earlier book on his grandparents
and their world.[4] Whether this status accounts (as Jablonka contends) for the
relatively and avowedly nonexperimental nature of the more theoretical and
methodological book under discussion is debatable.

It is curious that so little attention is paid to the role of oral testimony, oral
history, and the relations between history and memory in recalling the experience of events. This issue was very much at play in the earlier book on the
grandparents Jablonka "never had" and in his quest to find both witnesses
and documents that could inform him about a past he tried to recover. It is
also somewhat surprising that there are no extended, substantive footnotes
in the text that can themselves be seen as supplementary essays that open up
lines of thought, suggest alternatives to the dominant argument, and function in a critical way. Part of the surprise comes from the way Jablonka provides an excellent discussion of the possibilities and limitations of various
kinds of footnote, including an *éloge* of its possible literary and scientific
value: "If one wants to give again all its dignity to the note, it is possible
to make of it a literary object by disseminating the account (*le récit*) with
several levels of notes linked to the text: references, reflexive commentaries,
states of the question, learned discussions" (269).[5] Quite thought-provoking,
moreover, is the suggestion that one displace the center of gravity from the
narration and consecrate a part of the account to the research and thought
process itself, resulting in not only a historical account but a (meta)account
of historical reasoning as an intellectual activity (296–97). I would observe
that one might see this initiative not as "navel gazing" (as it would be for
many conventional historians) but instead as an attempt at cognitively responsible self-understanding and even as an elaboration of the substantive

---

4. Ivan Jablonka, *Histoire des grands-parents que je n'ai pas eus: Une enquête* (Paris: Éditions du
Seuil, 2012).

5. Intellectually, stylistically, and affectively, a substantive footnote can indicate that, at this point
in a text, one should stop, think critically, and quite possibly argue. It may also indicate the role of
what M. M. Bakhtin terms the "internal dialogization" of a text, involving argument with others or
with oneself in a manner that impedes hasty conclusions and wards off closure. Jacques Derrida has
insisted on the importance of the footnote as a crucial supplement to the main text that may both
elaborate it and challenge it or even function uncannily as its unconscious.

footnote into a condensed exploratory essay inserted into a narrative or other historical account.

A more obvious counter to Jablonka's insistence on the centrality of narrative, as well as to theories that try to reduce all other forms in history to a covert narrative (evident at times in Paul Ricoeur), is the status of a social-scientific model in which the crux of history is the explicit formulation and testing of hypotheses. This approach need not take the form of a largely discredited "covering-law" paradigm that Carl Hempel and others derived from a restricted idea of natural science and projected normatively onto history. It may take a more encompassing but still other than narrative articulation as at least one important model of legitimate history. Such a view has recently been advocated by William Sewell in an important line of thought of his *Logics of History: Social Theory and Social Transformation.*[6] At least in certain respects, Sewell's book and Jablonka's supplement and help to compensate for one another's limitations.

Despite criticisms one may make of it, Sewell's approach, unlike Jablonka's, has the merit of trying to retain what he sees as the genuine advances of the "cultural turn" and the importance of language, stressed in the work of various theorists, including for him Clifford Geertz and Ludwig Wittgenstein. But he warns that "cultural history's lack of interest in, indeed effective denial of, socioeconomic determination to me seems potentially disabling in an era when such determinations are so evidently at work in the world, including, it would appear, in our own conceptualizations of historical process" (347–48). It is debatable to what extent a focus on socioeconomic determinations, say, in nineteenth-century France, would illuminate problems in the current era of rampant commodification, "globalization," privatization, deregulation, out-sourcing, hedge funds, the merger of commercial and investment banks, bundled mortgages, credit default swaps, off-shore banking and laundering of money, the specific causes of the vast discrepancy between the poor or even the vast majority and the very rich (the "1%" or even the "1/10 of 1%" in the United States), and so forth. Still, in a seemingly paradoxical fashion, Sewell sees socioeconomic determinations themselves (as well as the role of power) in semiotic terms or by way of language games. "The state, in both its military and civil guises, is a network of semiotic

---

6. William Sewell, *Logics of History: Social Theory and Social Transformation* (Chicago: University of Chicago Press, 2005). Sewell's book takes the form of a collection of interacting essays, which at times go in different or even divergent directions. See also Victoria E. Bonnell and Lynn Avery Hunt, eds., *Beyond the Cultural Turn: New Directions in the Study of Society and Culture* (Berkeley: University of California Press, 1999) and Gabrielle Spiegel, ed., *Practicing History: New Directions in Historical Writing after the Linguistic Turn* (New York: Routledge, 2005).

practices. . . . In this respect it resembles the collection of language games we call capitalism" (344). One might rather argue that semiotic practices and "language games" (related to what Wittgenstein termed "forms of life") are indeed crucial dimensions of various signifying practices and play a role on multiple levels in the complex working of power as well as of socioeconomic processes in general. There is of course a danger in relying on unexamined binary oppositions, such as that between culture and materiality (reminiscent of superstructure and infrastructure)—oppositions that might be questioned in the interest of elaborating nondichotomous distinctions. And one need not deny the role of statistics with respect to certain truth claims without simply conflating or even postulating a necessary link between numbers and structures, as Sewell is prone to do.

Sewell's treatment of methodology does not arrive at a more basic form of theoretical inquiry that examines assumptions and the way they underlie more or less questionable assertions—something Jablonka seeks but at times may not deliver. The very relations between socioeconomic determinations and cultural or signifying practices might itself be better conceptualized in terms of the problem of articulations and disjunctions, including supplementary rather than dialectical relations in a totalizing sense that implies cumulative gain without loss in intellectual, existential, or historical processes. Socioeconomic forces may help to shape and place limits on cultural practices and events (such as the writing of a novel), but they do not simply determine them, unless one is willing to revert to an unproblematic idea of the relation of an economic or socioeconomic infrastructure to a cultural superstructure or to Pierre Bourdieu's more Durkheimian mode of extreme sociological reductionism.[7]

Not everything in society or in the relations of humans and other animals or the environment can be explained in delimited socioeconomic or power-political terms. However one construes them, a crucial aspect of the cultural and linguistic "turns" was attention to other forces and factors, including meaning, ideology, desire, fantasy, fanaticism, racism, terrorism, traumatization, and quasi-religious or postsecular forces, notably the sacrificial and quasi-sacrificial. The Nazi attempt to get rid of Jews cannot be accounted for in delimited socioeconomic or power-political terms, and at times the killing and abuse of Jews might be "counterproductive" in relation to both the economy and the war against the Allies. One question is whether what Saul Friedländer treats in terms of "redemptive anti-Semitism" has a broader

---

7. See Pierre Bourdieu's *Rules of Art: Genesis and Structure of the Literary Field*, trans. Susan Emanuel (1992; Stanford: Stanford University Press, 1996).

applicability with respect to other modes of prejudice and animosity, for example, in various genocidal initiatives involving "ethnic cleansing." Prejudice and racism in general are not purely socioeconomic or power-political issues, although very important dimensions of the former may well be intertwined with them and have socioeconomic and power-political consequences. Nor should the easily manipulated role of economic anxiety and relative deprivation obscure the force of prejudice, racism, and nostalgia for a putatively better or even "great" and glorious past (including for some even a Confederate and slave-owning past—or at least a time when having an African American president was unthinkable) in the election of Donald Trump.

I have intimated that not all facets of cultural activity, such as the "creation" of art or the writing of novels, are accountable in socioeconomic or political terms. Indeed much art and writing in the modern period has had an explicitly contestatory relation to key economic and political forces from commodification to racism, exploitation, war, and militarization. Moreover, it should be apparent from the preceding discussion that a focus or emphasis on culture need not imply a "lack of interest in, indeed effective denial of, socioeconomic determination." It may involve an attempt to provide an informed and thought-provoking understanding of certain problems—or even to compensate for an existing imbalance of attention and research—but in a manner that may recognize the importance of other problems, which one may even discuss in limited, admittedly inadequate terms. Hence I think one may criticize an intellectual or even a cultural historian for not offering extended treatments of texts or artifacts about which sometimes cavalier claims are made but not for having an inadequate analysis of capitalism and its development over time. Conversely, it would be implausible and unfair to criticize Marx for an analysis of Balzac that is at best very restricted, or Keynes for not offering a searching understanding of the novels of his "Bloomsbury" associate Virginia Woolf.[8]

One thing Jablonka brings out and instantiates is the prevalent desire for "the real," perhaps indicative of anxiety over increased virtualization and

---

8. One may note that Sewell's argument moves in several directions. One of the more challenging is formulated by Judith Surkis: "Sewell has argued for a view of culture not as total, but as possessing 'thin coherence'. . . . The dialectic between system and practice in his vision of 'thin coherence' coincides with a 'deconstructionist' perspective on meaning. 'Deconstruction,' he writes, 'does not deny the possibility of coherence. Rather, it assumes that the coherence inherent in a system of symbols is thin in the sense that I have described: it demonstrates over and over that what are taken as the certainties or truths of texts or discourses are in fact disputable and unstable. This seems entirely compatible with a practice perspective on culture.'" See Surkis, "Of Scandals and Supplements: Relating Intellectual and Cultural History," in *Rethinking Modern European Intellectual History*, ed. Darrin M. McMahon and Samuel Moyn (New York: Oxford University Press, 2014), 94–111, at 102–3.

digitalization as well as the role of seemingly abstract socioeconomic structures and processes where it is often difficult to assign responsibility to determinate agents. This desire is pronounced in the quest for origins, "roots," presence, and identity and has led recently to "reality television," which often (even beyond the likes of Jerry Springer and Donald Trump) illustrates the gap between desire and realization or achievement. Jablonka's own earlier book on the grandparents he never had is in its own careful, erudite way a quest for knowledge of his emotionally laden roots in "the real," however elusive the latter may at times prove to be.

Jablonka enumerates his own checklist of characteristics of literature or the literary (whose status might better have been explicitly presented as inevitably contestable): literature is *form* (as aesthetic beauty—but does this exclude explicit techniques of disarticulation, disfiguration, and distortion?), *imagination* (including fictions but not uncontrolled fantasy), *polysemy* (how does this relate to ambivalence, equivocation, ambiguity, and more radical dissemination?), *singularity* (as "the eruption of a self"—*un moi*—developed later in the text more fully than the other characteristics, in terms of permissible use of the first-person singular as well as an "autobiographical socio-analysis" rejecting the omniscient view-from-nowhere and situating the self and its perspectives, notably as researcher, witness, and self-critic [*contre-moi*]; 288–89). Finally (in an expressly tautological formulation), the literary is what is recognized and even consecrated by readers and institutions as *literature* (perhaps too rapid a move to reception) (245–47). These characteristics are condensed into a definition that is recognized as open to criticism but has the presumed merits of simplicity (enabling easy applicability) and plasticity (making it compatible with the social sciences): "*Literature is a text considered as such and that, by means of a form, produces an emotion*" (247). Curiously, "emotion" appears in the reduced definition but not in the list of characteristics. Toward the end of the book, one has another variation of the nature of "history-literature" as a neo-Ciceronian endeavor to prove, please, and move the reader (311).

Jablonka is also interested in the relations between historical thinking and fictional literature such as novels, which he understands in a certain and, I think, sometimes questionable as well as question-worthy manner. In seeing history or historical thinking as both social science and literature, Jablonka has the obvious goal of placing in question and getting beyond the opposition between literary art and history as science, an opposition that was and still is important for a significant set of historians and for a set of writers and literary critics as well. He stresses the importance of history as writing, that is, an attempt to write a text in a strong if somewhat vague sense specified to some extent by Jablonka's list of characteristics mentioned in the preceding paragraph. (He does not address the problem of teaching, but one assumes that it would be subject to the same criteria as writing, including an ability to address a varied audience.) In any case, history is more than mere representation or mimesis in which one "writes up" the results of research, often in a "scientistic," antiseptic manner. And Jablonka rejects two complementary theories of fiction: an autotelic or self-referential idea, found in post-Saussurian critics such as Roland Barthes and Michael Riffaterre, and a reflective or mimetic idea in which fiction mirrors reality, found, for example, in certain Marxists, sociologists, and historians.

Difficulties nonetheless arise in what precisely Jablonka means by his key terms and what he is offering as an alternative to what he rejects. "Truth," "reality" (or "the real"), "writing," and "text" are explored only in restricted ways, although truth is at one point seen in terms of Karl Popper's idea of hypotheses that withstand tests of falsifiability, thus rendering assertions or larger claims credible as the best available approaches to the truth. And truth seems clearly to include accuracy and the disclosure and debunking of falsehoods. Yet "truth" and "the real" retain a hazy penumbra, as does "science" itself. While the notions of writing and text might evoke the work of Derrida, they remain on the level of common sense, which makes them, like other dimensions of the account, readily "readable" and open to the lay public, but at times at the expense of critical inquiry into their meaning and implications, although such inquiry seems to be what Jablonka is calling for. The term *enquête* itself, which appears frequently as defining the nature of historical thought, is ambiguous in that it means "inquiry," "inquest," and "investigation." "Inquiry" (a key meaning of the Greek word for "history") is probably the most important meaning, but the latter two meanings point to judicial procedure and detective work in determining the truth, which also play a role in the argument. A comparable ambiguity (polysemy?) arises in the definition of literature as well as history in terms of *recherche*—research as well as search, at least suggesting the possibility of a quest (as in Proust, for example, or in Jablonka's own apparent quest for knowledge of, and contact with, his grandparents, who were victims of the Holocaust). Moreover, Jablonka stresses understanding (*compréhension*) and explanation as aspects of historical reasoning or thought but says little about interpretation and its relation to problems of reading. Does Popperian falsifiability apply to interpretations or even to responsive forms of understanding, or is their assessment more complicated, perhaps even essentially contestable? It is also unclear how the issue of values and normativity relates to "science" as well as to literature. Does Jablonka agree with the summary formula of Max

Weber whereby values in social science shape the questions we ask to the
past or the object of study but have no significant role in the answers we
give? Is this view simplistic and, if so, how does one conceptualize the problem? There is of course a long tradition of reflection on these issues at least
from Dilthey and Gadamer as well as Durkheim to deconstruction. Jablonka
touches on them in passing but does not formulate and explore them as
distinctive problems.

Jablonka's only reference to Derrida is with respect to what he sees as John
Searle's dismissal of Derrida because of the latter's obscurity (258). (This is
like reporting on a boxing match from the perspective of only one of the
contenders, whom the other would see as blurry-eyed. Derrida's piece on
Searle might rather be read as an essayistic probe and a serious joke in which
the problems of intentionality and the copyright are at issue, with Derrida
quoting all of Searle's essay in his own piece but in a manner that would
make a suit for copyright infringement seem ludicrous.)[9] Put in the brief-
est terms, in Derrida the text is reconceptualized as a network of instituted
traces, which encompasses not only texts in the ordinary sense but all modes
of inscription from markings and tattoos in so-called preliterate cultures to
statistical series and the genetic code. One benefit of this view is that it allows
for connections and articulations (explicitly sought in "complexity theory")
while obviously calling for specification on the level of nondichotomous but
variably strong-to-weak distinctions that must be defended in argument. In
time this view becomes linked to a posthumanistic approach that does not
dismiss everything done under the rubric of humanism but instead targets
anthropocentrism and the postulation of any decisive division or separation
between humans and other animals along with the reduction of all other
animals to the homogenizing category of "the" animal (here Derrida offers
the genial neologism "animot"). The problem becomes the noninvidious
exploration of the complex, tangled networks among humans and various
animals without denying their proximities and empathic relations. (I would
suggest that evolutionary theory should thus not be fixated on the endlessly
repeated quest for the shifting, elusive, and contestable criteria that set apart
the human being from even its closest relatives—often serving to justify
human uses and abuses of other animals, including factory farming, hunting, imprisoning, experimenting on, killing, and eating them. Evolutionary theory might rather emphasize forms of coevolution at times creating

---

9. Derrida's essay, which quotes Searle's, is "Limited Inc. abc," *Glyph* 2 (Baltimore: Johns Hopkins University Press, 1977), 162–254; reprinted in *Limited Inc.,* ed. Gerald Graff, trans. Jeffrey Mehl-
man and Samuel Weber (Evanston: Northwestern University Press, 1988).

symbiotic links between humans and other animals such as dogs, horses, and elephants.) Derrida also construes language or other modes of inscription as other than human inventions or indices of human exceptionalism. By contrast, what is prominent in Jablonka is an unquestioned humanism and an idea of the human or social sciences that arguably has characterized the Annales school since its inception, despite the admirable range of its interests and its desire to situate humans in broader ecological networks. One might argue that the latter tendency might lead to a rethinking of the often professed humanism of those affiliated with the Annales. Derrida may not offer a handbook for the *métier de l'historien*, and his work does not solve all problems in a rethinking of history. But one need not be an uncritical disciple to argue that it may at the very least help to set the stage for more critical self-understanding involving problematic but important distinctions, for example, between history or historical literature and fiction. And there is no reason to rule out a priori texts (including some of Derrida's) that enact a hybridization of historical understanding and deconstructive writing.

Jablonka appears to be a rising young star in the constellation of the Annales. And his own positioning within the Annales seems obvious, notably in his stress on cognition, problem-oriented research, and the status of history as a social science. But the attention and research devoted in the work of scholars in and around the Annales to the relations between history, literature, and fiction have not been pronounced, except in certain areas, such as the sociology of knowledge and the role of writers in society and politics (for example, in Gisèle Sapiro or Christophe Charle) and the history of the book (as in Roger Chartier and Robert Darnton). There are also some notable but relatively exceptional figures with a broad interest in the interactions between history and literature, including Christophe Prochasson, Philippe Carrard, Michel de Certeau, and Jacques Rancière (the last three of whom are referred to by Jablonka). Hopefully, Jablonka will help to give greater importance within the Annales and more broadly to the issues that concern him.[10] Yet he also tends to downplay, marginalize, or exclude certain issues,

---

10. The contested nature of an affirmative interest in the relations between history and literature, among a significant number of historians associated with the Annales school, is perhaps indicated in the wording and tenor of a notice I received on April 24, 2017, from the Société d'Histoire Moderne & Contemporaine with respect to a proposed roundtable on the topic "L'écriture de l'histoire: Sciences sociales et récit," being held in Paris on June 16, 2017: "The writing of history and its relations to literature are today the object of numerous publications whether in order to affirm the presence of forms of knowledge in literature (*'savoirs de la littératures'* [sic]), to extol (*prôner*) a history that would be 'literature,' or to affirm that literature would be better suited to account for history. These propositions, largely offered for plebiscite (*plébiscités*) by the media, also evoke lively critiques among historians. The roundtable will be the occasion to debate the question of narrative

which I mention later, in the manner prevalent in Annales historiography, even in recent, somewhat more open-minded avatars such as the more senior Chartier or Jacques Revel and the younger Antoine Lilti. One might see his initiative as a significant inflection of approaches prevalent in the Annales by attempting to supplement, expand, or at least make more explicit tendencies in Annales historiography that in fact combine social science and literature (or the literary) in at least restricted ways. Jablonka mentions a number of texts that would qualify, including texts by Fernand Braudel and Georges Duby. He also rather surprisingly takes Carlo Ginzburg and Arnaldo Momigliano not only as important and influential models of erudite historiography but as significant theorists, which is daring but not altogether convincing. But what the latter share with Jablonka is a summary dismissal of what is rather inadequately understood as the so-called linguistic turn as well as postmodernism, which are quite simply conflated by Jablonka (and others) on the basis of a marked absence of sustained critical analysis and specific references. In general, the stress on the interaction and mutual implication of history and literature may help to prod the Annales (as well as historians elsewhere) in certain directions, and Jablonka's plea not only for "history as a contemporary literature" but also for postdisciplinarity and hybridized texts may strike some resonant chords even if it may have, for obvious reasons, little chance of transforming the academy. Still, the nature and level of his argument, along with its significant silences or omissions, may be accommodated as a friendly amendment and not really threaten to contest or change orientations already evident in historians associated with the Annales, however loosely defined or seen as "splintered" the latter may have become.[11]

Indeed the linguistic-turn-cum-postmodernism is one instance where Jablonka's tolerance, intellectual curiosity, generosity, and openness to

---

(*le récit*) and the possible tensions in the inscription of the discipline within the social sciences in this respect (*à ce titre*), an inscription founded on a critical apparatus and an interpretive approach (*démarche*). The professional practices of historians, the role of empirical and theoretical work in writing, but also the weight of editorial constraints, are at the heart of reflection. The stakes are vast: they relate to the future of research in history, the possible reception of its specific discourse, and the relation of historians to the public sphere (*la Cité*)" (my translation).

11. It is noteworthy that Jablonka does not rely on the concept of *mentalité*, once a blazon of Annales historians with a strong interest in cultural history. One reason for its decline may well be that the concept was too broad and homogenizing to allow for a close, differential reading of specific texts or contexts. And a more interactive understanding of the relation of *mentalité* to texts (in both the ordinary and the Derridean senses) was not sufficiently developed. "Mentality" did not attain much purchase in the Anglophone world, and the trio of text (or signifying practice), context, and culture, promising less but arguably delivering more, has remained prevalent among cultural and intellectual historians.

alternative styles and orientations appear to break down.[12] And, in a rare specific reference receiving some commentary, Hayden White is strangely taken as the exemplar of the linguistically turning PoMo composite monster. The essence of the beast is the reduction of history to fiction and rhetoric, a dismissal or radical downplaying of the cognitive dimension (essence?) of history, and a purely linguistic pantextualism in which there is nothing outside the text (in the ordinary sense of the word). But there is little cause for concern because "today the linguistic turn is dead" (109), although Jablonka seems to fear its resurrection, since he spends so much effort in beating the dead being. In the form Jablonka presents it, the linguistic turn was in any case always at best a frightful if spectral zombie. Insofar as the linguistic turn involved a sustained concern for language in historical use as a very important signifying practice interacting with other practices (*langage* in contradistinction to Saussure's binary between abstract *langue* and instantiating *parole*), it remains a vital problem with much still to be done, for example, in the study of the nature and relations among various forms and institutionalizations of language use such as the historical, the religious, the philosophical, the literary, and so forth. And one may pose nonreductively the important problem of the relation of historiography to rhetoric and to fiction. Jablonka's book itself has a pertinent discussion of rhetoric and is in large measure an inquiry into historical, social-scientific, literary, and fictional uses of language that would have benefited from a sustained awareness of the problems in language use it was touching on. If one is going to provide a cogent critique of the so-called linguistic turn, conforming to Jablonka's own rules of method, I think one needs more careful, discriminating analysis of specific thinkers, groups, and texts—not a carte-blanche categorization and indictment of a clichéd sort that, alas, may amount to scapegoating, a procedure that is not in the least new or experimental.

As is the case with any significant, controversial thinker, one may find things to criticize (and much that has already been criticized) in Hayden White, such as his radical constructivism (reminiscent of Kant's understanding of the formative power of the mind via the categories), his affirmation of a rather Sartrean existential freedom of the historian in employing White's own set of more or less associated categories in "prefiguring" the past, and his insufficiently explicated shifts over time, for example, in discussing the limitations placed on constructions, notably of the Holocaust, by what can

---

12. Here his approach is reminiscent of those of Joyce Appleby, Lynn Hunt, and Margaret Jacob, *Telling the Truth about History* (New York: W. W. Norton, 1994), Gérard Noiriel, *Sur la "crise" de l'histoire* (Paris: Belin, 1996), and Richard Evans, *In Defense of History* (New York: W. W. Norton, 1997).

be convincingly established about the past. But, in one sense, White never took language as a serious problem, and his approach was predominantly formalistic and conceptual in nature. He nonetheless made a truly major contribution to a decidedly cross-disciplinary historiography and its relations with literature. In fact he made a number of points very close to Jablonka's on the state of the historical discipline and the relations between history and literature, including the desirability for history to compete experimentally with innovations in the novel, hence returning in a different way to interactions prevalent in the nineteenth century. And later in his career he did distinguish between literature and fiction. His knowledge of the history of rhetoric, like Jablonka's, was more capacious than his theory of the four tropes, which by the way he did not restrict to the nineteenth century in their applicability to historical writing. I would add that one of the more interesting analyses of White is by his close associate Hans Kellner, who presented and commended White's work as "a bedrock of order" and a "linguistic humanism."[13] I would add that there are discussions of the linguistic turn that would have made Jablonka's treatment more nuanced and informed, although I think it is largely the case that both "postmodernism" and "the linguistic turn" were used less as self-designations than as categories employed by critics often in a reductive manner to classify and at times castigate what they opposed, perhaps as a hostile phantom. Derrida did accept and defend "deconstruction" after it had become a term employed by others, but did not take up the banner of either postmodernism or the linguistic turn, although this did not prevent deconstruction from becoming perhaps the principal phantom-like and fantasy-laden demon conjured up by critics who might even see it as the end of historiography if not of civilization.[14]

---

13. Hans Kellner, "A Bedrock of Order: Hayden White's Linguistic Humanism," *History and Theory* 19 (December 1980): 1–29.

14. Informed accounts include Elizabeth A. Clark, *History, Theory, Text: Historians and the Linguistic Turn* (Cambridge, MA: Harvard University Press, 2004); François Dosse, *La marche des idées: Histoire des intellectuels—histoire intellectuelle* (Paris: Éditions La Découverte, 2003); Ethan Kleinberg, "Haunting History: Deconstruction and the Spirit of Revision," *History and Theory* 46 (December 2007): 113–43; and two insightful essays by Judith Surkis, "When Was the Linguistic Turn? A Genealogy," *American Historical Review* 117, no. 3 (2012): 700–22, and "Of Scandals and Supplements," in McMahon and Moyn, *Rethinking Modern European Intellectual History*, 94–111. In the latter volume, see also the comparably insightful analyses by Peter E. Gordon, "Contextualism and Criticism in the History of Ideas," 32–55; Tracie Matysik, "Decentering Sex: Reflections on Freud, Foucault, and Subjectivity in Intellectual History," 173–92; and Warren Breckman, "Intellectual History and the Interdisciplinary Ideal," 275–93. In his excellent analysis, Kleinberg provides many illustrations of historians, typically on the basis of limited if not secondhand understanding, construing deconstruction as quite simply incompatible with, if not the annihilation of, historiography. For a very well-informed and thought-provoking analysis of the phases of intellectual history over the last few generations, see

Also worth mentioning is that despite the range of his references, Jablonka restricts himself, with very few exceptions, to texts written in or translated into French. This tendency, which might be seen as provincial, is not uncommon in French scholarship, including that of the Annales, but it may be changing in a way that is worth furthering. It is unfortunate that Jablonka did not directly engage or at least indicate the existence of texts in English as well as in German (including other languages, however desirable, might be asking too much). Doing so would have been useful not only for professional historians but for the lay public as well. Indeed the extent to which those writing in French are referred to, discussed, and translated by those writing in English is altogether disproportionate to the limited traffic flowing in the other direction.[15]

Jablonka realizes the ways texts classified as fiction are not entirely fictive and may well address real problems in their own way, problems also of interest for historians and social scientists. Yet, perhaps as an effect of his upbeat enthusiasm, he pays relatively little attention to problems such as violence, trauma, and post-traumatic effects, including "haunting" revenants, problems that, as he at times realizes, have been very important in modern writing.[16] Does historical writing about such problems simply aim "to prove, please, and move the reader," or does it encounter other demands? Such writing may well be moving but also try to avoid kitsch sentimentality and other intrusive or manipulative procedures. It may involve attempts to prove or at least substantiate claims, but it may also be unsettling and even unpleasant. In any case, it may strive not to eliminate or obfuscate the effects of the sometimes traumatic events that called it into existence and that it tries to

Allan Megill and Xpeng Zhang, "Questions on the History of Ideas and Its Neighbors," *Rethinking History* 17 (2013): 333–53. The diverse literature on postmodernism is enormous, but one of the most useful texts remains Jean-François Lyotard, *The Postmodern Condition: A Report on Knowledge*, trans. Geoffrey Bennington and Brian Massumi (Minneapolis: University of Minnesota Press, 1979). Also worthy of mention as informed and critical is Steven Connor, *Postmodernist Culture: An Introduction to Theories of the Contemporary* (Oxford: Blackwell, 1989). It is interesting that Connor's book, published relatively close to the emergence and growing prevalence of controversies about postmodernism, makes no reference to Hayden White. Connor remarks that "increasingly, postmodernist works were represented, and came to represent themselves, as self-conscious, quasi-critical activities" (7)—a view that might incline one to see Jablonka's book as "postmodernist."

15. I would note for the record that none of my own work is mentioned by Jablonka. Nor is the work of others who have written on topics pertinent to Jablonka's book, such as Perry Anderson, Frank Ankersmit, Warren Breckman, Mark Bevir, Carolyn Dean, Peter Gordon, Lynn Hunt, Martin Jay, Ethan Kleinberg, Allan Megill, Samuel Moyn, J. G. A. Pocock, Anson Rabinbach, Michael Roth, Quentin Skinner, Joan Scott, Gabrielle Spiegel, Judith Surkis, and John Toews. The list could go on.

16. See, for example, my *Writing History, Writing Trauma* (2001; Baltimore: Johns Hopkins University Press, 2014 [with a new preface]).

address as best it can. Would it really be a commendation to call a book about genocide "pleasing"? Is the attempt to prove, please, and move the reader a principal reason why a homogenizing style, striving to realize classical ideals such as beauty and even balance, is not in fact suited to all problems?

The alternative to autotelic and reflection theories of the relation between history and fiction that Jablonka proposes relies in a crucial manner on so-called fictions of method. What this in effect amounts to is not so much a mutual interrogation or challenging interaction but an attempt at mastery of fiction by historical thinking as Jablonka construes it. History makes use of fiction in a controlled and perhaps instrumental manner but does not seem questioned by works of fiction. Fiction passes muster only insofar as it furthers cognition and its ways and means in saying the truth about the real. Obscured or omitted here is the way fiction as well as history or social science may understand "reality" in a critical manner and probe ideological constructions of it that may misleadingly pass as knowledge. Fiction may also employ performative language and even play more or less surrealistic variations on what is taken to be real in ways that do indeed bring about the alienation or estrangement effects that Jablonka affirms as important in history. Despite its supposed reliance on reflection or mimetic theory, so-called critical realism at times touched on these issues. (The term has been applied by Georg Lukács to the novels of both Honoré de Balzac and Thomas Mann.) And the interaction between fiction and history was addressed in an other than Saussurian manner, which bracketed the referent and focused only on signifier and signified, by M. M. Bakhtin, whose work was critical of Saussure and quite important for some historians, including Natalie Zemon Davis, whom Jablonka mentions, as well as for critical theorists such as Julia Kristeva and Tvetan Todorov, whom he does not. Bakhtin saw the novel as a "baggy monster" that interacted with other forms from poetry to what Jablonka terms "literature of the real" such as memoirs and journalism. Bakhtin also stressed the role of dialogization and responsive understanding, not identified with literal dialogues but typically associated with exploratory, mutually questioning, internally self-questioning, and not simply objectifying orientations. While Jablonka is inclined to exclude the ludic from historical thought, in Bakhtin one has the interplay of the serious and the ludic in forms of praise-abuse operative in literature such as the Menippean satire and certain novels (those of Rabelais and Dostoevsky in particular), and arguably in history or social science as well. (Following Goethe as well as echoing Nietzsche, Mann referred to art as "jesting in earnest" or serious play.) One of Bakhtin's genial insights was the way the social carnival, which to some significant extent became less prominent over time (but not as much as Bakhtin seemed to think), was displaced as the carnivalesque into literature in the form of "reduced" laughter and irony. This form of irony was not simply suspensive, supercilious, or evasive but could have strong critical effects both in fiction and in social science, for example, in Marx's *Eighteenth Brumaire*. There is no mention of Bakhtin and only three not very crucial references to Marx in Jablonka. Today is their work also "dead"?[17]

Also absent or at least not prominent in Jablonka is close, sustained attention to what poses threats to the attempt to tell the truth about the real. Here one has the problem not only of the workings of ideology in historical thought and writing but also the role of psychoanalysis in inquiring critically into the way ideology, fantasy, and forms of scapegoating and violence may rely on suppression, repression, dissociation, projection, condensation, displacement, secondary revision, and related processes. The latter should at least be taken as "hypotheses" that may jeopardize if not disconfirm assertions or arguments. Indeed psychoanalysis is crucial in an investigation of affect and emotion, and the challenge is to rethink it as in large part a historically pertinent, critical-theoretical social science, based on a notion of the inherently social, "implicated" nature of the never fully autonomous (but nonetheless responsive and responsible) self or *moi* (*vide* the key concept of transference). Jablonka does mention the problems of subject positions and the implication of the observer in the observed, but they could be developed further and informed by psychoanalytic modes of inquiry. Moreover, the important psychoanalytic dimension of the work of Michel de Certeau and Saul Friedländer among others is not so much as indicated.[18]

---

17. On these issues, see my *Rethinking Intellectual History: Texts, Contexts, Language* (Ithaca: Cornell University Press, 1983), esp. chaps. 8, 9, and 10.

18. In early 2017, dimensions of the early Trump administration led to a turn to George Orwell's *1984* (published in 1949). The novel was being read as prescient "literature of the real"—but a real in which fantasy, fabrication, and the big lie were prominent features. Orwell's *1984* even became, in its posthumous rebirth, a best seller on Amazon. Orwell's depictions of the possibly nonexistent, televisual "Big Brother," his regime of mendaciousness, manipulation, and surveillance, and the emergence of "Newspeak" specializing in falsification and fake news, resonated with the reality-TV persona of Donald Trump and the dark role of principal White House advisers, notably Stephen Bannon, Stephen Miller, and General Michael Flynn, who shared a propensity for conspiracy theory, scapegoating, and an apocalyptic "clash-of-civilizations" view of Islam as the terroristic enemy, as well as an affinity with the extreme or "alt-right" views propagated by Breitbart Media. In a January 27, 2017, article in the *New Yorker* (www.newyorker.com/news/daily-comment/orwells-1984-and-trumps-america [accessed January 30, 2017]), Adam Gopnick wrote that "the single most striking thing about [Trump's] matchlessly strange first week [as president—DLC] is how primitive, atavistic, and uncomplicatedly brutal Trump's brand of authoritarianism is turning out to be. We have to go back to '1984' because, in effect, we have to go back to 1948 to get the flavor. There is nothing subtle about Trump's behavior. He lies, he repeats the lie, and his listeners either cower in fear, stammer in disbelief, or try to see how they can turn the lie to their own benefit. . . . Trump's

I would also note that the exemplar in the use of "fictions of method" for Jablonka curiously seems to be Claude Lanzmann's *Shoah,* where, in Lanzmann's words, there is "the obstinate effort ('obstination') to not understand" and where "blindness is 'clairvoyance' itself" (214). Yet, for Jablonsky, "a fiction of the real" (215) presumably is a path to knowledge as well as at least limited understanding and relies on reasoning (and, I would assume, critical judgment). The analysis of Lanzmann is brief at best. But what is not observed is that Lanzmann's stated goal, indeed the object of his quest, is to have victims "incarnate" or relive "the truth" with respect to their traumatic past experience. And his own relation to victims, such as the barber Abraham Bomba, is, I think, one of unmediated identification, which, in Lanzmann's supposed quest for "the truth," induces him to pursue intrusive questions and to persevere in prodding the victim to become retraumatized by reliving an unbearable past—a past that can be incorporated by Lanzmann and passed on as an incarnated present to the viewer of his film. Not disclosed to the viewer is the fact that the scene with Bomba takes place in a rented barbershop with extras who do not know the language (English) in which the exchange takes place. The shop has walls covered with mirrors that do not show the presence of a camera, which would seem to function as a participatory illusionistic device rather than as a self-conscious alienation effect. Under Lanzmann's direction, Bomba enacts hair-cutting gestures similar to those he performed on women in Treblinka. Everything would seem staged to induce the traumatizing reliving of the past and facilitate identification in the filmmaker and the viewer.

Unmediated projective or incorporative identification is not compassion or empathy, which requires an emotional rapport involving empathic unsettlement but also a certain distance and a respect for the other as other in his or her difference. Lanzmann's approach is closer to what in psychoanalysis is understood as acting out (*passage à l'acte*). Lanzmann (as he himself acknowledges in the 2015 documentary, *Spectres of the Shoah*) has no interest in survivors and their stories or attempts to come to terms with the past,

lies, and his urge to tell them, are pure Big Brother crude, however oafish their articulation. They are not postmodern traps and temptations; they are primitive schoolyard taunts and threats. . . . Resentment comes before reason. Conservative intellectuals, as a reading of the *Times* each day reveals, turn out to share these resentments far more deeply than they value the rational practices." Yet Trump (along with many of his followers in the Republican Party) does have his conservative critics. See, for example, David Frum, "How to Build an Autocracy," in the March 2017 issue of *The Atlantic*, https://www.theatlantic.com/magazine/archive/2017/03/how-to-build-an-autocracy/513872/ (accessed February 5, 2017). See also inter alia the writings and public appearances of Jennifer Rubin, opinion writer for the *Washington Post*, former Republican National Committee chairman Michael Steele, and Richard Painter, former chief White House ethics lawyer under George W. Bush.

and he intentionally excluded certain witnesses (such as Wladyslaw Bartoszewski) who did not relive or reincarnate the past but instead recounted
and analyzed it (and in Bartoszewski's case, without denying extensive Polish anti-Semitism, provided evidence of at least limited Polish assistance for
Jews despite the threat of draconian punishment by Nazis—something that
is, like the more complicitous or at least problematic dimensions of Primo
Levi's "gray zone," absent in *Shoah*). It would also be pertinent to analyze
the relations between *Shoah* and the earlier film *Pourquoi Israel* and the later
Tsahal, as well as Lanzmann's recent autobiography (*The Patagonian Hare,*
2012) and documentaries that at times include footage excluded from *Shoah*.
One might also plausibly argue that, especially in *Shoah* combined with his
influential, rather apodictic commentaries on it, Lanzmann did much to sa-
cralize the Holocaust and that his notion of "art" as involving incarnation
involved a secularized displacement of the sacred. One may well acknowledge Lanzmann's major achievement in *Shoah,* the power of its disconcertingly haunting evocations, and its ability to conjure up the hallucinatory cries
of victims through a nonrepresentational approach. But if any or all of my
critical comments are cogent, how can the film be taken as the epitome of
secular historical understanding via a "fiction of method"?[19] There is quite
a distance between Lanzmann and Primo Levi as chemist and writer who

---

19. On Lanzmann, see my *History and Memory after Auschwitz* (Ithaca: Cornell University Press,
1998), chap. 4, "Lanzmann's Shoah: Here There Is No Why." See also the documentary *Spectres of the
Shoah* (2015), where Lanzmann tries to justify his interrogation of Bomba by appealing to his quest
for "the truth" and his feeling that Bomba was his "brother," which raises the questions of how one
should undertake a quest for the truth or treat one's brother. I think the issue is not whether Lanzmann is sadomasochistic—a charge he rejects—but whether he gives way to unmediated projective
and incorporative identification that enables intrusive questioning at times appearing to take the
form of an inquisitorial technique. Note as well that there are many ways to view and try to understand or interpret Lanzmann's *Shoah*. At the time I published my discussion of it, I thought the most
prominent approach in the literature was (and at times may still be) based on a more or less uncritical
acceptance of Lanzmann's self-understanding and, like it, may at times have noted the documentary
and testimonial aspects of the film but stressed, sometimes exclusively, its status as a cinematic work
of art to be analyzed and evaluated on aesthetic grounds. (A striking instance of the approach I was
trying to question appeared, fortuitously enough, in the journal in which a version of my piece was
first published. See Ora Gelley, "A Response to Dominick LaCapra's 'Lanzmann's *Shoah*,'" *Critical
Inquiry* 24 [1999]: 830–32. See also my rejoinder in the same volume, "Equivocations of Autonomous
Art," 833–36.) Without denying the relevance of cinematic or aesthetic criteria, I contended that a
restricted or autonomous aesthetic conception of the film might well encrypt and conceal a more
religious response that could function to further the sacralization of the Holocaust, which at times
has been put to contestable political uses and abuses. I would further observe that a distinctive (postsecular?) way to view the film is in terms of a ritual of mourning and a memorial to the victims of
the Nazi genocide. This view may possibly serve a politicized sacralization of the Holocaust, but it
may also run counter to politicization understood as an instrumental distortion and degradation of
the process of mourning.

resisted identification and whose analytic prose combined reason and emotion or Claude Lévi-Strauss as analyst, commentator, and at times ironically self-critical participant-observer in *Tristes Tropiques* [293–94), both of whom Jablonka admires and explicates briefly but well. Lanzmann would also seem distant from Georges Perec, who insisted in Brechtian fashion on the explicit role of alienation effects that countered tendencies toward unmediated identification.

In general, a shortfall of Jablonka's book is the paucity of extended critical analysis of texts or other artifacts such as films that might indeed pose questions both to the book's fast-paced, free-flowing style and to its arguments or "hypotheses." (A reason Samuel Beckett gave for his turn to writing in French was the desire to slow down his intellectual and compositional practice.) One writer to whom Jablonka makes perceptive intermittent reference is Georges Perec, who is found to be exemplary in writing novels that, while employing fiction, nonetheless count as "literature of the real," for example, with respect to Perec's childhood and his relation to the Holocaust. Moreover, Perec imposed on himself rules of method that indicated how artistic freedom interacted with discipline and formal constraints:

> The procedures that he elaborates, the rigorous exercise book of burdens (*cahier des charges*) he imposes on himself, the systems of constraints in which he inserts himself, from the lipogram in E of *La disparition* to the polygraphy of the knight (*chevalier*) in *La vie mode d'emploi,* stimulate the narrative and verbal imagination in the manner of a fiction pump (*pompe à fiction*): one gives oneself rules in order to be "totally free." (255)

Moreover,

> at the beginning of the 1960s, Perec had not yet written about the disappearance of his parents; but he was already influenced by the literature-truth (*littérature-vérité*) of Robert Antelme, "this man who narrates and who questions, [. . .] who uproots their secrets from events, who refuses their silence"—beautiful definition of historical reasoning. The postrealism of Perec goes beyond nineteenth-century realism in making literature an operation that places the world in order, an obstinately lucid exhaustion (*épuisement*). His first book would be *Les choses,* which numerous critics would read as a sociological essay in the cover of a novel. (229)

Jablonka evidently feels an affinity with Perec on personal and intellectual levels.

Jablonka notes that Perec stated in 1969, the year that *La disparition* appeared, that he had been "a student in the school of Brecht: I am for coldness, the step back *(le recul)*" (303). Jablonka gives, in one of his few extended analyses, a conception of Brecht and the alienation effect that provides one of the clearest insights into what he defends in history, social science, and the literature of the real:

The only effect that the researcher *(le chercheur)* may claim is the distancing (or "alienation") effect, the *Verfremdungseffekt* of Brecht, this procedure made up of humor, of irony, of warning, of disillusionment, and of complicity. In the theater, the *V-Effekt* motivates the spectator to consider the scene with "an investigative and critical eye": lively illumination, visibility of the sources of light, the off-set play of the actors, placing the public on trial *(prise à partie du public)*. The room, cleared of all magic, does not create any "hypnotic field." Brecht posits explicitly a parallel between the distancing effect and the scientific view. One and the other constituted a "technique of systematic suspicion" with respect to everything that seems to go without saying: the actor should place between himself and the present "this distance that the historian takes in the face of events and behaviors of the past." The fact of refusing all mystification *(mystique)* does not prevent one from fully living the theater; simply, the emotions are of another nature. (303)

Perec and Brecht as read by Jablonka serve as telling instances of what the latter valorizes not only in history and social science but also in literature of the real that may have fictional features. But does this reading enable one to encompass the variety of overtures in modern literature or fiction? Despite certain affinities with Brecht, does Flaubert, for example, do more to disorient than to illustrate Jablonka's understanding of historical reasoning and "fictions of method"? Flaubert's seemingly precise descriptions and explorations of events tend to wander off in bewildering directions, destabilize expectations, point to disorder in the world, or defy the imagination (for example, the bizarre description of the hat of Charles Bovary, the opaque world of the sacred in *Salammbô*, the collapsing private and public "spheres" in *The Sentimental Education*, even more so the heteroclite "temptations" of Saint Anthony, or the self-imploding quest for knowledge of Bouvard and Pécuchet).[20] How do these initiatives nonetheless have a probing relation to

---

20. On Flaubert, see Jonathan Culler, *Flaubert: The Uses of Uncertainty* (Ithaca: Cornell University Press, 1974). See also my *"Madame Bovary" on Trial* (Ithaca: Cornell University Press, 1982) and *History, Politics, and the Novel* (Ithaca: Cornell University Press, 1987), chap. 2 (on *The Sentimental Education*).

an attempt to tell the truth about the real, challenge the reader to consider her or his own position with respect to the destabilizing problems and dilemmas explored in the text, and arguably be said to provide a critical reading of the times? The question could also be raised about numerous authors Jablonka does not discuss or at times even mention, for example, Beckett, Blanchot, and Celan (whose writings may be uncannily and disconcertingly moving but do not prove or please). Adorno is mentioned only once (258) in the same breath as Derrida and treated similarly, here with respect to Karl Popper's defense of "simple and clear" language in contrast to "intimidating gibberish (*galimatias*), 'brilliant opacity' being the refuge of triviality, if not of error." Without being an obscurantist or advocate of gibberish and opacity, Adorno did affirm the validity of certain difficult uses of language in their resistance to easy understanding and commodification, did not send Hegel or Marx packing as "totalitarian" exponents of a "closed" society, valued Beckett with his dislocations of "reality" and enigmatic asperities over Sartre and transparently committed literature, and put forth a sharp critique of Brecht.[21]

One important current in modern literature, at times in the same texts in which "real" problems are addressed, is a quest not simply for creation ex nihilo (as Jablonka contends) but for a radically transformed world or even for transcendence as well as the experience of, or encounter with, its failure or collapse. Here, however critically or skeptically one responds to it, one has inter alia a desire for situational overcoming of what is currently taken as "the real." At times one may have a longing to get beyond or outside of history and to awake from its "nightmare," as Joyce has Stephen Dedalus put it in *Ulysses*. One also finds what might be termed a traumatic writing of disaster along with an exploration of the abject and at least hints of a negative sublime rising from the ashes. The sublime may even displace the sacred, giving literature a postsecular dimension that comes in the wake, absence, or unavailability of traditional religion and may gesture toward an unrepresentable beyond or *à-venir* (in Derrida's term). The quest for a totally other albeit blank utopia may even emerge as a contestable counterpoint to secular, "immanent" history. In the above respects, it is unclear what Jablonka makes of Jonathan Littell's *Les bienveillantes* (mentioned on p. 235) as fictional

---

21. See, for example, Adorno's 1962 essay "Commitment," in *The Essential Frankfurt School Reader*, ed. Andrew Arato and Eike Gebhardt (New York: Continuum, 1985), 300–318. See also Gene Ray's defense of Brecht's "dialectical realism" against Adorno's critique: "Dialectical Realism and Radical Commitments: Brecht and Adorno on Representing Capitalism," *Historical Materialism* 18, no. 3 (2010): 3–24.

literature extensively referring to and incorporating history but having other problematic dimensions, including a putative "rigor" that Littell, however questionably, associated with Bataille, Blanchot, and Beckett.[22] More generally, there is every reason in a critical and self-critical form of historical thinking to treat texts as significant events and as "hypotheses" that require careful inquiry and not simply passing mention or use as illustrative allusions. An interruption of the flow of a fast-moving narrative might itself be seen as a valuable alienation or distancing effect that prompts critical reflection.

I do not want to end with the impression that Jablonka's book is not to be taken seriously and admired. The book offers abundant food for thought for readers whom it will inform, impress, and perhaps, in its own evident and admirable enthusiasm for history and literature, inspire to think further about the questions it raises. Other readers may well take exception to my own comments or critiques and find other lines of thought or possibilities in Jablonka. His book is written with brio in what might be seen as a stylistic combination of the ardor (*fougue*) of Lucien Febvre in *Combats pour l'histoire* and the *roman-fleuve* flow of Fernand Braudel's prose in his classic on the Mediterranean in the age of Philip II. Its goals are altogether commendable, and, despite possible disagreements one may have over specific issues, it raises very important questions, opens many significant avenues of inquiry, and seeks a desirable interaction between historical and literary approaches.

---

22. For my own attempt to analyze this novel along with Saul Friedländer's *Nazi Germany and the Jews*, see "Historical and Literary Approaches to the 'Final Solution': Saul Friedländer and Jonathan Littell," *History and Theory* 50 (February 2011): 71–97, a version of which is reprinted as chap. 4 of *History, Literature, Critical Theory* (Ithaca: Cornell University Press, 2013). For a criticism of my approach, which is based on what I find to be a rather indiscriminate notion of the role of irony in the novel, see Dabarati Sanyal, *Memory and Complicity: Migrations of Holocaust Remembrance* (New York: Fordham University Press, 2015), chap. 5.

CHAPTER 6

What Use Are the Humanities?

I shall conclude with a cross-disciplinary topic touching on the public sphere and open to understanding and debate in a diversified audience. The public significance of the topic is indicated by insistent emphasis on so-called STEM fields (science, technology, engineering, and mathematics) along with the downgrading of the humanities. Kentucky Republican governor Matt Bevin argued that students majoring in French literature should not receive state funding for their college education. North Carolina Republican governor Patrick McCrory (defeated in 2016), apparently oblivious to erotic innuendo, proposed that higher-education funding should not be "based on butts in seats, but on how many of those butts can get jobs." Senator Marco Rubio, Republican from Florida, has called for more welders and fewer philosophers, although, to the best of my knowledge, Rubio himself has not demonstrated noticeable competence as either.[1] STEM areas are of obvious importance.[2] But the stem is not of much value

---

1. See "Love for the Humanities Dwindles," *The New Mexican,* February 29, 2016, A-6.

2. Equally important are support and respect for a variety of positions in the economy, including that of welders, as well as the provision of training or retraining for workers who are either entering the economy or losing jobs in other areas, such as coal mining—jobs that cannot be recreated by magic or by promises that are seeming expressions of concern. It is clearly desirable to offer training, education, and outlets for as many people as possible in positions of their choice, which would obviously require very significant restructuring of the current economic and social situation.

without the rest of the plant. Crucial is the ability to validate facts, critically analyze defective arguments, and understand the nature of civic responsibility in a diverse democratic society—arguably skills that certain members of Congress have not recently displayed.

The seeming crisis in the humanities was signaled by the appearance of a blue-ribbon report in 2013, entitled *The Heart of the Matter: The Humanities and Social Sciences for a Vibrant, Competitive, and Secure Nation.* The report had fifty-two important signatories and two co-chairs, the president of Duke University and the ex-CEO of Exelon (a major defense contractor), and was commissioned by a bipartisan foursome of two senators and two members of the House of Representatives. I think the basic, implicit question of the report is how those with a humanistic education can compete with the STEM disciplines, succeed in existing society, and be of use in contributing to national strength and competitiveness. This pressing concern, prevalent or indeed dominant in contemporary ideology both here and abroad, is not one on which I shall focus. But I urge readers to examine the report, which was issued by the American Academy of Arts and Sciences. My own view is that a report such as this may well further some of the least desirable aspects of modern education and general culture that place a premium on tactical or instrumental rationality geared to getting ahead and winning, to the detriment of forms of education that develop informed, critical judgment not conflated with mere subjective opinion or even bias.

I would note that natural scientists often have two vastly different discourses. One is highly specialized and bears on their research. The other usually points to the results or payoffs of that research, say, rockets in rocket science or the increase in crop production in agriculture. Humanists often strive for greater integration and communication between their discourses. And, at least among the general public, the question of usefulness would in all probability seldom arise with respect to the natural or even the social sciences. The question might rather be how one could avert certain dangerous uses or abuses of these fields (resulting in, for example, the deployment of doomsday bombs and deadly drones, techniques of total surveillance and control, and food endangered by the reliance on harmful pesticides). That the question of usefulness, as well as of employability, is so readily and prevalently posed about the humanities might be interpreted as symptomatic of a defensive posture as well as of a feeling that the humanities are essentially of no real use, whether positive or negative. The response to this orientation may be difficult in a business-and-success-oriented, technologically avid society. One may nonetheless argue that the humanities may not be of short-term use or deliver immediate, technological payoffs (although literature or philosophy majors may of course find jobs in communications, go to law school, or enter financial services). The "use" of the humanities might be seen as more indirect and long-term.[3] As is often said, the humanities contribute to the quality of life. The fact that people in retirement return to the study of humanistic subjects is testimony simultaneously to their appeal and to their marginality in our culture. (However, on the less marginal end of the spectrum, one might also mention the role of cultural activities such as concerts, lectures, and plays not only in choice retirement areas, such as Naples, Florida, or Santa Fe, New Mexico, but, in seemingly paradoxical fashion, in ghettos and concentration camps, for example, Terezin or Theresienstadt, as brought out in Doug Schulz's 2012 film, *Defiant Requiem*.) One index of the significance of the humanities at a university is the existence and role of a humanities center from a broom-closet operation to a spacious and well-equipped facility with offices, fellowships, and adequate support for its activities.

The pursuit of the humanities is more than a sign of their function as status symbols, "cultural capital," or occasions for a cultural suntan. It is an indication of their value as components of a life that is more than one-dimensional. If you are bright and have a good education, you have a fair chance to make a significant amount of money in our extremely deregulated and skewed society. The nature and role of the humanities at their best go beyond use value (and its complement in a utilitarian or capitalistic frame of reference: exchange or moneymaking value). The humanities at least gesture in the direction of generosity, liberality, and gift-giving. The latter would seem to be one important meaning of "liberal" in the term "liberal arts," and the humanities are liberal arts par excellence. And while they go beyond narrowly conceived use value or practicality, they are not entirely useless, for they may foster critical and self-critical understanding and create bonds, sometimes very durable bonds. (They may create bonds or a sense of intimacy with texts and other artifacts or works of art and at times with people or other creatures.)[4] In brief, they are both good to think with and good to live with.

---

3. A similar point might be made about basic research in the sciences, which itself is often underfunded in comparison with more immediately useful or applicable orientations.

4. William Blake's *Auguries of Innocence* is particularly effective in stressing bonds with other beings as well as prompting outrage over their abusive treatment. The poem begins with the famous verses "To see a World in a Grain of Sand / And a Heaven in a Wild Flower / Hold Infinity in the palm of your hand / And Eternity in an hour / A Robin Red breast in a cage / Puts all Heaven in a Rage." The poem continues with a powerfully evoked catalogue of abuses to which humans have subjected other animals. See *Blake's Poetry and Designs,* selected and edited by Mary Lynn Johnson and John E. Grant, 2nd ed., Norton Critical Edition (New York: Norton, 2008), 403–5.

A spirit of liberality, generosity, and gift-giving can be proposed as crucial to the humanities—crucial not in some dogmatic or exclusive sense (this spirit may in fact also characterize significant aspects of work in the sciences) but in a sense that stipulates what is important and relatively distinctive but continually open to debate and contestation. For the latter qualities—debate and contestation—may also be seen as crucial to humanistic understanding and exchange, and argument or even polemic, as well as the telling of engaging yet also critical, self-critical, and carnivalesque stories or narratives, can be undertaken in a liberal, generous spirit. One might contend that an intelligent, informed, spirited critique is a better gift than a conventional encomium (although this point may be more readily acknowledged by the giver than the receiver of the critique!).

Liberality, generosity, or gift-giving is not identical with ethical or moral goodness. The latter depends on the nature of the gift, and liberality may be conjoined with forms of excess that may be harmful, for example, deregulated competition linked with domination, exploitation, and extreme discrepancies in income and wealth. In another register, one might mention gifts of death in Derrida's term with respect to sacrifice—which Georges Bataille took (and dubiously celebrated) as a preeminent form of useless expenditure or wasteful excess. And a quest for justice, bound up with compassion and judgment that limit excess, may also be understood as a defensible component of humanistic (or "posthumanistic") inquiry. Moreover, investigation of a problem in the humanities need not be seen as a zero-sum game or competition, since the recurrently debatable question is the nature and relative value of contributions to problems that do not lend themselves to a definitive solution or first-time discovery. It would be misguided even to ask the question of who discovered language or other signifying practices, such as music or art, although one may of course raise the question and debate the issue of who or what counts as the exponent of innovation or "creativity" in these areas. Language and signifying practices in general are posthumanistic in that humans did not simply invent or create them, and they are both limiting and enabling in what they permit one to do. The extent to which they are unique to, or even distinctive of, humans is a recurrent source of contention and rethinking over time. Note also that important dimensions of poststructuralism have both led up to and been integrated into varieties of posthumanism, notably the questioning of essentialism, of totalization, and of human exceptionalism in favor of a stress on decentering and the deconstruction of binary oppositions. Also prominent in poststructuralism has been the contestation of boundaries (including those between disciplines) and the need for a rearticulation of reconceptualized, problematic distinctions in contrast to rigid binaries. I have indicated the particular importance in the recent past of the radical questioning of a total or radical dichotomy between humans and other animals—a dichotomy that is typically conjoined with anthropocentrism and a questionably essentializing, exclusionary form of humanism.

As Jacques Derrida more than intimates in his extended project of tracing and deconstructing the long history and displacements of metaphysics in the West, one may also argue that basic problems in the humanities are repeated (and repeatedly thought about) with variations over time, and temporality itself from a humanistic perspective is arguably this very process of repetition with variation or change, at times abrupt, decisive, revolutionary, or even traumatic change. (However it is construed or misconstrued, "modernity" is often understood as marking one such traumatic swerve, break, or "shock" experience but not necessarily a total cut or rupture with respect to the past. Indeed the idea of a total break or creation ex nihilo, at least in sublunary affairs, may well be an apocalyptic illusion or perhaps a post-traumatic symptom.)

Here a crucial distinction is that between problems and puzzles. A puzzle (or puzzle-like "problem") may be solved, and its solution has a more or less immediate use value. (How does one build a more efficient engine, devise a faster way of accessing the Internet, or operate an older printer with a new Apple computer—Apple being one of the all-time leaders in planned obsolescence?) Puzzles have a place in all studies, including the humanities (for example, the dating of a document, the identification of an allusion, or the digitizing of an art collection—indeed puzzles are central in much of the technically oriented, often very useful, but sometimes technocentric and change-obsessed digital humanities in general). But as important, even more important, are problems into which one inquires and which one may argue about, elucidate, or even deepen, and in certain ways work through but not solve or totally transcend. If asked to propose a single (albeit long-winded) statement to designate what is crucial to the humanities, I would offer the following: the study of basic, indeed cross- or even transdisciplinary problems that are not narrowly utilitarian but instead allow one to intervene in, or contribute to, an open, questioning, and self-questioning process of inquiry. The self is "transferentially" implicated in that process and its relation to others and to the past in ways that may enable possible, and possibly more desirable and durable, futures. How should one understand the terms of this "definition" of what is crucial as well as liberally empowering in the humanities?

Cross-disciplinary is not simply interdisciplinary in that it does not merely combine existing disciplines (say, history and literature) to investigate and provide better answers to existing questions. It inquires into problems that themselves cut across existing disciplines, may be treated with different disciplinary emphases or inflections, and perhaps even suggest the need for more flexible if not newer disciplines, subdisciplines, or institutional units such as programs and departments. What are some recurring cross-disciplinary problems of humanistic significance that may be elucidated but not solved as if they were puzzles? Without pretending to be all-inclusive and exhaustive, one might mention violence, victimization, mourning, trauma, and oppression but also justice, gift-giving, trust, compassion, responsibility, agency, community or institution building, and laughter, as well as the sacred and sacrifice. One may of course think of other problems—temporality and improvisation or the human-animal relation, for example. Sacrifice is particularly knotty from an ethical and political perspective, since it typically conflates oblation (or gift-giving) and victimization, with the victim as the gift to a higher being or even as an offering when there is no belief in a determinate higher being or personalized deity. Indeed one speculation is that such a deity was the result of sacrifice once the perhaps misguided question was raised, to whom is one offering this sacrifice? Sacrifice need not imply belief in a god, but it may retroactively help to generate gods if one assumes that a gift must be offered to some being or entity as recipient. And sacrifice may be seen as transcending ethics and justice, hence taken as a form, perhaps a paradigmatic form, of excess or sacralized, even divine violence. Sacrifice may be displaced into secular contexts in often distorted, obscure, and disavowed ways, appearing in the form of a cult of violence or a belief that through violence (even victimization, including self-victimization) one may regenerate or redeem the self or the group. Sacrifice is often seen as an ecstatic, sublime activity or even as the road to redemption. (I have argued that this point may well apply to the Nazis and their abuse of victims—abusive treatment seen as cleansing or purifying the community of contaminating aliens and sometimes even experienced in an elated, intoxicating way.)[5]

---

5. See, for example, my *Representing the Holocaust: History, Theory, Trauma* (Ithaca, NY: Cornell University Press, 1994), *Writing History, Writing Trauma* (2001; Baltimore: Johns Hopkins University Press, 2014 [with a new preface]), *History and Its Limits: Human, Animal, Violence* (Ithaca, NY: Cornell University Press, 2009), and *History, Literature, Critical Theory* (Ithaca, NY: Cornell University Press, 2013).

How could one possibly solve such problems and processes as trauma, victimization, sacralization, sacrifice, trusting, assuming or ascribing responsibility, justice, gift-giving, and excess? One can at best work on and to some extent through them in a manner that more or less "usefully" expands the possibility of accentuating whatever may be judged to be desirable in them and eliminating, diminishing, or at least counteracting what is judged to be undesirable. Hence, with respect to sacrifice, I have suggested that the normative challenge is to valorize the gift while disengaging it from, and counteracting, victimization. (But should one call this challenge humanistic or posthumanistic, since it concerns not only humans but also other animals?)[6] I think that what we term the humanities should and at times does bear on relations with other than human beings. Ethical, political, and at times legal issues are applicable to the activities of enterprises involved not only in the killing or capture of animals but also in such activities as drilling and

---

6. One may observe a close but often unnoticed correlation between two fundamental works of an important figure for Jacques Derrida, Georges Bataille, and Claude Lévi-Strauss among others: Marcel Mauss. The first work (published in 1898 with Mauss's close collaborator Henri Hubert) is *Essai sur la nature et la fonction du sacrifice* [Sacrifice: Its Nature and Functions], and the second (published in 1925) is *Essai sur le don* [The Gift]. Crucial to both works is the role of a fundamental ambivalence: that of the sacred, which can be both pure and impure (or sanctifying and dangerously contaminating), and that of the gift, which can be both gratifying and threatening (emblematized in the ambivalence of the German word *Gift*, meaning both "gift" and "poison"—what Derrida discussed in terms of the cure/poison ambivalence of the Greek *pharmakon*, posing the problem of the proper dosage). The gift is dangerous in that it must be reciprocated with increased largesse, which reaches its excessive extreme in the potlatch that seeks to crush one's rival with largesse so great it cannot be returned. In a sense, gift exchange reverses the principle of capitalist exchange in that one seeks not profit, by which one takes more than one gives, but honor, power, and prestige that may nonetheless reach a hubristic extreme, notably when the gift is not given to a rival but arrogantly destroyed in a holocaust or thrown into the sea. And the sacrifice is dangerous not only for its victim but for the sacrificer who may become (self-)destructively overcharged with religious power and in a sense radioactive, raising the problem of how to exit safely from the sacrificial scene. I have indicated that in sacrifice there is a questionable conjunction of the gift and victimization in that the victim is the gift or offering and the gift is the victim in a gift of death. The gift may even be a sacrifice, as in the case of the Gallic chief Mauss discussed in a supplementary essay—the chief who is unable to reciprocate in kind and so offers to his rival the one thing he has of comparable value to the gift he received: his own life. A difference between Mauss's works on sacrifice and on the gift is that the first is uncritically situated within a sacrificial "logic" of which it tries to make sense, while the second (unlike Bataille) takes a critical distance on hubristic potlatch as the "monster child" of the gift system, putting forth a judgment (treated favorably by Derrida in *Given Time I: Counterfeit Money* [Chicago: University of Chicago Press, 1992], 64–65) in favor of "amiable rivalry" that is not excessive but rather allows the gift cycle to continue in creating valuable social bonds and even in providing a normative model applicable in the criticism of a one-dimensional, exploitative, instrumentally "rational" capitalistic logic. I intimate above that a comparable critique of sacrifice would involve a disambiguation of the gift and the victim, with a critique of victimization and a valorization of liberality in gift-giving, implying that a seemingly neutral and often anthropocentric attempt simply to "make sense of" or "find meaning in" sacrifice (often ignoring the animal victim or construing it only as the occasion for a meditation on one's own mortality) is misguided and itself open to criticism.

fracking. The latter activities have divided the American government along with the Army Corps of Engineers as well as many American citizens, on the one hand, and, on the other hand, indigenous peoples trying to protect sacred sites, recently at issue in the conflict between proponents of the South Dakota oil pipeline and the Standing Rock Sioux with their indigenous and nonindigenous supporters. If the conflict runs true to historical form, as now seems highly probable with the change of political administrations, pipeline proponents will win another pyrrhic "victory" even at the expense of indigenous rights and religious practices, not to mention possible if not probable oil leaks endangering the purity of water systems.[7]

A recent cross-disciplinary problem that has risen to prominence, notably in its relation to extreme events (such as rape, abuse, and genocide), is trauma. Trauma studies or trauma theory may be employed in questionable ways, and one should not simply participate in or repeat its ideological construction as a key that opens all locks, for example, as "original sin" or as the "big bang" at the "origin" of all culture. Nor should one take it as an imperialistic threat to an interest in other problems that may nonetheless have significant interactions with inquiry into trauma and its effects.[8] But trauma and the post-traumatic not only cross disciplinary boundaries within the humanities, applying to humans and to other animals. They even involve the sciences and social sciences (neurophysiology, social psychology, psychoanalysis, psychiatry, narrative medicine). One might argue that, like trauma, most significant problems in the humanities are precisely those that are not simply "trendy" (as some have misleadingly seen the study of trauma itself). To see a problem as merely trendy is ostensibly to deny or downgrade its significance—to see inquiry into it as merely "talk," trauma talk, say, in the sense Heidegger prejudicially referred to idle chatter or *Gerede* (in his time and place, a term of denigration typically applied to Jews or the French). It is also to misleadingly situate oneself or one's group and its approach as the real thing and the foundation of an unproblematic identity, say, as a true historian, philosopher, or literary critic. Yet significant problems are not "owned" by any given humanistic discipline but often studied, at times with

---

7. See Steven Mufson, "A Dakota Pipeline's Last Stand," *Washington Post,* https://www.washingtonpost.com/business/economy/a-dakota-pipelines-last-stand/2016/11/25/35a5dd32-b02c-11e6-be1c-8cec35b1ad25_story.html (accessed November 26, 2016).

8. For example, the contemporary media, including the reporting of news, may rely on fast-moving sound-and-sight bites that allow little if any time for in-depth study or critical analysis. Thus trauma and its effects may be treated in superficial, often sensationalistic, and repetitive ways (epitomized in the endlessly recurrent images of the terrorist attacks on the Twin Towers or the coverage of devastating bombings and other forms of violence in the Middle East and elsewhere).

unsettling or uncanny effects, in various disciplines, including disciplines not generally seen as humanistic. They are also the problems that are not confined to the academy but have a bearing on the so-called public sphere and the larger society. However questionable it may be as an adequate explanation, it is interesting that Cornelius Gurlitt told *Der Spiegel* that he kept for half a century and still wanted to keep the 1,406 paintings stolen by the Nazis and handled by Gurlitt's part-Jewish father (Hildebrand) because he (Gurlitt *fils*) loved nothing more in life than his pictures. And a small sign of success for an author is to have his or her books stolen from the library.

A similar point about cross-disciplinarity might be made about specific texts, artworks, artifacts, and media that are studied in the humanities. What discipline "owns" the works of Plato, Cervantes, Vermeer, Goya, Freud, Virginia Woolf, Federico Fellini, Hannah Arendt, or Pablo Picasso (one of the painters in Gurlitt's horde)? One or another may be studied more in one discipline than in another. But would a scholar in art history or visual studies be justified in dismissing a discussion of Vermeer or Picasso in literature or history?[9]

Here I would refer briefly to a coup that befell me a number of years ago. I was reading the classifieds in the *Ithaca Journal* and ran down the list from firewood to futon and, once the anomaly registered, returned to the reference to Freud. I called the number for Freud and found a recent graduate in psychology whose close relative, in a flash of uninformed generosity, mistakenly thought that the entire *Standard Edition* would be a welcome graduation present. Having learned the lay of the land in a psychology department not friendly to the study of psychoanalysis, the recent graduate was selling her gift, boxes unopened, for half price—an offer I could not refuse. There is a certain sense in which the understanding of Freud implied here is accurate. Freud is not a psychologist in any ordinary sense, individual or social. He is best understood as a critical theorist, as he was in the Frankfurt school (whose orientation in this respect, as in quite a few others, I take seriously). More generally, as Freud's stock went down in psychology, his work was picked up and used in at times creative ways in the humanities. His role in France, in good part via Jacques Lacan, has been widespread, even on

---

9. Freud is a particularly interesting case, since he may be claimed by psychology even if his works are not studied in that discipline. I would also note that some ancient historians and social scientists at Cornell were very upset when the late Martin Bernal strayed outside his field of modern Chinese studies. Obviously, you may argue about Bernal's theses but not deny the thought-provoking nature of his work, notably *Black Athena* and ensuing discussions of it.

a relatively popular level.[10] And Freudian concepts, however understood or misunderstood, have permeated languages in many areas, including North and South America. As indicated earlier, I attempt to rethink crucial concepts in Freud with special reference to history, society, and culture. I have stressed that there is a basic social dimension to Freud's thought, as in the concept of transference that involves an elementary implication of self and other with the tendency to repeat. And working through as a process of articulation has a crucial social and political dimension and may be ineffective when restricted to the individual not having significant involvement in social and political roles.

What is distinctive about basic humanistic artifacts or texts, including Freud's, is the way their significance exceeds any given discipline—one form of excess that may well be defended. As I intimated, basic humanistic artifacts may be appreciated, read, or studied not only across disciplines but also outside the academy. Indeed the degree to which they enter the public sphere is an index of general culture, including the richness and diversity of a culture that combines such interests with prevalent forms of popular and media culture. Popular media themselves are enlivened, enhanced, and at times critically challenged by a sustained relation to so-called high or elite culture—and vice versa. Just as Walter Benjamin would not be Walter Benjamin without both an intimate knowledge of traditional high culture and arresting insights into popular culture, so Monty Python or the Beatles would not be what they are without a comparable interaction between the high and low or elite and popular. Whether intentionally or not, no song is more "Heideggerian," indeed a hymn to *Gelassenheit*, than "Let It Be." And the erudition displayed and parodied in Monty Python is often remarkable.[11] I would also mention the recently rediscovered music of Sixto Rodriguez, in certain ways as remarkable as that of his more famous contemporary Bob Dylan. Rodriguez is featured in the documentary *Searching for Sugarman*. His two albums from the early 1970s are *Cold Facts* and *Coming from Reality*. Quite stunning is the story of his virtual neglect until recently in his insecure homeland (where he has lived for over forty years in the same modest house

---

10. See, for example, Sherry Turkle, *Psychoanalytic Politics: Jacques Lacan and Freud's French Revolution* (New York: Basic Books, 1978) and Camille Robcis, *The Law of Kinship: Anthropology, Psychoanalysis, and the Family in France* (Ithaca: Cornell University Press, 2013).

11. One should also take note of the informed, carnivalesque, at times hilarious role of comedians, for example, those on *Saturday Night Live,* in critically satirizing the inanities, ineptitudes, and dangerous initiatives of Donald Trump and his entourage (as well as parodying propensities of Hillary Clinton and Bernie Sanders during the campaign).

in Detroit) as opposed to his cult status and role as a political inspiration for anti-apartheid forces in South Africa. The general point is that both elite and popular culture tend to become involuted, mannered, and even mindless to the extent their range of reference and concern remains insular.

One of the manifest deficiencies of news and talk shows during the 2016 presidential campaign was the creation of a self-centered bubble enclosing uncritical furtherance of uninformative and at times uninformed "debate" involving a series of fast-talking spin doctors, often egregious yet endlessly repeated misstatements or even falsehoods if not lies that at times remained unchecked and unchallenged (especially in "real time"), and an obsessive concern for presenting a presidential campaign on the model of a horse race or other competitive sports event seeking the highest possible ratings. Trump's inaugural address in Washington, DC, on January 20, 2017, had a relatively small crowd, estimated at approximately 250,000, especially when compared not only to Barack Obama's 2009 audience of some 1.8 million but also to the estimate of more than 500,000 people (some estimates are over a million) at the women's protest march the day after the inauguration (in addition to very large crowds at many protest marches in other cities in the United States and around the world). When questioned about Press Secretary Sean Spicer's January 21 media-hostile and fiery repudiation of what he questionably saw as a low estimate of the audience at the Trump inaugural, Trump surrogate and senior adviser Kellyanne Conway on MSNBC's *Meet the Press* of January 22 referred to Spicer's use of "alternative facts." This was met by host Chuck Todd's assertion that the so-called alternative facts were simply falsehoods.[12] Todd's reaction was in line with the postcampaign

---

12. The interview is available at http://www.nbc.com/meet-the-press/video/meet-the-press-jan-22-2017/3456842 (accessed January 23, 2017). See also Chris Cilizza, "Sean Spicer Holds a Press Conference. He Didn't Take Questions. Or Tell the Whole Truth," *Washington Post,* January 21, 2017, https://www.washingtonpost.com/news/the-fix/wp/2017/01/21/sean-spicer-held-a-press-conference-he-didnt-take-questions-or-tell-the-whole-truth/?utm_term=.f619da1ee4bb (accessed January 22, 2017); and Jon Swaine, "Trump Presidency Begins with Defense of False Alternative Facts," *The Guardian,* January 22, 2017, https://www.theguardian.com/us-news/2017/jan/22/donald-trump-kellyanne-conway-inauguration-alternative-facts (accessed January 23, 2017). Conway, like Alice in Wonderland, also had a notion of alternative meanings. Whenever the issue of making public Trump's tax returns is raised, she claims that the issue was thoroughly "litigated" during the campaign. In fact, it was not litigated at all. Depending upon the source, it was brought up repeatedly, evaded repeatedly, falsely promised by Trump that it would be subject to disclosure after the election, and is still in abeyance. Conway returned to and "re-spun" the question of what was meant by "alternative facts" in an interview of July 23, 2017, with Brian Stelter on CNN's *Reliable Sources.* To elucidate her defense of Spicer's assertion that Trump had the largest crowd "period" for his inauguration speech, she offered the subjective "judgments" that a glass was half-empty or half-full or that it was cloudy or sunny (on a day when it was partially both). Stelter was apparently so taken aback that he offered no resistance to these wildly irrelevant examples.

tendency of certain journalists to eschew euphemism and respond critically to what had often been allowed to pass without real-time fact-checking or critical comment during the campaign. One might even plausibly conclude that the principle in understanding the unprincipled Trump could almost be the following: suspect him and his entourage of doing, wanting to do, or having done whatever it is that he accuses his targeted opposition or enemy of doing, from "fake news" and "crookedness" to surveillance and more or less "conspiratorial" attempts to shape policy through unofficial actors that replace or circumvent competent career professionals.

One of the greatest casualties of the 2016 campaign was the state of discourse in the public sphere, including the earlier discussed distinction between accuracy, fact, and truth, on the one hand, and falsehood, lie, and obfuscation, on the other. The frequent media "meme" about Trump has been that with him we are in uncharted waters. In my judgment, we are rather in very troubled waters, and Trump is unable or unwilling to read and abide by long-standing, readily available charts. A particularly dangerous thing about Trump is that he has no sense of limits and feels he can get away with anything. And he has associates, including both paid surrogates and prominent members of the Republican Party, who seem willing to support or encourage his excesses and provide excuses or justifications for them. If he takes offense at critics, he retaliates not in some measured manner but with a massive overdose of what he projects onto or thinks he sees in them. At best he has a severely impaired "mechanism" of self-censorship and self-control. He profits greatly from the prevalent notion of a post-truth or post-fact society, which is seemingly clever but altogether predictable as a sequel to a long series of ill-assorted and ill-defined "post" labels. But this use of "post" is particularly misleading and harmful. It even seems to write off truth and fact as parts of a bygone age. Much in the rhetoric and practice of Trump and his surrogates has been antithetical to the spirit of the humanities (as well as the posthumanities), while their propagandistic, manipulative animus against elites tapped into what has long been seen as a widespread anti-intellectualism in American culture, including the devaluation of the humanities and the forms of critical thought they convey.

"High" culture and its "elites" were derided by Trump surrogates as "anti-populist" forces, often associated with the Northeast and the West Coast (which were largely responsible for Clinton's popular victory by almost 3 million votes), their people and institutions (notably universities and even the media), and their supposed distance from the ordinary people whose voice Trump pretended to be. (Evidently, despite his castle-like Fifth Avenue tower and long history of living the high life in the Big Apple, he was not a member of one of the New York elites.) But a prominent feature of high cultures not only in modernity or postmodernity but across the ages has been their variable interaction with popular cultures, including the popular carnivalesque culture of contestation and laughter (an important motif in the work of Mikhail Bakhtin).[13] The difficulty in this respect is not the existence of "canons." The latter exist even in popular culture.[14] It may well be the case that the unfortunate possibility, even in serious exponents of high culture, is insularity as well as the process of canonization, when a canon is used for exclusionary and discriminatory social and political purposes, and texts or artworks become the analogues of school ties. But this possibility is not a necessity or a foregone conclusion. It may be insistently countered by those who do not dichotomize or draw invidious distinctions between dimensions or "levels" of culture.

A criterion of a humanistic approach is a certain relation to its past, including canons as institutions that help constitute that past and pose problems for revising or riffing on it. A science (as well as a scientistic idea of social or human science) may rest on the belief that whatever is essential to it that comes from the past has been integrated into the present state of the discipline. (Here the understanding of knowledge is cumulative and basically progressive.) Hence a physicist qua physicist may not experience a professional need to read Newton or Einstein, a biologist to read Darwin, or even a social scientist to read Durkheim or Weber. These figures are studied in intellectual history or perhaps in science studies, which straddles (like much of history) the social sciences and the humanities. One might well argue that a well-educated biologist should in fact read Darwin. But such a claim would relate to a broader, quasi-humanistic or "liberal" understanding of what a well-educated biologist as a scholar and an intellectual should be. (By the same token, a well-educated humanist should have at least basic literacy in the sciences and social sciences.) But, without ever having read Einstein or Darwin, a scientist could win the Nobel Prize for a contribution based on relativity or evolutionary theory. Such a state of affairs would be unacceptable, or

---

13. If Trump can be seen as a carnival figure, it is not the people's fool who unmasks hypocrisy and oppressive power characterizing "strong men" that Bakhtin termed people eaters. It is rather the authoritarian buffoon and con artist devoid of humor (especially when self-directed) who hypocritically and oppressively uses ridiculing, barbed sarcasm to bully and humiliate scapegoated others while counting on the gullibility or duplicity of his supporters. During the campaign, Trump famously (or infamously) observed that he could shoot someone on Fifth Avenue without shaking the faith of his devoted followers.

14. There was even a canon of Trump talking points and pivot-and-project tactics, disseminated among Trump advisers and the surrogates who quickly became TV personalities.

at least raise eyebrows, only if natural sciences were to be defined in broader sociocultural and intellectual terms that would make certain intellectual or cultural "externalities" more internal to the definition of the discipline. These internalized externalities might of course also include the role of critical responses to forms of experimentation (notably on other animals) and to possible "uses" of discoveries, at times in extremely destructive ways. Some natural scientists or others in the STEM disciplines may indeed see what they do in such expanded terms, but I doubt whether this vision is part of the definition or even the prevalent self-understanding of these disciplines. However, I may be and indeed hope I am or will in time be proved wrong.

What has often been understood as the humanistic relation to the past assumes the past is not simply past but in significant ways still part of the present with implications for the future. Only a narrowly objectifying and positivistic notion of history presents the past as sharply separated from the present and future. Aspects of the past, including its canonical texts or artifacts, may well be criticized but must also be known and play a key role in the present state of inquiry. For in the humanities the very way the past and its artifacts are read, critically reread, and responsively understood (or "riffed on") is constitutive of learning processes and renewal in the present. (Here examples abound. Renaissance figures offered revisionary readings of antiquity, Protestants of the Bible, Marx of Hegel, Joyce of Homer and Flaubert, Beckett of Joyce along with the Cartesians and Flaubert, Lacan of Freud, and so on, with many complications and variations.) Moreover, the relation to the past, its processes, and its artifacts is self-implicating. The observer is implicated in the object of observation in a way that cannot be confined to one, easily bracketed dimension of research (for example, with respect to the observation of very small particles in physics). Self-implication extends throughout the entire range of significant inquiry, and in the humanities the small, seemingly insignificant, easily bracketed detail or research area may be the site of displacement of the most valorized, affectively charged problems, something of course underscored not only in Freud but also in Derrida's notion of the dangerous supplement.[15]

As noted earlier, in psychoanalysis a self-implicating relation to the other is addressed in terms of transference. And I have indicated that transference

---

15. Here I shall mention two little, easily overlooked details in Flaubert and leave the reader to think about them. It seems striking that, despite its temporal frame, there is no mention of the revolution of 1848 in *Madame Bovary*. Does Emma Bovary's suicide take its place? And there is a narrative gap in *The Sentimental Education* that covers the entire Second Empire (1851–1870). Is this an indication of Flaubert's alienation from the period and his desire to evade or erase its characteristics?

may be understood as a social, self-implicating aspect of psychic processes more generally. Active both in animosity or hatred and in affection, care, or love, transference is one important force in relations between self and others. For Freud its templates were forged in early childhood, which, in view of the pronounced vulnerability and impressionable nature of infants and young children, is of course a strong possibility. But a ground for transferential relations may also come in one's later encounters with a bully or a helping hand, an abuser or a care giver, an antagonist or a supporter, a friend or a foe, or even in a striking brief encounter that for some reason remains imprinted in both psyche and soma. Such experiences may be both significant in themselves and carry over into other relationships that bring them back or trigger comparable responses.[16]

The implicated observer or inquirer tends to displace and repeat, on a basic level, processes active in, or projected onto, the other or the object of research. Hence, for example, the student of the Holocaust confronts the "transferential" problem even on the elementary level of naming or terminology, for especially in emotionally charged, value-laden areas of study, there are no neutral or innocent terms. If one uses "Holocaust," one may stir the sediment of sacrificialism, for (as is well known) etymologically the term refers to a burnt offering. But the wearing away of a sacrificial connotation may be a beneficial effect of prevalent usage and banalization of the term. (Here we have a possible value in rendering a term banal.) If one resorts to "final solution," one repeats Nazi terminology, and the use of scare quotes is a necessary precaution that may be ignored or misread. "Shoah" bears witness to the role of the media in modern culture, for (to the best of my knowledge) its use was not widespread before the appearance of Claude Lanzmann's important film in the mid-1980s, and the term may have an exoticizing potential for those who do not know Hebrew. Even Nazi genocide (seemingly the most neutral of terms) still seems to grant a proprietary hold over the genocide to the Nazis and, however unintentionally or remotely, realize their desire to totally dispose of Jews (including the question of how Jews should be named and remembered even after their hoped-for elimination—a museum in Prague was to be dedicated to this form of appropriative remembrance). On the other hand, Jewish genocide or the term Jewish martyr (used

16. Some commentators have noted that Donald Trump's prejudicial and aggressive words and behavior had a strongly disturbing effect on them, at times evoking a traumatic memory of abuse and enabling or seeming to authorize hateful, prejudiced, and at times violent orientations in others. See, for example, Rebecca Solnit, "From Lying to Leering: Donald Trump's Fear of Women," *London Review of Books*, January 19, 2017, 3–7.

even by Levinas) may be complicit with a dubiously sense-making sacrificial perspective. More generally, I think the subject position assumed by many historians tends to be that of the bystander, which deceptively seems closest to objectivity. (The bystander is to varying degrees often complicit in what happens in phenomena such as abuse and genocide.) The point here is not to foster nominalism or engender terminological disarray but to indicate the necessity of careful qualification and the need to be sensitive to one's "transferential" implication in processes. Of course the question of how to work out a defensible subject position or set of positions is difficult and essentially contested, especially with respect to highly charged problems.

The broader challenge is to elaborate or work through a relation to the past rather than to think one can transcend it through a purely objectifying methodology or through a decisive leap or creation ex nihilo. Perhaps combined with one of the former orientations, one may also blindly and even compulsively repeat, in a more or less displaced fashion, its processes, at times with fatalistic, negative results. Such a caveat indicates the limitations of attempts at full objectification of the other whereby self-implication (or transference) is disavowed or denied but often acted out in uncontrolled, unacknowledged fashion.[17] But it also signals the crucial importance of careful, indeed meticulous research and close reading that may check inevitable projective and repetitive tendencies that are especially insistent to the extent a problem is still alive and pressing. (This point casts a different light on the role of contextualization without making it tantamount to historical understanding, although one may argue that it is a necessary condition of the latter. In any case, contextualization furthers defensible objectivity by countering projection or reprocessing, which to some extent is inherent in an implicated or transferential relation.) The problems I have signaled in relation to the Holocaust are prevalent in history, especially in the case of extreme, traumatizing events such as genocides, and pose particularly insistent challenges not only to the humanities but to all related forms of research and understanding.

At their most demanding and promising, the humanities are on the cusp between critical thought and liberality, generosity, or gift-giving as well as on the threshold between humanistic and other forms of understanding, including the scientific and social-scientific. And the gift in question cannot be seen as going in a one-directional sense from the human to the other.

_____

17. Uncanny conjunctions and double binds are quite prevalent, notably including the fascination with the virtual or digital, on the one hand, and, on the other, the quest for authenticity, reality, roots, and origins (often pursued digitally via Ancestry.com).

For one thing, it depends on the differences within the human, especially including those brought about by being a human animal—from a certain perspective, a problematic kind of hybrid or compromise formation. Moreover, the horizon of humanism may well be "posthumanistic" or other than exclusively humanistic in a specific sense. Along with such crucial, widely acknowledged issues as race, class, sexuality, and gender (all of which have been intimately bound up with questions of victimization and its relation to survivorship, resilience, and agency), one should also stress the role of species, which may well be in the process of becoming a major concern in a critical and self-questioning "humanistic" approach. The concern for species is a vital component of an interest in broad ecological issues. More generally, it may be plausible to argue that the humanities have traditionally had "the" animal as their covert scapegoat, which global studies may itself repeat, however inadvertently, even when the values asserted are purportedly universalistic or at least worldwide. The other-than-human animal has typically been the constitutive other of humanism and the humanities, and it may now be commonplace to contend that there has been a recurrently displaced but compulsively repeated quest to find the essential criterion (or theologian's and philosopher's stone) that decisively separates the human from other animals (or postulates the essentially human as transcendent with respect to the animal, including the animal within). This elusive criterion of humanity, which often functions as a disavowal of the animal in the human, has taken many forms—creation in the image and likeness of God, soul, spirit, reason, freedom, language, and so forth, often downplaying what brings us closer to other animals, not only animal languages—about which we are learning more—but the capacity to be aggressive yet also to suffer, empathize, be traumatized, be victimized, be resilient, be trusting, or be joyful. Perhaps one should begin inquiry with suspicion concerning any quest for the presumably essential, dichotomizing difference or set of differences between humans and other animals.

In any case, what has become increasingly obvious is that the differentiating criteria of the human can never be established with the decisiveness and, more arrestingly, with the invidious and exploitative consequences with which such criteria have been overtly or covertly put forward. The genuine problem may lie not simply in the elusiveness of the object of the quest but in the misguided nature of undertaking the quest itself. As indicated earlier, that misguided quest for the cuttingly decisive criteria of the human seems typically to involve invidious, self-congratulatory, prejudicial investments that may serve to justify unacceptable uses and abuses of other animals. This realization, which cannot be avoided by a one-dimensional, exclusionary, self-defeating insistence on human rights or confined within an anthropocentric conception of animal "rights," should bring about a decisive shift in the self-understanding of the humanities (or posthumanities), whose nature and implications are, I think, in the process of emerging. It reopens the question of the relation between humanistic, scientific, and social-scientific disciplines. It is clearly a basis on which the humanities will have to be extensively rethought and in whose terms—ideally both just and generous—its other crucial concerns will have to be reconfigured, in certain ways from the ground up. In a word, what is crucial to the humanities may now require a posthumanistic orientation that counters the hypocrisy of a human dignity and status at least implicitly based on a binaristic scapegoat mechanism whereby what goes on all fours cannot by definition be taken as having dignity. Such a "posthumanistic" orientation, while not being antihuman or antihumanistic, does entail a thoroughgoing critique of anthropocentrism along with human exceptionalism and extends the field of concern to other-than-human beings and to the differences within the human as well.

Posthumanism has become increasingly prevalent in the work of scholars formerly identified as humanists, although attention to it in historiography is still quite limited. Its range encompasses not only other animals but other nonhuman beings such as cyborgs, robots, and the entities in the expanding field of artificial intelligence (AI). Equally limited in the inquiries of historians is a prominent concern that has arisen along with posthumanism: the postsecular. It shares with posthumanism the at-best self-questioning coherence as well as the openness to innovation of the various "post" orientations that posthumanism and postsecularism follow and may recapitulate or rethink.[18] The postsecular is obviously related to religion and to the question of secularization. Religion has been many things, but it is typically a nonhumanism in that it gives the human being a subordinate place with respect to higher spiritual powers. In monotheisms, these powers culminate or are condensed in the theocentric notion of God. But in various traditional or indigenous religions, a God-being or totally other, transcendent Other is not a forceful presence, if it plays a significant role at all. More important are spirits or spiritual beings that may have a higher status than humans (and often are seen as closer to nonhuman animals) but are bound up with other beings in ways that impose limits on human assertion and the exploitation of nature, particularly with respect to sacred sites imbued with spiritual forces. In

---

18. See my discussions of the postsecular in *History, Literature, Critical Theory*, esp. chap. 5. See also the thought-provoking essay-review of this book by Allan Megill, "History, Theoreticism, and the Limits of 'the Postsecular,'" *History and Theory* 52 (February 2013): 110–29.

the West, religion has of course persisted despite the rise of secularity. It has often been an imposing presence whose continuing role has until recently not been sufficiently recognized by those affirming an Enlightenment project, important aspects of which many (including myself) would still want to affirm.[19]

The relation of the postsecular and the religious is vexed. The postsecular often seems to be a threshold phenomenon, both similar to and different from more traditional religions. Secularization itself took diverse forms. The clearest was the secularization of church property. But, in more contested, less obvious, and more thought-provoking ways, secularization raised the question of the extent to which seemingly secular processes or phenomena are more or less disguised displacements of religion. Displacement entailed repetition and disguise with more or less prominent changes or variations. Many important figures, including Karl Löwith, Carl Schmitt, Hans Blumenberg, and Sigmund Freud, have addressed the question of the extent and ways secular phenomena, such as the sovereign nation-state, could be understood as a displacement of the religious. Especially with reference to the thought of Joachim of Flora, Löwith seemed to postulate a virtual identity between religious and secular concepts, notably in the case of meaningful, well-nigh providential stages of history (as in Hegel and Marx) as well as the more apocalyptic idea of a final stage ending in a decisive, revolutionary break in time (say, absolute knowledge or the classless society). Schmitt made the famous assertion that "all significant concepts of the modern state are secularized theological concepts" (36). Blumenberg distanced himself from identity-based notions of secularization but nonetheless conveyed a specific idea of displacement in the concept of "reoccupation" (or *Umbesetzung*, which may be compared with Freud's use of *Besetzung*, translated in the *Standard Edition* as "cathexis"). For Blumenberg, formerly religious constructs, even buildings such as churches or chapels, were reoccupied by more secular constructs, as a church might become an asylum or a concept of divinity be ascribed to the legitimation of a king and even to a charismatic leader. Blumenberg stressed difference, although reoccupation involved repetition with change, and the relation between the two was variable. His emphasis on difference became accentuated when he varied his formulation to indicate that over time the same or similar questions might be raised but the answers to them were original. (This formulation recalled Max Weber's debatable idea that values shaped the questions social scientists posed to the past but did

---

19. See Jürgen Habermas, "Notes on a Postsecular Society," *Sign and Sight*, June 18, 2008, http://www.signandsight.com/features/1714.html (accessed May 17, 2009).

not affect the "scientific" answers to them.) The concepts of displacement and *Besetzung* were crucial in Freud and not invariably decidable in terms of whether repetition or change was dominant. Generally, Freud emphasized disguised repetitions and reinvestments of affect bringing more or less significant differences. But, somewhat hyperbolically, Freud wrote to Wilhelm Fliess: "By the way, what have you to say to the suggestion that the whole of my brand-new theory of the primary origins of hysteria is already familiar and has been published a hundred times over, though several centuries ago? Do you remember my always saying that the medieval theory of possession, that held by ecclesiastical courts, was identical with our theory of a foreign body and the splitting of consciousness?" (90). Others pursued this line of inquiry further, including Jacques Derrida, notably in terms of a "hauntology" displacing ontology.[20]

"Religion" itself is notoriously variable in meaning and difficult to understand, especially with respect to the unfamiliar religion of others where habitual practice no longer conceals problematic issues (such as drinking Christ's blood or eating his body in the mass). With respect to traditional or "archaic" societies hitherto classified in Christianity as forms of paganism, it is even open to question whether certain constellations of practices, including what are termed myths and rituals, are sufficiently similar to what are ordinarily seen as religions (such as the monotheisms) or as modern myths and rituals (at times forms of falsification or conformity drawing a perhaps unearned increment from association with other forms termed religious or spiritual). In any event, one may point to many phenomena in "modernity" that are not simply secular, aside from the now evident, continuing role of historical religions and their progeny. Max Weber made frequent appeal to the role of "charisma" (the gift of grace) as a force in society that could not be reduced to instrumental rationality and often seemed to operate in other

---

20. See Karl Löwith, *Meaning in History: The Theological Implications of the Philosohpy of History* (Chicago: University of Chicago Press, 1949); Carl Schmitt, *Political Theology*, trans. George Schwab (1922; Cambridge, MA: MIT Press, 1985); Hans Blumenberg, *The Legitimacy of the Modern Age*, trans. Robert M. Wallace (1966; Cambridge, MA: MIT Press, 1983); Marie Bonaparte and Anna Freud, eds., *The Origins of Psychoanalysis: Letters, Drafts, and Notes to Wilhelm Fliess, 1887–1902* (Garden City, NY: Doubleday, 1957); and Jacques Derrida, *Specters of Marx: The State of Debt, the Work of Mourning, and the New International*, trans. Peggy Kamuf (1993; New York: Routledge, 2006). See also my *Representing the Holocaust: History, Theory, Trauma* (Ithaca: Cornell University Press, 1994), chap. 6, "The Return of the Historically Repressed." For a comparison of the psychoanalyst with the shaman and the exorcist, see, respectively, Claude Lévi-Strauss, *Structural Anthropology*, trans. Claire Jacobson (New York: Basic Books, 1963), chap. 9, "The Sorcerer and His Magic"; and Michel de Certeau, *The Possession at Loudun*, trans. Michael B. Smith, foreword by Stephen Greenblatt (1970; Chicago: University of Chicago Press, 2000).

than rational ways. Yet it was a source of power and even authority that extended from divine-right kingships to leaders in modern mass movements and established regimes. Charisma may be secularized but not amount to the narrowly secular. It may account for attachment to, even adulation of, leaders, even ostensibly hollow figures, whose appeal is not a matter of rational self-interest and may even run counter to it. It is remarkable that even Donald Trump has been seen as charismatic despite his manifest limitations and business failures. The fact that he was able to withstand scandal after scandal and rise from the ashes has been taken by supporters as a sign of his election and savior-like status (rather than as an indication of his good fortune and one's own bad judgment).

The sublime is another phenomenon prominent in modern notions of quasi-transcendental force of such magnitude that it blocks the understanding, may be linked with a near-death experience, exceeds the limits of the beautiful, often comes with fear and trembling (or traumatic impact), and may reduce one to silent awe. Yet it is also seen as the highest peak of the aesthetic experience and may be sought elsewhere in life, including in politics.[21] It is typically the most elevated encomium one may attribute to a performance or artifact. And it is arguably the more secular or postsecular side of the sacred or perhaps of transcendent holiness. The sublime came into prominence in the thought of figures such as Edmund Burke and Immanuel Kant. (T. E. Hulme ironically literalized displacement in defining Romanticism as "spilt religion.")[22] The sublime was a keynote of the Romantic movement, which has arguably persisted as a beacon for many in and around poststructuralism. The sublime is related to valorized excess and the transgression of limits (recalled even in the commonplace notion that an art object or a performance is "out of this world"). Appeals to the sublime have also been active in at times valorized conceptions of trauma, which itself is

---

21. One way of understanding Edmund Burke's critique of the French Revolution (as well as the connection between his often dissociated early and later work) is that it misguidedly sought a political sublime instead of keeping the sublime more safely contained within the aesthetic and the religious.

22. Quoted by M. H. Abrams in *Natural Supernaturalism: Tradition and Revolution in Romantic Literature* (New York: W. W. Norton, 1971), 68. In treating the relations of Romanticism to religion, Abrams emphasizes gentle displacements without significant disruption, sublime disorientation, and irony or humor (evident in Carlyle's *Sartor Resartus* but not in Abrams's discussion of it). More focused on the sublime and the problematic in Romanticism (and giving a more prominent place than Abrams to the German Romantics) is the approach in Jean-Luc Nancy and Philippe Lacoue-Labarthe, *L'absolu littéraire: Théorie de la littérature du romanticisme allemand* (Paris: Éditions du Seuil, 1978), containing excellent selections from the German Romantics and philosophical Idealists. Nancy and Lacoue-Labarthe are probably the two foremost French disciples of Derrida and have developed his approach in creative ways.

often taken as a mode of excess that is quasi-transcendental, takes one out of the ordinary, and leaves one speechless. As intimated earlier, the sublime / trauma diptych demands sustained attention and, in my judgment, careful criticism.[23]

A perplexing issue is whether and how the posthuman is combined with the postsecular or, in apparent contrast, represents an intensification of a secularity hostile to, or in any event decisively different from, religion as well as various forms of spirituality. In the latter eventuality, the posthuman would be oriented toward seeming paradigms of the secular such as natural science and machines such as computers. Of course there have been post-secular or even religious aspects in, or bound up with, science, including biology, for example, in a figure such as Pierre Teilhard de Chardin. Chardin (like Michel de Certeau) was a Jesuit. He had impeccable scientific credentials yet construed divinity as the motivation of the evolutionary process leading to some unknown Omega Point or Singularity.[24] For those who wanted to dispense with God or pointed to his death, the human being might assume a divine or quasi-divine status. The divinization of the human being occurred in many forms: in a religion of reason or of humanity (prominent in the French Revolution and later in Auguste Comte), in Feuerbach's transformative criticism of Hegel (based on the interiorization by humans of what was presumably alienated and projected onto God), in Durkheim's approximation if not conflation of society and divinity, or more simply in the human assumption of the sovereign position once held by God and divine-right kings.[25] Up to the present day, a familiar phenomenon is the narcissistic, ultranationalistic, scapegoating, authoritarian ruler (or "con man") who takes him- (usually not her-) self to be God or God-like. Such a figure may have a cult-like following of true believers, willing to affirm or support whatever the ruler or leader puts forth, however outlandish it may be.

To the best of my knowledge, those interested in posthumanism have not generally explored the question of its possible or actual relations with the

---

23. Attention and criticism may be found in many of my publications, including *History, Literature, Critical Theory*. In alluding to the character Jacques Arnoux's production of kitsch articles of religious devotion (for Flaubert in many ways emblematic of modernity), the novelist, in *L'éducation sentimentale*, referred to "le sublime à bon marché" (the sublime at a bargain-basement price). On what I have treated as traumatropisms (transforming the traumatic into the sublime), see *History and Its Limits*, chap. 3.

24. See, for example, *Christianity and Evolution*, trans. R. Hague (New York: Harvest, 1974).

25. On Durkheim and his predecessors, notably with respect to the secular and the religious, see my *Emile Durkheim: Sociologist and Philosopher* (1972, 1985; Aurora, CO: The Davies Group, 2001), esp. chap. 6, "The Sacred and Society."

postsecular. Yet this is a question that warrants inquiry.[26] Indeed the larger problem may well be the complex formed by the posthuman and the post-secular. Even Derrida, arguably a key inspiration for posthumanism, turned in his later career in a contestable direction: a messianicity without messianism, involving an affirmation of *une attente sans attente* or waiting without an expectation of arrival. This is a waiting for what is unexpectedly to come (*à venir*) but is not identifiable with a given being or state of affairs.[27] The allure of an apocalyptic blank utopia is at play in various influential thinkers, for example, Giorgio Agamben and Slavoj Zizek. Zizek supported the election of Donald Trump (as, in their own ways, did many of his supporters) because he saw Trump as the bringer of "real" change, of something radically different that would shake up the status quo, departing from familiar neoliberalism and (hope against hope) leading to desired (yet on arrival perhaps not really desirable) transformation.[28]

One finds an apprehension, perhaps a desire, for a big-bang apocalypse or "singularity" in certain posthumanists (for example, Nick Bostrom), and it seems at times to have postsecular resonances as an adventitious, radically transformative advent.[29] One may recall Heidegger's quasi-religious invocation of the *Ereignis* (the Event or perhaps the Singularity) and, after his involvement in Nazism, his posthumously reported, apocalyptic assertion that only a god can save us. It is unclear just how prevalent an apocalyptic, posthumanist-postsecular view might be. Clearer is the way it readily feeds

---

26. But see J. Benjamin and Hava Tirosch-Samuelson, eds., *Transhuman Visions and Technological Imaginations* (Wiesbaden: Springer VS, 2016), esp. chap. 2, "Manifestations of the Posthuman in the Postsecular Imagination," by Elaine Graham. For Graham, the attention to the posthuman is focused not on other animals but on machines, cyborgs, and artificial intelligence, an approach that usefully supplements my own emphases.

27. See, for example, John D. Caputo, *The Prayers and Tears of Jacques Derrida: Religion without Religion* (Bloomington: Indiana University Press, 1997) and Jacques Derrida and Gianni Vattimo, eds., *Religion* (1996; Stanford: Stanford University Press, 1998), esp. 1–78. For a very different approach attempting to validate liberal Catholicism, see Charles Taylor, *A Secular Age* (Cambridge, MA: Harvard University Press, 2007) as well as the highly critical review of Martin Jay, "Faith-Based History," *History and Theory* 48 (February 2009): 76–84.

28. See the critique of Agamben in my *History in Transit: Experience, Identity, Critical Theory* (Ithaca: Cornell University Press, 2004), chap. 4; and *History and Its Limits*, esp. 164–75. On Zizek, see, for example, *Vice News*, November 30, 2016, https://news.vice.com/story/far-left-philosopher-slavoj-zizek-explains-why-he-suppored-trump-over-clinton (accessed Dec. 9, 2016). For a broader discussion, see "Epilogue: Recent Figurations of Trauma and Violence: Tarrying with Zizek," in my *History, Literature, Critical Theory*, 148–64.

29. See, for example, Bostrom's "Transhumanist Values" of 2003, http://www.nickbostrom.com/ethics/values.html (accessed Dec. 10, 2017). For an informed and incisive discussion of Bostrom, see Raffi Khatchadourian, "The Doomsday Invention: Will Artificial Intelligence Bring Us Utopia or Destruction?," *New Yorker*, November 23, 2015, 64–79.

into what might be seen as latter-day variations of what Max Weber analyzed in his renowned and controversial *Protestant Ethic and the Spirit of Capitalism* (1905), to wit, evangelical and fundamentalist forms of Christianity that may combine rapacious exploitation of the environment and pious if not sanctimonious otherworldliness, even an ecologically threatening end-of-days theology.

Certain issues call for further discussion with respect to posthumanism, especially the relations between the posthuman and the postsecular. One issue is how extreme or complete a break with the past and with varieties of humanism (and historiography) is sought by advocates of posthumanism. As explicitly noted, I think the points made and the concerns expressed in the present chapter would carry over into a posthumanistic perspective. But I have a critical response to more unguarded apocalyptic tendencies that may even harbor desires to transcend procedures for substantiating assertions—procedures that are necessary to critically check mythmaking and a wayward idea of "alternative facts."[30] But I would be more affirmative concerning other dimensions of the postsecular, especially a "sacred" respect and caring for others, the need for rituals such as mourning as well as for nonexploitative carnivalesque practices without a scapegoated butt, and a normatively regulated network of relations linking humans, other animals, and the environment.

I shall conclude with a few controversial, important, but, I hope, far from original remarks. In the recent past one does not, in my judgment, need particular theoretical or critical insight to realize that something is radically out of joint in contemporary social and economic systems, notably in the United States, where the sheer amount of wealth and resources makes a different system possible and even necessary. The financial and real-estate crisis beginning in full force in 2008 had devastating effects that have not run their course, and the lack of basic remedies increases the chances of recurrence, which the election of Trump, bringing right-wing, "libertarian" policies of

---

30. See my "Rethinking History and Resisting Apocalypse," in *Manifestos for History*, ed. Keith Jenkins et al. (London: Routledge, 2007), 160–78. I would not dismiss carefully framed alternative or "as-if" histories or provocative narratives informed by warrantable assertions about what indeed occurred in the past. An important literary, historically informed, counterfactual narrative is Philip K. Dick's *The Man in the High Castle*, in *Four Novels of the 1960s* (1962; New York: The Library of America, 2007), 1–229. It offers a vision of a world in which the Japanese and the Germans have won World War II. The sobering, still pertinent question that seems (as early as the 1960s) to emerge from the novel (including its counterfactual novel within the novel that indicates what actually happened—the victory of the Allies) is whether either eventuality makes all that much difference. Another way to put the point is to ask whether and to what extent the fascists may have lost the war but have done much to "win" its aftermath.

deregulation and privatization, will no doubt aggravate. This crisis has made more prevalent a sensitivity to the vast gap of wealth and income between the uppermost 1% or so and the rest of the population along with a series of discrepancies that run throughout the social and economic hierarchy. Here "Occupy Wall Street" had a strong and telling point to make, and the 2015–16 primary campaign of Bernie Sanders may have signaled the genesis of a broad social and political movement aiming at basic structural changes. Sanders helped make people familiar with certain aspects of blatant inequality.[31] A recent *Forbes* survey has the 400 wealthiest individuals in America possessing as much wealth as the lower 60 percent of the population. Earlier Congressional Budget Office statistics released in August 2016 had the top 10 percent of families holding 76 percent of wealth, with everyone else in the top 50 percent accounting for 23 percent, leaving only 1 percent for the entire bottom half of the population.[32] Moreover, there is a massive discrepancy between the top 200 CEOs' average income (some $15 million a year) and that of the average employee. In 1965 the difference was presumably not hundreds of times but closer to twenty times. Attention to the "bottom line" and a putative fiduciary responsibility to shareholders and their profit margin have overwhelmed if not obliterated a concern for the welfare of workers as well as for the state of the environment and society as a whole. Lobbyists for CEOs have militated against a bill that would not regulate but simply compare CEO income to that of employees. And investors, who supposedly vote with their dollars, do not have the right to regulate CEO

---

31. In his renowned book, *Capital in the Twenty-First Century*, trans. Arthur Goldhammer (Cambridge, MA: Harvard University Press, 2013), Thomas Piketty signaled the continued relevance of Karl Marx's critical analysis of capitalism and the adverse effects of the "free" market. For Piketty, Marx's basic logic was confirmed by the concentration of private wealth and the dichotomy between the small percent of the very wealthy and the very large percent of others, many of them quite poor, that has intensified particularly since around 1980 in the United States, Europe, and Japan. As Louis Menand pointed out in his concise and lucid analysis, "Sanders's proposals to reduce inequality are straight out of Piketty: tax wealth and give more people access to knowledge" ("He's Back: Karl Marx, Yesterday and Today," *New Yorker*, October 10, 2016, 90–97, at 97). Indeed, one problem in the campaign of Hillary Clinton (who, whatever her shortcomings, including complacency about a seemingly certain victory, was nonetheless a scapegoated victim of exaggerated and typically projective accusations of "crookedness," Wall-Street ties, and self-centered ambition) was not to have appealed more insistently both to key aspects of Sanders's proposals and to the underplayed, adverse ramifications of a Trump presidency (for example, not only in terms of his much discussed and almost self-evidently dubious character but also in terms of unreliable health care, increasingly skewed distribution of wealth and income, prejudicial immigration policy, and erratic governance). Important parts of the Sanders agenda were nonetheless in Clinton's platform, which was often ignored in coverage by the media fixated on Trump's antics and Clinton's emails.

32. See Jean Sahadi, "The Top 10% Hold 76% of the Wealth," *CNN Money*, August 16, 2016, http://money.cnn.com/2016/08/18/pf/wealth-inequality/ (accessed May 7, 2017).

incomes. Some CEOs have received incredible "packages" on retirement (in the case of the CEO of United Technologies, a major defense contractor and the parent company of Carrier, a reported $172 million, and in that of Rex Tillerson, Trump's secretary of state [who downsized the department with its diplomatic activities to the point of making it dysfunctional], a reported $180 million from Exxon). Senator Bernie Sanders's invocation of democratic socialism (instead of a new New Deal) may have misfired rhetorically in a largely hostile American context, but it was substantively on the right track. A new New Deal would offer a revised mixed economy composed of truly competitive markets, effective governmental agencies regulating them, free public education including college, and a system of "safety nets," such as universal health care and Social Security.

The CEO, bank executive, or hedge-fund manager who makes hundreds of times more than the income of the average employee, and particularly one who made a fortune from the far-from-accidental collapse of the housing market (notoriously including Steven Mnuchin, Trump's secretary of the treasury), has become a literal and symbolic instance of inequity in society.[33] Reminiscent of the worst abuses in pre-revolutionary old regimes is the way those most responsible for the financial and housing crisis have by and large been treated leniently or gotten away with unacceptable if not criminal

---

33. See David Dayan, "Wilbur Ross and Steve Mnuchin—Profiteers of the Great Foreclosure Machine," *The Nation*, November 30, 2016, https://www.thenation.com/article/wilbur-ross-and-steve-mnuchin-profiteers-of-the-great-foreclosure-machine-go-to-washington/ (accessed December 1, 2016). See also Dayan's book, *Chain of Title: How Three Ordinary Americans Uncovered Wall Street's Foreclosure Fraud* (New York: New Press, 2016). Mnuchin, a billionaire hedge-fund manager, worked for seventeen years at Goldman-Sachs. Termed by Senator Elizabeth Warren "the Forrest Gump of the financial crisis," he was the head of an investment team that bought the predatory lender IndyMac, which Mnuchin as CEO renamed OneWest. It foreclosed on over 36,000 mortgages, using fraudulent procedures. In a July 2009 deposition, OneWest vice president Erica Johnson-Seck under oath admitted she signed 750 unread foreclosure documents a week, spending no more than thirty seconds on each. She has the distinction of being the only executive to be jailed (on a five-year term) for foreclosure fraud. Wilbur Ross, Trump's head of the Department of Commerce and seen by some commentators as one of his better picks, made his billions largely as a corporate raider, buying up failing companies and "restructuring" them by firing workers, shipping jobs offshore, and navigating the companies through bankruptcy. (See, for example, Chris Arnold of NPR in an article dated January 18, 2017, http://www.npr.org/templates/transcript/transcript.php?storyId=510472440 (accessed January 23, 2017). Ross also profited from the foreclosure process through one of the companies he pulled out of bankruptcy, American Home Mortgage Servicing (or AHMSI). In light of these nominations as well as others, Trump's campaign "promise" to "clean up the swamp on Wall Street" and counteract the effects of the financial crisis of 2008 seems like one more instance of empty and deceptive rhetoric. But the appointments of Mnuchin and Ross resonated with Trump's view, expressed during the campaign, that he was "smart" to make money in a down market and even not to pay taxes, which of course required shifting burdens to those less able to afford them and taking advantage of the desperate condition of others.

behavior—not indicted or punished but even rewarded with bonuses and higher salaries in the wake of the destruction they were instrumental in inflicting.[34] And one of the bitter ironies of recent history is that Donald Trump, one of the chief beneficiaries of an ability to play the system to his own narcissistic advantage, was taken at his empty word by many of the dispossessed and genuinely disadvantaged who saw him as their spokesperson and savior.[35]

Especially in this larger context, the corporatization of the academy is a real problem, including the extremely high salaries and perquisites of

---

34. A pertinent book here, among many others, is Gretchen Morgenson and Joshua Rosner, *Reckless Endangerment: How Outsized Ambition, Greed, and Corruption Created the Worst Financial Crisis of Our Time* (New York: Macmillan, 2011). For a study that indicates how the concept of the Anthropocene may be diversionary, how capitalism over the past five centuries has reduced nature to an instrumental status and commodified it, and how capitalism is incompatible with sound ecological practices in what he terms the age of the Capitalocene, see Jason Moore, *Capitalism in the Web of Life: Ecology and the Accumulation of Capital* (London: Verso, 2015)

35. Senator Jeff Flake, Republican from Arizona, has offered a low-key but at times pointed analysis of the way his party has abandoned genuinely conservative principles and over time paved the way for a "populist" president who undermines conservative values. For him, the GOP, in supporting Trump, suspended its critical faculties and has been in a state of denial concerning an emperor who has no clothes. Calling on his fellow GOP members of Congress to speak out and stand up to unacceptable dimensions of the president's behavior, he argues that Trump's words and actions have contradicted conservative principles and go in dangerous directions, such as the embrace of "alternative facts" and of destabilizing policies both domestically and abroad. See Flake's *Conscience of a Conservative: A Rejection of Destructive Politics and a Return to Principle* (New York: Random House, 2017). Flake's appeal initially had relatively little uptake among his fellow Republicans in Congress, and Flake himself did not consistently act in ways that conform to his argument. (For example, he voted for all four versions of the Republican health-care act.) But his stated position may be a sign of growing dissension in at least more moderate segments of the party. Trump has threatened to support a candidate who "primaries" Flake for his Senate seat in 2018, but Flake has announced that he is not seeking reelection. In the aftermath of Trump's controversial responses to the far-right demonstrations of August 11 and 12, 2017, in Charlottesville, Virginia, Senator Bob Corker of Tennessee, a heretofore strong supporter of the president (and someone also not standing for reelection), declared on August 17: "The President has not yet been able to demonstrate the stability nor some of the competence that he needs to demonstrate in order to be successful." Quoted in Jeremy Herb, *CNN Politics*, August 18, 2017, http://www.cnn.com/2017/08/17/politics/bob-corker-criticizes-trump-charlottesville/index.html (accessed August 18, 2017). The same day Senator Tim Scott of South Carolina asserted that Trump's changing responses had "compromised" his "moral authority." On August 18, various sources reported that Stephen Bannon had been dismissed from his exceptional advisory position in the White House. Bannon, however, felt unleashed and militantly asserted that he would return to his redoubt at Breitbart where he could still have the support of billionaire Robert Mercer. From that position, he would further an ethnonational, anti-immigrant, "America-first," so-called populist agenda against "globalists" and moderates, both in the White House (presumably including Jared Kushner and H. R. McMaster) and beyond it, notably in Congress. And he would miraculously dissociate the sovereign's two bodies by continuing to support (a transcendent?) Trump but attacking a failed or dead Trump presidency. See, for example, Jonathan Swain, "Bannon, Backed by Billionaire, Prepares to Go to War," *Axios*, August 18, 2017, https://www.axios.com/bannons-next-move-2474479917.html (accessed August 18, 2017).

corporate-like, top-level administrators and the very large number of underpaid staff and non-tenure-track faculty, along with the problem of unemployed or underemployed PhDs, especially in the humanities. The very
question of the usefulness of the humanities seems a deceptive diversion if
not an aspect of scapegoating in light of this state of affairs—scapegoating
that has seemed to become a widespread and often uncriticized dimension
of contemporary life. One need not be able to provide a model of a fully
justifiable social and economic system to see that the current state of affairs is riddled with severe problems, and it appears obvious that extreme
deregulation favors the rich and powerful (notably large corporations) and
has a negative impact on the disadvantaged and the disempowered. Here one
might invoke a principle that may be derived from Rousseau: no one should
be so rich as to be able to buy another, or so poor as to be constrained to sell
him- or herself. Such a principle may seem so basic as to obviate the need for
any special expertise, humanistic or otherwise, in recognizing its force and
legitimacy.[36]

Open to debate would be the specific implications of the proposed principle, notably in the contemporary context. Arguably, one implication is
that in a just society there should be both floors and ceilings for wealth and
income in the interest of the general good. This would require redistribution that is reasonable and effective, including a significant tax on income
and wealth above a certain level, in contrast to the Republican plan to take
from the less advantaged to give even more to the rich while hoping, in the
face of historical evidence to the contrary, or perhaps deceptively pretending
that tax cuts for corporations and the wealthy will simply "trickle down"
to the lower and middle classes because of economic growth. It is debatable whether the trickle-down theory is specious or "trumped-up" enough
to count as another big lie that only gains credibility through propagandistic
repetition and appeals to authority. Less debatable is that running up a massive budget deficit through major tax cuts benefiting primarily corporations
and the wealthy (of course including Trump and his family) may be used as
a pretext to justify spending cuts aimed at paring down if not taking apart
government, including regulative agencies along with Social Security, Medi-
care, and Medicaid—the New Deal "entitlements" serving as safety nets for

36. For a concise account of Rousseau's views on the pernicious effects of extreme inequality,
see David Lay Williams, "Should We Care about Inequality? Let's Ask a Philosopher," *Washington
Post,* March 28, 2014, https://www.washingtonpost.com/news/monkey-cage/wp/2014/03/28/
should-we-care-about-inequality-lets-ask-a-philosopher/?utm_term=.06fac88dad1a (accessed January 6, 2017). See also Williams, *Rousseau's Platonic Enlightenment,* foreword by Patrick Riley (University Park: Pennsylvania State University Press, 2007).

the vulnerable (but often misconstrued by far-from-generous opponents as handouts to the lazy and improvident). In any event, the prevalent idea that growth (along with small government except for the military and the police) is the principal or even the only concern and that progressive redistribution is irrelevant or worse would not be cogent at a time when pressing issues prominently include a massive divide between rich and poor, pollution and ecological damage (including global warming), and the threat of endless wars along with the imposition of a police state. A further requirement would be the need for deliberative bodies, such as Congress, in which narrow-minded self-interest and power-hungry, at times hypocritical, big donor–subservient legislators do not prevail. With a modicum of political imagination and will, one might also envision a populism serving people, notably the underprivileged, and not bound up with a hollow, "charismatic" leader and a self-defeating politics of self-aggrandizement, resentment, and, for some, despair. However "unrealistic" it may appear in a given context, one may still affirm both a sense of legitimate limits (especially with respect to self-aggrandizement whether individual or collective) and a commitment to basic values and desirable goals.

In a review of recent works on the effects on the economy and society of the use of robots to replace workers, the noted author and journalist Elizabeth Kolbert makes observations that indicate that certain initiatives may not be written off as unrealistic but seen as reasonable responses to contemporary developments, including the ill-advised nature of initiatives by Trump and his administration.[37] She notes that operations moving back to the United States will not do much for employment, since they are largely automated. "This is a major reason that there is a reshoring trend; salaries are no longer an issue once you get rid of the salaried" (88). (Note that this is a point made and celebrated by the environmentally dangerous, deregulating, big-business-oriented EPA secretary Scott Pruitt concerning workers and jobs within the United States itself.) Kolbert notes that Martin Ford, in his 2015 *Rise of the Robots: Technology and the Threat of a Jobless Future,* "worries that we are headed toward an era of 'techno-feudalism.' He imagines a plutocracy shut away 'in gated communities or in elite cities, perhaps guarded by autonomous military robots and drones.' " But unlike the older feudalism, the underclass would not be exploited but superfluous. Ford "recommends a guaranteed basic income for all, to be paid for with new taxes, leveled, at least in part, at the new gazillionaires" (88). I would add that the risk even

37. See "Rage against the Machine: Will Robots Take Your Job?," *New Yorker,* December 19 and 26, 2016, 84–88.

for the very wealthy is that an underclass may come to realize that they have little to expect of Trump and his like and may well engage in either revolt or random violence, possibly against the callous well-to-do. Or they may be recruited for paramilitary groups or for standard police and military forces assigned to maintain "law and order," incarcerate "criminals" (at times in privatized prisons and including hapless drug offenders), chase down and expel the undocumented, further the emergence of a police state, and fight endless wars around the globe.

Kolbert also observes that, to one degree or another, just about everyone writing on the topic comes to similar or related conclusions concerning necessary reforms. Jerry Kaplan, in his 2015 *Humans Need Not Apply: A Guide to Wealth and Work in the Age of Artificial Intelligence*, proposes that "the federal government create a 401(k)-like account for every ten-year-old in the U.S. Those who ultimately do find jobs could contribute some of their earnings to the accounts; those who don't could perform volunteer work in return for government contributions" (88). Others prefer the idea of a negative income tax that would offer the unemployed a minimal living, and the underemployed cash supplements.

It is debatable whether the scenarios Kolbert discusses are utopian or dystopian or simply a search for a way out of a rather hopeless bind. Perhaps a more promising possibility lies in seeking forms of employment less likely to be entirely performed by robots or "labor-saving" devices. One area is of course education, notably teaching in schools other than the charter establishments promoted by superrich, big campaign donor, and remarkably uninformed Secretary of Education Betsy DeVos. Such schools would be supported by public funds and staffed in part by retrained or newly employed people displaced by automation and related forms of economic "progress." Another is greater funding for the arts and humanities where people could pursue activities (maybe even the study of art, dance, history, or literature—not excluding French literature!) currently subordinated to the economic-and-STEM orientation of "developed" countries. It might be far-fetched but conceivably desirable to entertain (if only as a thought experiment) the possibility of widespread support for cultural and intellectual development of a sort that did not amount to a zero-sum, win-or-lose game and might call on talents and proclivities other than those exemplified in the current U.S. administration.

As intimated earlier, one may empathize with and compassionately try to understand those of Trump's supporters who had genuine grievances, felt the establishment of the Democratic Party, including its candidate, had let them down, and wanted to lodge at least a strong protest, while still criticizing the way they turned to what did not offer a real response to their grievances but might well exacerbate them. (But do Trump himself and some of his more cynical supporters warrant empathy or only the type of understanding that critically investigates their deceptive procedures and attempts to counteract them?) In any event, it makes little sense to make the kind of protest against the way the ship of state is being handled that itself may well contribute to running it aground.

In many ways, Trump, his associates, and their modus operandi are hostile to the qualities I have tried to propose as crucial to a humanistic (or posthumanistic as well as humane) approach. It would be difficult or even impossible to make convincing sense of the amazing success of Trump and his dangerous, vulgar, self-serving bravado without at least a qualified appeal to an affectively and ideologically shaped propensity to support what deceptively pumps up one's ego, solidifies one's identity, either reinforces one's narrowly construed self-interest or caters to one's discontent, and feeds misguided resentment as well as prejudice but does not further one's enlightened self-interest or pass muster with one's critical judgment. Trump's success also resonates with the rise of authoritarian and even neofascist political leaders in other parts of the world and with more or less comparable events in the not-too-distant past. A plausible commonplace is that people want to believe in something, and many remained faithful to the end (sometimes beyond the end) even to a Hitler or Stalin.

Without appealing to problematic comparisons, one may nonetheless contend that straits must be dire for someone in the contemporary United States to take Trump as a personal savior. Along with factors mentioned earlier, this willingness indicates that the concept of a legitimation crisis may in certain ways apply not only to the Trump presidency but more broadly to important American institutions and practices, such as the economy, the media, and the political system, including an at times dysfunctional Congress and electoral college. The entire Trump phenomenon makes one sensitive to the shortfalls of overly theoretical discourse and to the limits of approaching problems in an extremely abstract or high-altitude manner. Here the humanities are not a panacea. Yet the humanities, leavened by critical thought, have a point insofar as they are both attentive to detail and address underlying assumptions and frames of reference that shape one's understanding and bear on specific issues, often in a manner that remains uninvestigated. Understood in a certain way, the humanities, opening the way to the posthumanities, may at least help to point in desirable directions and stimulate critical thought that more fully comes to grips with problems that link the past and the present in an attempt to further the possibility of a less mean-spirited, hateful, or prejudice-laden, and instead more livable future. I think that a significant number of people in the United States and elsewhere believe that a primary goal of life is not always to win, vanquish others, or try to amass as much wealth as possible. It is rather to do everything one can to be able to live and to die in a society at least a little more just, generous, and compassionate than the one into which one was born.

INDEX

CPSIA information can be obtained
at www.ICGtesting.com
Printed in the USA
LVHW052151060519
616814LV00003B/403